Restaurants of Detroit

Seventh Edition
By Molly Abraham

Designer, editor
Ken McDonald
Copy editors
Esther Allweiss Tschirhart
Helene Lorber
Cover photo
John Luke
Illustrations
James Denk

Published by
The Detroit Free Press
321 W. Lafayette Blvd.
Detroit, MI 48226

Copyright 1995   Detroit Free Press

Manufactured in the United States of America.

ISBN 0-937247-65-0

On the cover

The two-story dining room of Acadia, located across the street
from the Palace of Auburn Hills.

Introduction

This is not restaurant review by committee. The opinions expressed here are my own, one person's take, arrived at after a minimum of two, and in many cases, several visits to a given restaurant.

If your favorite place isn't found in these pages, or — heaven forbid — you disagree with a particular rating, there is no one to blame but me. And even though my taste might not parallel yours, the consistency of a single point of view ought to help you decide on a destination as you flip through the pages.

I rate restaurants using a four-star method. I classify pricing by estimating the cost of an average dinner for each person, without wine, cocktails or tip. Here's what the price ratings indicate:

Reasonable	$10 or less
Moderate	$15 to $25
Expensive	More than $25

What I have attempted to do in this edition of our Free Press guide is present a sampling of the best and most interesting dining possibilities in the metro Detroit and Windsor area. A handful of places farther afield is included, too.

There are as many (or more) little, offbeat places as big deal restaurants. Though I don't look for just my own personal favorites, I do have a fondness for the kind of place where the proprietor is at the door or in the kitchen.

The restaurants differ in style, ambition, price range and menu, ranging from the modest to the elaborate. You'll find very few chains mentioned and few hotel restaurants. This is not intended to be the phone book. It is a selective list of some 300 restaurants, hopefully wide-ranging enough to give an overview of what the area has to offer.

The fact that Detroit is not a tourist town is to our advantage when it comes to the restaurant scene. Tourist traps don't make it here. The restaurants have to be able to satisfy their local clientele, people who return again and again, not those in town for a night or two and gone before the credit card bill comes due. And that's to the good.

The rating of each restaurant is based on the quality of food, service and setting, with more weight given to food and service than to decor. Still, atmosphere is important, too. I don't think most of us want to go to restaurants that make no effort toward providing a pleasant, comfortable setting.

I try hard not to compare one restaurant to another, but to come up with a rating based only on how well a place accomplishes what it sets out to do. To receive four stars, the top rating, a restaurant does not have to be an upscale, over-the-top kind of place. It simply — though it's never simple — has to excel at what it does. Much easier said than done.

Molly Abraham

This book is dedicated

to Jarvis McMorris (1970-1994)

and all the other hard-working people

behind kitchen doors.

Acadia

I can't imagine a more perfect setting for the talents of chef Brian Polcyn than this woodsy, two-story dining room, where the flame-spewing ovens in the open kitchen are part of the oak, pine and glass setting.

Polcyn's solid, Midwestern approach, brightened with the touch of spice contributed by his Mexican mother, and the sturdy contours of the arts-and-crafts-inspired restaurant, are exactly right for each other.

☆ ☆ ☆ ☆

3800 Lapeer Road, Auburn Hills. (810) 373-7330.

Hours: 11 a.m.-10 p.m. Mon.-Thu., 11 a.m.-11 p.m. Fri., 5-11 p.m. Sat. Closed Sun. except when there is a major event at the Palace of Auburn Hills. Closed on major holidays except Mother's Day and Easter.

Nonsmoking: 85 percent.

Full bar. Major credit cards.

Moderate.

The restaurant across the street from the Palace of Auburn Hills was built in just three months in late summer and fall of '92, with Polcyn in partnership with the Becker brothers, Bruce and Charles.

While a few things remain from the original menu — the wonderfully earthy wood-roasted potato, mushroom and leek soup and the thin-crusted grilled vegetable pizza, for instance — the current approach is less tricky.

Dishes are straightforward, attractively but not fussily presented on designer plates of black and white porcelain. Polcyn has a rather architectural approach in composing the plates, without making them look outlandish.

Choices are reasonable, not overwhelming. Sometimes, however, people look at the list of a dozen entrees and say, "I can't find anything I want." Polcyn's reply: "What do you want? I'll make it for you."

I can't imagine not being satisfied with an array that might include grilled or wood-roasted salmon, whitefish with crispy fried fennel, glazed mahimahi on fried rice with Chinese vegetables, baby back ribs, pork loin chop with housemade baked beans, and beef tenderloin with "smashed" potatoes. The latter are the house mashed potatoes, which include skins; they are, indeed, wonderful. Other choices include pastas (in half or whole portions) and great little pizzas that many people share as appetizers.

The menu is a work in progress, changing with the seasons but based on colorful, fresh ingredients. Polcyn says he wants the food to be ever-evolving, but the theme is consistent. Count on a couple of red meat dishes, pork, chicken, ocean fish and some lake fish.

Impeccable salads come with entrees: several varieties of greens from bitter to sweet served in a drizzle of balsamic vinaigrette that leaves only a trace on the plates. Breads are superior, too, from the crisp, spicy focaccia to the herb-flecked rolls and wheat bread in rustic twig baskets that fit the setting perfectly.

Breads are housemade, as is virtually everything, down to the fresh fruit sorbets, ice creams and puddings on the dessert list in the hands of pastry chef Sue Miller.

While Acadia is basically a casual restaurant with an informal feeling, it has lots of refinements: big linen napkins, handsome tableware, a waitstaff in long-sleeved, dark cotton shirts and green, rust and brown vests with dark trousers for a variation on the usual look.

The background music changes with the lineup at the Palace, where attractions range from NBA basketball to rodeos and rock concerts. The variety at the Palace keeps Polcyn and staff hopping to keep up with what very different audiences want.

That's just fine with the chef, who is without a trace of snobbism. "You have to listen to your customers," he says.

Ah Wok

41563 W. 10 Mile Road, Novi.
(810) 349-9260.

Hours: 11 a.m.-9:30 p.m. Mon.-Thu., 11 a.m.-11 p.m. Fri., 4-11 p.m. Sat., noon-9:30 p.m. Sun. Closed major holidays.

Nonsmoking: 75 percent.

Full bar.   Major credit cards.

Moderate.

Chef Pak Lai learned his craft from the late, talented Gam Moy, patriarch of the Moy family that runs this 22-year-old restaurant. Lai has chalked up a number of years of service upholding Moy's standards.

Peter and George Moy and George's wife, Grace, continue the family presence.

And like other restaurants where the owners are on hand, it makes a big difference. At this well-run place, offerings range from very familiar dishes, such as beef with snow peas, to whole steamed fish with ginger and garlic sauce.

Two especially popular dishes involve shrimp: honey walnut shrimp on a bed of peapods, and house shrimp with sweet and sour sauce and vegetables. Main courses may be ordered a la carte, or as complete dinners including soup, eggroll, dessert and tea for $1.50 extra.

Akasaka

What might appear to be just another strip-mall storefront is much more. It has housed the crisp, clean quarters of this serene spot, done up in shades of rose, gray and rust, since 1988.

Proprietor Tomiko DeMeere carries on cheerfully without the partners who were with her in the beginning. They've moved on to the bigger Cherry Blossom in Novi.

Since then, the 20-seat sushi bar has become even more popular. It always was the restaurant's central core. Also available are many other Japanese standbys, from appetizers like gyoza (pan-fried pork and chicken dumplings) to teriyakis, tempuras and an array of noodle soups.

**37152 Six Mile Road, Livonia.
(313) 462-2630.**

Hours: Lunch, 11:30 a.m.-2 p.m. Mon.-Sat.; dinner, 5:30-10:15 p.m. Mon.-Thu., 5:30-10:30 p.m. Sat., 4:30-9:30 p.m. Sun. Closed major holidays.

Nonsmoking: 50 percent.

Full bar.   Major credit cards.

Moderate.

Alban's

Under the same roof with a wine shop and carry-out deli, this has developed over the years into a full-scale dining spot. Not surprisingly, wines are spotlighted. Each chef's special includes a wine recommendation, and the Cruvinet houses another eight reds and eight whites.

The menu features some pasta dishes as well as Kansas City steak, along with such perennials as prime ribs, shrimp salad and deli-style sandwiches. It's the kind of variety that appeals to both a business and family clientele.

There's a nice blend of informality with such niceties as fresh flowers on the vinyl-clothed tables and a woodsy ski lodge setting.

**190 N. Hunter, Birmingham.
(810) 258-7588.**

Hours: 11 a.m.-11 p.m. Mon.-Thu., 11 a.m.-midnight Fri.-Sat.; brunch, 11 a.m.-2:30 p.m. Sun., dinner until 9 p.m. Closed Christmas Day and New Year's Day.

Nonsmoking: 70 percent.

Full bar.   Major credit cards.

Reasonable.

America

The reworking of the short-lived Avenue Diner takes as its theme the wealth of regional dishes served throughout the United States. The premise fits the plush diner setting well. After all, what could be more American than the passenger trains that criss-crossed America 50 years ago?

Chef Elizabeth Sollish is in charge of an a la carte menu that includes such dishes as fried green tomatoes, Texas barbecued shrimp with black bean polenta and mushroom pie with tomatillo salsa.

The combinations are unpredictable and unhackneyed. Main courses include Wisconsin veal medallions in apple cider sauce, Pacific Northwest salmon with spicy slaw made of daikon radishes and Indian duck with mustard greens and cracked black pepper sauce.

Food is arranged architecturally on the white plates. That, too, fits the room with its nice architectural details, such as the barrel-vaulted ceiling and slick surfaces, as well as a Barney Judge mural with a warm '30s feeling.

Though the room has a dressy look, guests don't have to dress up. The atmosphere is casual, with blue-shirted servers dashing about in their Statue of Liberty print ties and dark trousers.

Most table settings include an American cookbook, to underscore the direction. The menu changes seasonally and reflects the harvests within the USA. It's a winning concept.

The wine list is completely American, too. Not so the list of single-malt Scotches. But we can forgive that, now can't we?

America's Pizza Cafe

Thin-crusted pizzas thrust in and out of wood-burning ovens on paddles are served in cheerfully upbeat settings. The concept has been very successful for Mike and Marian Ilitch, who certainly know their way around a kitchen. These outposts take the Little Caesars approach one step further for those who want to go beyond tomato sauce and pepperoni and into something a little more upscale.

The menus also offer a range of salads and pasta dishes and what I suspect some people love best: warm, garlicky breadsticks. The settings differ slightly from one location to another but all are casual and comfortable, with paper napkins and bare-topped tables.

Newest and biggest of the cafes is the spot in downtown Rochester.

**Fox Theatre Building,
2239 Woodward Ave., Detroit.
(313) 964-3122.**

Hours: 11 a.m.-10 p.m. Mon.-Thu., 11 a.m.-midnight Fri., noon-midnight Sat., noon-10 p.m. Sun.

**24459 Telegraph Road,
south of 10 Mile Road, Southfield.
(810) 352-5588.**

Hours: 11 a.m.-11 p.m. Mon.-Thu., 11 a.m.-midnight Fri.-Sat., noon-10 p.m. Sun.

**129 S. Main, Royal Oak.
(810) 544-1001.**

Hours: 11 a.m.-11 p.m. Mon.-Thu., 11 a.m.-1 a.m. Fri.-Sat., noon-10 p.m. Sun.

**401 Main Street, Rochester.
(810) 656-0373.**

Hours: 7 a.m.-11 p.m. Mon.-Thu., 7 a.m.-1 a.m. Fri.-Sat., 8 a.m.-10 p.m. Sun.

Nonsmoking: 50 percent.
Full bar.   Major credit cards.
Reasonable.

Andiamo Ristorante

7096 E. 14 Mile Road, west of
Van Dyke, Warren. (810) 268-3200.

Hours: 11 a.m.-11 p.m. Mon.-Thu., 11 a.m.-midnight Fri., 4 p.m.-midnight Sat., 2-9 p.m. Sun. Closed Thanksgiving, Christmas and New Year's Day.

Nonsmoking: 50 percent.

Full bar.   Major credit cards.

Moderate.

Two chefs, at least in this case, are definitely not one too many. The combo of master Aldo Ottaviani in the kitchen with Jeff Kay has been surprisingly successful.

Aldo — who ran his own establishment for more than 30 years on the east side of Detroit — is, of course, from the old school. The younger Kay appreciates his colleague's traditional Italian style, and he adds a fresh approach that brings tried-and-true dishes up to date.

Theirs is a from-scratch kitchen. Pastas, breads, sauces — even the spumoni — are made right here. In contrast to the tradition in the kitchen, the setting is slickly contemporary.

Attesting to the popularity of the Andiamo approach has been the addition of a big banquet area, with its own, separate kitchen.

The menu is extensive, and goes well beyond pastas with a list of chicken, veal, fish and beef selections.

Ann Sayles Dining Room

As befits the menu, the plain, unsophisticated setting just east of Greenfield Road doesn't even try for ambience other than unpretentious comfort. The focus is on the hearty food served to a loyal, repeat crowd, many of whom remember when food like this was on family dinner tables most nights.

☆ ☆ ☆

4313 W. 13 Mile Road, Royal Oak.
(810) 288-6020.

Hours: Lunch, 11:30 a.m.-2:30 p.m. Tue.-Sat.; dinner, 4:30-8 p.m. Tue.-Thu., 4:30-8:30 p.m. Fri.-Sat., noon-8 p.m. Sun. Closed Mon., Christmas Eve, Christmas Day, New Year's Day and Fourth of July.

Nonsmoking: 75 percent.

Full bar.   MC and Visa.

Reasonable.

Like the basic American recipes handwritten on scraps of paper and passed along from owner to owner since the '20s, the saga of the Ann Sayles Dining Room has been pieced together from the stories told by loyal customers.

Mike Farero, who took over in '86, says his wife, Patricia, patiently listened to the stories told by the old-timers to glean the history now printed on the menus.

Of course, the informants didn't always agree on the precise details. But they do know that it all began sometime during the Roaring '20s and, amazingly, survives today with much the same style. Walk into Ann Sayles, and you know you have found a restaurant unlike any other in the area.

Patrons no longer write out their orders in pencil on little slips of paper and hand them to the waitress. The cottage curtains are gone.

But from the fruit cup to the banana cream pie, the parsley boiled potatoes to the crushed cornflake-encrusted banana salad with celery seed dressing, things are pretty much the same as they've always been.

Some patrons eat at Ann Sayles almost every day — except the traditional closed-on-Mondays. If they come in three or four times a week, well, that's pretty much par for the course at this throwback to gentler times.

Of course, it's a mature crowd. Some take several minutes to make it from the door to their table, sinking gratefully into their chairs, to be greeted by their favorite waitress, cheery as always.

Some patrons wave away the menu. They know it by heart. Roast turkey ($8.50) is so perennially popular it's available every night, accompanied by little paper cups of jellied cranberry sauce, bland bread dressing, pale gravy. With all white meat, 50 cents extra. It is the real thing.

Ann Sayles, whose restaurant was known as Ann Sayles Tea Room until the arrival of the liquor license in 1972, surely would be pleased to know that much more than her name survives. This restaurant is remarkably true to the spirit of that American institution known as the tearoom, even though the bill of fare now includes drinks stronger than tea.

"Classic American cuisine" say the business cards stacked at the cashier's counter where people pay their checks. But that's wrong. Simple, plain, straightforward cooking is what goes on here. It is basic soups, like navy bean and vegetable; iceberg and tomato salads; vegetables like lima beans and corn. It's mashed potatoes and apple pie. It's wonderful, yeasty dinner rolls.

The spice level, if any, is very, very gentle. Just like the price structure.

Antonio's

**20311 Mack Avenue at Lochmoor,
Grosse Pointe Woods.
(313) 884-0253.**

Hours: Dinner only, 6-10 p.m. Tue.-Fri., 5-10 p.m. Sat., 5-8 p.m. Sun. Closed Mon. and major holidays.

Nonsmoking: 33 percent.

Beer and wine. AE, MC and Visa.

Moderate.

The epitome of the small, romantic restaurant, Antonio's is invisible from the street in its quarters in a small, discreet shopping plaza. Nonetheless, it has managed to attract a loyal clientele to its 40-some seats for a number of years now.

Partners Antonio Scerri and Brian Sammut share the duties, with Scerri running the dining room, Sammut in the kitchen. An appropriately brief menu of Italian dishes is supplemented with such daily specials as Sicilian veal chop steamed in white wine, salmon with fresh basil or perhaps tri-colored tortellini (green, white and red, of course) with a choice of sauces from creamy tomato to Alfredo.

Italian bread, fresh green salads and the classic side dish of pasta are served with meat and seafood entrees.

The terra cotta walls, skylight and pastel floral curtains and tablecloths lend a courtyard feeling to what is truly a hideaway setting.

Antonio's Italian Cuisine

After seven years of dishing up pasta, veal and chicken dishes, Antonio Picano has really settled in. The menu is working well, so why change it, he asks rhetorically.

Why, indeed? He's got winners in his linguine, fettuccine, lasagna and ravioli, served with mixed green salads and warm garlic sticks, as well as such specialty dishes as chicken Aldo (named for his cousin Aldo), which combines sauteed chicken with Alfredo sauce and pasta. The setting is upbeat, with its framed photographs of Italy, but due for an update.

☆ ☆ ☆

2505 E. 14 Mile Road, east of Dequindre, Sterling Heights. (810) 264-5252.

Hours: 11 a.m.-9:30 p.m. Mon.-Thu., 11 a.m.-10:30 p.m. Fri., noon-10:30 p.m. Sat., noon-9:30 p.m. Sun. Closed major holidays

Nonsmoking: 75 percent.

Full bar.   Major credit cards.

Reasonable.

Appeteaser Cafe

Backed up by the young chefs he calls his "culinary Fab Five," chef/proprietor Chris Angelosante has prospered in this quaint small town since 1979. For some time now, the menu has returned to the original format: an a la carte assortment that gives customers the choice of going with lighter, less expensive choices or something more substantial.

In any case, he has managed to keep the price structure well below what other restaurants of this quality are asking.

335 N. Main, Milford. (810) 685-0989.

Hours: Lunch, 11 a.m.-5 p.m. Mon.-Sat.; dinner, 5-11 p.m. Mon.-Thu., 5 p.m.-midnight Fri.-Sat., 3-10 p.m. Sun.; brunch, 10:30 a.m.-2:30 p.m. Sun. Closed major holidays except Easter Sunday and Mother's Day.

Nonsmoking: 75 percent.

Full bar.   Major credit cards.

Reasonable.

The array includes some perennially successful items: coconut shrimp and coconut chicken with sweet and sour sauce; the soup sampler that allows diners to taste any three of five soups on the menu; the Gorgonzola burger, and grilled vegetable salad with soy vinaigrette and black beans.

There are at least eight dinner specials each night, typified by grilled pickerel with horseradish crust and Atlantic salmon with pistachio nuts and tomato saffron sauce.

The modestly priced Sunday brunch buffet — under $10 — is an especially popular feature.

Armando's

4242 Vernor, Detroit.
(313) 554-0666.

Hours: 10:30 a.m.-3:30 a.m. Sun.-Thu., 10:30 a.m.-4 a.m. Fri.-Sat. Closed Thanksgiving and Christmas Day.

Nonsmoking: 50 percent.

Full bar.   Major credit cards.

Reasonable.

Armando may be the name, but the place on Vernor that bears it has been the domain of Serafina Hernandez since the mid-'80s. She came to Detroit to visit her daughter, stopped by the restaurant to say hi to then-proprietor Armando Galan, and ended up buying the place.

Wouldn't Serafina's be a great name for a Mexican restaurant? Serafina doesn't think so. She's happy with the name that was on the building when she first saw it. And the restaurant she runs with the help of her daughter Cecilia has managed to find a real niche.

It is one of the few Mexican restaurants popular with both the neighborhood people, who come in for carryouts, and the business crowd, who sit at tile-topped tables for quick lunches.

Armando's is less touristy than the Mexican Town spots a little farther east. Yet it's more accessible than some of the obscure neighborhood cantinas that aren't on the salsa trail. A nice combination.

I especially like the friendliness of the place, the sound of the Spanish being spoken all around, and the little dishes of bean dip and pico de gallo that come to the tables along with chips and the house hot sauce.

There's no doubt in my mind that the $4.95 luncheon buffet is one of the best deals in town. It is regularly replenished with fresh cheese enchiladas, tacos and burritos. There are also very good carnitas, pieces of seasoned deep-fried pork, and guisado de puerco, tender chunks of pork stewed with onions, green peppers and tomatoes. Each day one special dish is added to the buffet — most Fridays it is fish stew that the regulars swear by. Other days you might find a Cuban gumbo made with pork, okra and sweet plantains; sauteed beef tongue, or corn tortillas rolled around a filling of chicken, beef or pork.

The Hernandezes, who emigrated from Havana in the mid-'60s, have talked about adding more Cuban dishes. Somehow, though, they never seem to get around to it.

Arriva Italia

The sheer size and dramatic decor of this Italian restaurant are somewhat daunting. It seats 300 on the main floor alone. The feeling is more that of nightclub than restaurant, but that's deceiving.

6880 E. 12 Mile Road, west of Van Dyke, Warren. (810) 573-8100.

Hours: Lunch, 11 a.m.-4:30 p.m. Mon.-Fri.; dinner, 4:30-11 p.m. Mon.-Thu., 4:30 p.m.-midnight Fri., 5 p.m.-midnight Sat., 4-9 p.m. Sun. Closed Thanksgiving, Christmas Eve, Christmas Day and New Year's Day.

Missing: 55 percent

Full bar.   Major credit cards

Moderate.

All the glitz cannot obscure the fact that chef Bill Hall's kitchen is the focus. Hall's name may not end with the requisite vowel, but he has been an avid student of Italian cuisine for many years. He lived in Italy, soaking up atmosphere and skills. He continues to research the cuisine, especially the peasant dishes he considers that country's greatest food.

Appetizers range from baked stuffed baby eggplant to polenta and sauteed tagliatelle with four cheeses, prosciutto and pinenuts. In addition to pastas, salads are also offered in two portion sizes.

The side dish of pasta served with such main courses as sauteed veal with mushrooms and white wine or sauteed perch with fresh sage and lemon changes regularly. Chances are slim it will be spagetti with meat sauce.

There's too much imagination in the kitchen for that.

For those who want more than just food, Arriva has dinner shows on a regular basis, and there's also a downstairs jazz room with entertainment on Wednesday by the Johnny Trudell sextet and on Friday and Saturday by Alexander Zonjic.

Asian Garden

☆ ☆ ☆

37702 Van Dyke at 16½ Mile Road, Sterling Heights. (810) 978-0110.

Hours: 11 a.m.-9 p.m. Mon.-Thu., 11 a.m.-10 p.m. Fri.; noon-10 p.m. Sat., noon-9 p.m. Sun. Closed major holidays.

Nonsmoking: 65 percent.

No bar.   MC and Visa

Reasonable.

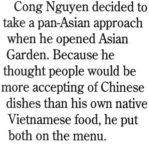

Cong Nguyen decided to take a pan-Asian approach when he opened Asian Garden. Because he thought people would be more accepting of Chinese dishes than his own native Vietnamese food, he put both on the menu.

To further enhance the theme, he decorated the front window with the shoji screens and bonsai and bamboo plants of Japan — silk ones rather than live — and borrowed the Japanese custom of presenting a hot, damp towel before food is served.

Nguyen is an accountant by trade, and that's a boon in the tough restaurant business.

In two dinner visits, it wasn't possible to delve too deeply into the extensive Chinese menu, but I did manage to try several of the dishes on the Vietnamese side. That list has steadily expanded as people have become more comfortable with Vietnamese cooking. It's a cuisine that is lighter and more delicate than Chinese, with clean, sometimes nearly invisible sauces, and well-balanced spiciness.

My favorite of all was the soft-shell crab (cua lot rang muoi), two crispy crabs enhanced with finely chopped red and small green hot peppers and browned bits of garlic accented with an intricately cut tomato. It is served as an entree but also works well as a shared appetizer.

Another interesting dish from the Vietnamese side of the menu is Lucky Spicy Beef (bo luc lac), well-marinated chunks of tender beef, again in a very light sauce sparked with sweet onion slices. And still another: a crispy roast chicken (ga duc lo) cut into beautiful white chunks.

The Chinese menu includes all the favorites, from sweet-and-sour chicken to moo shu pork, as well as such esoteric stuff as squid with spicy black bean garlic sauce and a number of tofu, vegetarian and noodle dishes.

Vietnamese coffee, a strong French roast with chicory, is an especially popular drink with Nguyen's fellow Vietnamese.

Shiny white walls accented with light wood, well-chosen pieces of Asian art and tables covered with fresh white paper give the room a crisp, polished look. Housekeeping standards are high.

Ayse's Courtyard Cafe

Turkish food has been a rarity locally. To the best of my knowledge, this is the only place to find it in the metro area. The 20-seat spot not far from the North Campus of the University of Michigan is immaculate and attractive with its patterned wallpaper, big windows and classical music in the background.

☆ ☆ ☆

1703 Plymouth Road, Ann Arbor. (313) 662-1711.

Hours: 11 a.m.-8 p.m. Mon.-Thu., 11 a.m.-9 p.m. Fri.-Sat. Closed Sun. and major holidays.

Nonsmoking: 100 percent.

No bar.   No credit cards.

Reasonable.

When Ayse (pronounced Eye-she) Uras opened the cafe, she expected it to be predominately carry-out. But not so. "People came in and sat down, so we started serving them," she says, and she continues to do so, using real china and flatware, not the throwaways that might be expected.

The room itself, boasting a baker's rack filled with Turkish imports including hot pepper sauce, jams and candy, is a model of cleanliness. I can well understand why people didn't just rush out with their bags and boxes. It's simply a pleasant place to sit and enjoy the fragrance emanating from the tiny kitchen.

What's cooking? Perhaps red peppers stuffed with a delicate mixture of rice, ground beef, mint, dill and flat-leaf parsley — herbs that, along with coriander and crushed red pepper, are prominent in this cuisine.

Among the typical main dishes are spicy lamb, beef or vegetable stew, meat pizzas called lahmacun, and meat-stuffed eggplant. Soups are notable, including ezo, a blend of yogurt, tomato, mint and vermicelli; lentil; and yogurt, dill and cucumber.

Other staples include cheese, spinach and potato pastries (borek); a changing array of vegetarian side dishes, and salads ranging from lentil to baby eggplant.

Everything is displayed in a glass-enclosed case. Diners simply browse the case and choose what they want. The food is served to their table, along with Turkish juices or soft drinks, iced tea and, of course, strong Turkish coffee in tiny cups.

Uras is the first in her family to be a restaurateur. Her husband, Mehmet Uras, teaches mechanical engineering at Wayne State University.

Bamboo Garden

☆ ☆ ☆

**2600 N. Saginaw Road, Midland.
(517) 832-7967.**

Hours: Lunch, 11:30 a.m.-2 p.m. weekdays; dinner, 4-8:30 p.m. Mon.-Thu., 4-9:30 p.m. Fri., 5-9:30 p.m. Sat., noon-8 p.m. Sun. Closed New Year's Day.

Nonsmoking: 80 percent.

Full bar.　　　　MC, Visa and Discover.

Moderate.

Carl and Evangeline Chow's attractive restaurant has a dressy look, with its dark mahogany furnishings set off by burgundy fabric, fresh flowers and white linens. And the menu measures up to the expectations aroused by the setting, offering four regional cuisines of China, though perhaps there's a little more emphasis on the dishes of Sichuan since the two top chefs are from that area.

Fairly regular trips to China keep the Chows up to date on what the chefs in their homeland are doing. But when it comes to wine, they are strictly USA, spotlighting both Michigan and the Pacific Northwest.

A good wine list in a Chinese restaurant? Rare, but it happens. And it's happened here.

Bangkok Cafe

☆ ☆

**323 W. Nine Mile Road, Ferndale.
(810) 548-5373.**

Hours: 11 a.m.-10 p.m. Mon.-Sat. Closed Sun. and major holidays.

Nonsmoking: 40 percent.

Soft drinks only.　　　No credit cards.

Reasonable.

The reassuringly modest price structure at this spot on Ferndale's Nine Mile Road is just one of the reasons why it is so popular. It's certainly hard to beat prices like $4.75 for vegetable curry or $6.50 for a seafood and red curry dish called Three's Company, with its shrimp, scallops and crabmeat, green peppers, bamboo shoots and mushrooms.

For just an extra $1, main dishes come with one of the three house soups — the Thai version of hot and sour, sizzling rice, or the coconut milk-based tom kha gai. Amazingly enough, since the place opened in 1990, some prices have never changed. Others are up only a matter of 25 or 50 cents.

The long, narrow setting is casual, noisy but attractive. The open kitchen along the west wall is, of course, the nerve center of the place. Diners seated at tables on either side of the kitchen, or on a canopied pine deck opposite the kitchen, seem to love watching the flames erupt around the woks.

It's just part of the experience of Thai, a cuisine that has become one of the area's favorites.

Bangkok Cuisine

The Sterling Heights spot is the grandaddy of all the Thai restaurants in the area. It was the first to make its mark and survive on a long-term basis. In the process of introducing Thai food to the area, it spawned several more restaurants and probably will continue to do so.

Proprietors Montree and Somnuk Arpachinda also are involved in the Bangkok Express franchises in Farmington, Southfield and Waterford. It all started in 1983 in this surprisingly attractive hideaway in a modest shopping strip in Sterling Heights. The addition of beer and wine a few years back gave the location an added boost. Beer is especially good with the spicy fare.

No beer, though, in the former Big Boy in downtown Rochester, which became the second Bangkok Cuisine in '94. It's something of a tropical bird in a cage of canaries, but you can say that about the original, too.

☆ ☆ ☆

2240 Metro Parkway at Dequindre, Sterling Heights. (810) 977-0130.

Hours: Lunch, 11 a.m.-3 p.m. weekdays; dinner, 5-9:30 p.m. Mon.-Thu., 5-10:30 p.m. Fri., 4-10:30 p.m. Sat., 4-9:30 p.m. Sun. Closed major holidays.

727 N. Main Street, Rochester. (810) 652-8841.

Hours: 11 a.m.-9:30 p.m. Mon.-Thu., 11 a.m.-10:30 p.m. Fri., noon-10:30 p.m. Sat., noon-8:30 p.m. Sun. Closed major holidays.

Nonsmoking: 80 percent in Sterling Heights, 90 percent in Rochester.

Beer and wine in Sterling Heights only.

AE, MC and Visa.

Reasonable.

The now-familiar menu is the same at both places and includes a la carte appetizers and soups, ranging from spring rolls to the classic coconut milk and chicken soup, tom kha gai. There are numerous stir-fries and curries involving beef, pork, chicken and fish, as well as vegetables and fried rice.

About half the dishes are starred as hot and spicy, but there are cooler dishes. The best Thai meals include both spicy and bland dishes.

Most dishes may be ordered with a choice of meats or seafood as one of the ingredients. For instance, if you decide that string beans, baby corn, bamboo shoots, eggplant and hot curry (gan pha) sounds good, you may order the combination with chicken, beef, pork, squid or catfish. A mix of basil leaves and sweet peppers (pad baia gra prow) may be chosen with minced chicken, beef, pork or mussels.

Sauces are light here. They range from Thai chili sauce to green or red curry, sweet-and-sour, mushroom and coconut.

It's important to let the server know exactly how hot you want the food. On one occasion when our table asked for medium spice level, we got mild. In fact, the dishes were disappointingly bland.

One veteran of many Thai meals advises next time to make sure the word "hot" is conveyed to the server in no uncertain terms. Some servers just can't seem to accept that non-Thais are ready for the typical spicing level.

Some key words on this and other Thai menus include *gang,* which means curry; *pad,* which is saute; *pak,* vegetables; and *prik,* peppers. Knowing these few words can simplify the task of choosing from an array of unusual-sounding offerings.

Bangkok Express

254 W. Nine Mile Road, Ferndale.
(810) 545-8760.

Hours: 11 a.m.-8 p.m. Mon.-Thu., 11 a.m.-9 p.m. Fri.-Sat. Closed Sun. and major holidays.

Nonsmoking: 60 percent.

Soft drinks only.　　　　No credit cards.

Reasonable.

The words "fast food" take on new meaning at this tiny outpost of fiery Thai food. Al Ly and his staff will dish up pad Thai or a seafood saute almost as quickly as you can order it at the counter in front of the open kitchen.

The 28-seat spot has been around for nearly 10 years. Though it is completely basic and has few amenities, it offers a satisfying experience.

Unless you're the one standing over those flaming woks on a hot summer day.

Bangkok Tiger

The Dearborn spot came first. My Hang and Lee Say, from Laos but with some time spent in Thailand, opened it in a budget-style motel after working in the kitchen at Bangkok Cuisine in Sterling Heights.

The second spot came a couple of years later, when they transformed a former Taco Bell. Score another for the Thai food craze, which continues to sweep the area. Both restaurants are down-to-earth and unpretentious. Menus are relatively brief at lunch, more extensive in the evening.

Lunch is an especially good value, because soup is complimentary. Those who wish to add $1 to the price of the main dish receive fried rice and a garlic chicken wing. In the evening, the menu is completely a la carte.

☆ ☆

**25125 Michigan Avenue, Dearborn.
(313) 274-2450.**

Hours: 11 a.m.-10 p.m. Mon.-Thu., 11 a.m.-11 p.m. Fri., noon-11 p.m. Sat., 4-10 p.m. Sun. Closed major holidays.

**13360 Eureka Road, Southgate.
(313) 284-2928.**

Hours: 11 a.m.-9:30 p.m. Mon.-Thu., 11 a.m.-10:30 p.m. Fri., noon-10 p.m. Sat., 4-9 p.m. Sun. Closed major holidays.

Nonsmoking: 50 percent.

Soft drinks only.   Major credit cards.

Reasonable.

The Bank 1884

The fact that Marilyn and Tony Berry's restaurant is in a building with a historic designation is just one reason to visit. The food can stand on its own — in fact, it probably will surprise a lot of people with its quality.

The building opened as the Winsor Snover bank on July 18, 1884. But other "traditions" here include the sourdough bread direct from the source, San Francisco, an all-premium bar that also stocks the "designer water of the moment," and wonderful fish and seafood dishes. Walleye is a particular favorite. Daily specials augment the printed menu, and desserts are freshly made, just like everything else. This is Port Austin's pride.

☆ ☆ ☆

**8646 Lake Street, Port Austin.
(517) 738-5353.**

Hours: Memorial Day to Labor Day, 5-10 p.m. Tue.-Sun.; May, Sept. and Oct., 5-10 p.m. Fri.-Sat. Closed Mon. and Nov.-April.

Nonsmoking: 50 percent.

Full bar.   AE, MC and Visa.

Moderate.

Beverly Hills Grill

31471 Southfield Road, between 13 and 14 Mile roads, Beverly Hills. (810) 642-2355.

Hours: Breakfast, 7 a.m.-11 a.m. Mon.-Thu., 8 a.m.-4 p.m. Sat., 8:30 a.m.-4 p.m. Sun.; lunch, 11 a.m.-4:30 p.m. weekdays; dinner, 4:30-11 p.m. Mon.-Thu., 4:30 p.m.-midnight Fri.-Sat., 4-10 p.m. Sun. Closed major holidays.

Nonsmoking: 66 percent.

Full bar.   Major credit cards.

Moderate.

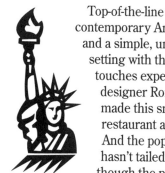

Top-of-the-line contemporary American fare and a simple, uncluttered setting with the witty touches expected of designer Ron Rea have made this small restaurant a major hit. And the popularity hasn't tailed off even though the place is several years into its run.

Unlike some spots that are packed in the early going, then as quickly deserted by their fickle clientele, Bill and Judi Roberts' airy spot just continues on, undisturbed by competition.

Patrick Roettele is the current chef, dishing up a menu that usually has some surprises chalked on the board. He also sticks with perennially attractive dishes, such as Creole rock shrimp on angelhair pasta, corned beef hash with eggs, and turkey Reubens at lunch, and shrimp scampi, an array of Caesar salad interpretations and roasted chicken with mashed potatoes at dinner.

Breakfast is especially winning, including classic eggs Benedict, cinnamon French toast, the breakfast burrito with fennel sausage, and scrambled eggs.

The setting is casual and patrons' garb runs the gamut from aerobics gear to drop-dead chic.

Bev's Caribbean Kitchen

1232 Packard Avenue, Ann Arbor. (313) 741-5252.

Hours: 11:30 a.m.-9 p.m. Tue.-Sat., 2-7 p.m. Sun. Closed Mon. and major holidays.

Nonsmoking: 100 percent.

Soft drinks only.   No credit cards.

Reasonable.

It's not easy to find island fare in Michigan. This spot, aromatic with allspice, hot peppers, nutmeg and mango chutney, is a true oasis. Beverley Taylor-Glaza is a Jamaican who prefers to use the word Caribbean to describe her fare, because she wants to attract those from other islands as well as her own.

From the brightly painted exterior to

the cheery green cafe curtains in the window, and with the pulsating background music and those tantalizing aromas, there's plenty to like about Bev's tiny corner.

Many people order her sandwiches of jerk chicken or pork, the highly spiced hot-and-sweet meat on hard-dough bread. They are hard to resist. Also wonderful are the curries of chicken or goat, the gently fried sweet potatoes, and roti (flatbread wrapped around potatoes, ground chickpeas and meat or vegetables).

Tiny salads of lettuce, carrot, red cabbage and tomato come with most dishes. Island soft drinks include ginger beer, and guava, mango and sour sop nectars.

In a place so small, there's no room for real plates and cutlery, so disposables are used for those who stay as well as carry out. Five stools pulled up to a counter in the window constitute the seating availability.

In suitable weather, many people tote their food to Burns Park or one of the vest pocket parks in the area.

Big Daddy's Parthenon

It was bound to be a huge hit. The menu offers dishes in the Greektown tradition: lamb chops, shish kebab, roast lamb, moussaka, stuffed grape leaves, calamari, lemon chicken, and on and on — and people in the northwest area don't have to drive miles to get them.

6199 Orchard Lake Road, north of Maple, West Bloomfield. (810) 737-8600.

Hours: 11 a.m.-midnight Sun.-Thu., 11 a.m.-1 a.m. Fri-Sat. Closed Christmas Day.

Nonsmoking: 80 percent.

Full bar.   AE, MC and Visa.

Moderate.

This is Greektown in the suburbs, and people love it. Partners Tommy Peristeris, formerly of Greektown's New Parthenon, and Rick Rogow obviously struck a nerve with their menu and the Ron Rea-designed setting done up in bright blue and white and decked out with a mural of the Parthenon and maps of the Greek islands.

At Big Daddy's, the Greek salad, spinach pie, tomato-sauced rice and the obligatory overcooked green beans — all the dishes that have kept Greektown going for lo, these many years — retain their appeal.

The menu stays the same all day. While at first glance, it doesn't look that expensive, prices are erratic. Five lamb chops at $21.95, with just potato or rice and vegetable as accompaniments, could be called steep. So could shrimp over rice at $16.95. Yet, there are many dishes in the $7-$8.95 range.

This is a see-and-be-seen place, noisy and bustling most of the time with a multi-generational crowd. Who am I to criticize such obvious success?

Big Fish; Big Fish Too

Big Fish ☆ ☆ 1/2

700 Town Center Drive, Dearborn.
(313) 336-6350.

Hours: 11 a.m.-10 p.m. Mon.-Thu., 11 a.m.-11 p.m. Fri.-Sat., 1-9 p.m. Sun. Closed Thanksgiving, Christmas, Labor Day and Memorial Day.

Nonsmoking: 70 percent.

Full bar.   Major credit cards.

Moderate.

Big Fish Too ☆ ☆ 1/2

14 Mile Road corner of Stephenson Hwy., Madison Heights.
(810) 585-9533.

Hours: 11 a.m.-11 p.m. Mon.-Thu., 11 a.m.-midnight Fri.-Sat., 3-9 p.m. Sun. Closed Christmas and New Year's Day.

Nonsmoking: 65 percent.

Full bar.   Major credit cards.

Moderate.

Now, what do you suppose would be the specialty at restaurants called "Big Fish?" Right.

These Chuck Muer restaurants have seasonally changing menus of fresh fish and seafood. Alternates are pastas — Muer restaurants spotlight pastas, too, and have for some time — and there's always a steak on the menu for the unreconstructed meat eaters in the crowd.

While the settings are bright and casual, especially at Big Fish Too, they are not nearly as informal as they were in the days when these places were known as family taverns. The decor was upgraded a couple of years ago, and while not as plush as the flagship Charley's Crab in Troy, both places now offer a little more atmosphere.

Like the settings, today's more ambitious menus are not interchangeable. Hugely popular dishes in Dearborn are the potato-encrusted whitefish and crabcakes. In Madison Heights, crowd pleasers are the parchment-encased hollow linguini noodles cooked with fish stew, San Francisco style and rotisserie lobster.

The trimmings are notable here. Three different salads, from house to cole slaw, are offered with dinner, the famous Muer hot bread is served until guests say "Stop," and fresh vegetables come along with most dishes.

Billingsgate

Originally a circa-1906 church, this picturesque structure surrounded by gardens in the farm country village of Horton was an antique shop when Raymond and Cynthia Holland bought it in the mid-'80s. They saw it as a getaway-style restaurant that would draw people from the city.

And they were right. People drive miles to dine in the unusual setting, with its hand-carved woodwork, stained glass and antique furnishings. Tables are set on the main floor and in the choir loft.

At first the Hollands served only on weekends, but another evening has been added to the schedule. On Thursdays, the three-course meal is $16.95, chosen from a list of soup, salad, eight entrees and four desserts.

More elaborate five-course meals are served the other nights at $29 (plus tax and gratuity). On those days, the choice is among three appetizers, two salads, four entrees and three desserts. The menu changes monthly, but always includes a beef, poultry, fish or seafood choice as well as a vegetarian dish.

Cynthia Holland researches a library of cookbooks to come up with ideas for the dinners, which are leisurely affairs. No one is rushed. Because of the pace and style of preparation, there are no provisions for small children.

☆ ☆ ☆

101 Main Street, Horton.
(517) 563-2943.

Hours: Dinner only, 6-8 p.m. Thu., 5:30-9 p.m. Fri.-Sat., 1-6 p.m. Sun. Closed Mon.-Wed. and major holidays.

Nonsmoking: 90 percent.

Full bar.   AE, MC and Visa.

Moderate.

Bill's Duck Inn

Bill and Pat Allen built their restaurant around a collection of duck decoys and wildlife memorabilia. The theme extends to baskets, print fabrics, brass and glass, lending a cozy, small-town air to the place.

The quintessential American menu ranges from frog legs, perch and pickerel to pork chops. This lineup looks unchanged from decades ago — even though the place itself is just 11 years old. Clam chowder on Fridays? Eighteen-

 ☆ ☆

7200 S. River Road, Marine City.
(810) 765-3210.

Hours: 11 a.m.-10 p.m. Mon.-Thu., 11 a.m.-11 p.m. Fri.-Sat., noon-10 p.m. Sun. Closed Christmas Day.

Nonsmoking: 60 percent.

Full bar.   Major credit cards.

Reasonable.

ounce cuts of prime rib? Surf and turf? Of course.

Dinner accompaniments include a choice of potato, salad, bread and a vegetable du jour.

One specialty, not surprisingly, is the roast duck dinner for two ($29.95, including a choice among a number of dressings and glazes). Strictly for plan-ahead types, it must be ordered 24 hours in advance.

Blackjacks Saloon

 1/2

656 Pitt Street West, Windsor, Ontario. (519) 252-2121.

Hours: 11 a.m.-11 p.m. Mon.-Sat., 4-11 p.m. Sun. Closed Christmas Day, Dec. 26 and New Year's Day.

Nonsmoking: 50 percent.

Full bar.   AE, MC and Visa.

Reasonable.

Paul Lavender, who successively ran Traiteurs and then Traiteurs Bistro in the west-side Windsor neighborhood known as Old Towne, now prefers to call the area the "Casino District."

And that explains the name on the oddly shaped little building he's now very glad he hung onto while engaged in other pursuits. While it may sound like a belly-up-to-the-bar kind of place, it's much more comparable to the quiet and food-oriented Traiteurs Bistro than it is to a gamblers' hangout. The dining room is tastefully done in deep terra cotta and soft yellow with linen-covered tables. The bar is more casual with its dark wood paneling.

Fans of Traiteurs will find some of the old dishes on the menu — things like baked Camembert cheese and steamed mussels — but this time the approach is a little less French, a little less Mediterranean than before.

While a grazing style is prominent — more than a dozen appetizers lead off the dinner menu — many solid dishes are there, too. These include steaks, pan-seared tenderloin with mustard cream sauce and grilled marinated lamb chops.

Other options are the quintessential Canadian fish and chips (the spicy chips are irresistible), salmon with mustard glaze, pork schnitzel with apple sauce and the ever-popular chicken Caesar salad.

Each entree is teamed with appropriate accompaniments, such as grilled vegetables, rice pilaf, mixed greens or good home fries.

Particularly notable, of all things, is that ubiquitous bar snack, chicken wings. Lavender came up with a spice mixture while he was with the Chinese carry-out company, Ho Lee Chow, and it gives the wings real character. It's a blend of teriyaki sauce, fresh ginger, garlic, sesame oil, hot chili paste and white pepper.

In warm weather, the patio, with its view of the Detroit skyline, is an especially nice place to dine.

Blue Nile

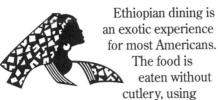

Ethiopian dining is an exotic experience for most Americans. The food is eaten without cutlery, using bread to scoop up the meat or vegetable stews heaped on it. The circle of spongy bread called injera is both plate and part of the meal.

A communal injera platter is shared by those who dine together. In Detroit, traditional chairs are made of carved wood with goatskin-covered cushions just 18 inches off the floor. They are pulled up to tables that resemble woven baskets. Proprietors Seifu Lessanework and Felli Mekasha brought furnishings from their homeland and these add wonderful flavor to the experience.

Dinners are served as complete entities, with one version spotlighting meat ($14.90), the other meatless ($11.90). Spice levels range from moderately spicy to bland.

☆ ☆ ☆

508 Monroe Street, Detroit. (313) 964-6699.

Hours: 5-10 p.m. Mon.-Thu., 4-11 p.m. Fri.-Sat., 3-9 p.m. Sun. Closed Thanksgiving, Christmas and New Year's Day.

Nonsmoking: 80 percent.

Full bar. Major credit cards.

Moderate.

317 Braun Court, Ann Arbor. (313) 663-3116.

Hours: 4-9 p.m. Tue.-Thu., Sun., 3-10:30 p.m. Fri.-Sat. Closed Mon. and Thanksgiving, Christmas and New Year's Day.

Nonsmoking: 100 percent.

Soft drinks only. Major credit cards.

Moderate.

Blue Pointe

The daily-changing menu focuses on fresh fish, seafood and Italian dishes. Pan-fried catfish, pickerel baked in a crust of Italian seasonings, manicotti and veal Parmesan are typical of the fare. Dinner includes a choice of two among soup, an especially nice green salad, spaghetti and potato. It's a fine value.

David Muer, a distant relation of the Muer seafood family, has certainly proven himself in 12 some years at this

17131 E. Warren, just east of Cadieux, Detroit. (313) 882-3653.

Hours: Lunch, 11 a.m.-4 p.m. Tue.-Fri.; dinner, 4-10 p.m. Tue.-Thu., 4-11 p.m. Fri.-Sat., 2:30-10 p.m. Sun. Closed Mon. and Christmas and New Year's Day.

Nonsmoking: 55 percent.

Full bar. Major credit cards.

Reasonable.

location. East side families have been coming here since it was Lambardi's (source of the Italian dishes), but in Muer's hands it has steadily improved over the years.

The service staff is friendly and competent, the decor simple, the aspirations well within the grasp of everyone involved. While certainly not an exciting, see-and-be-seen place, Blue Pointe has many good qualities and doesn't try to be anything but what it is. Every neighborhood should have a restaurant as solid as this one.

Boodles

☆ ☆ ☆

935 W. 11 Mile Road at I-75, Madison Heights. (810) 399-5960.

Hours: Lunch, 11:30 a.m.-4:30 p.m.; dinner, 4:30-11 p.m. Mon.-Thu., 4:30 p.m.-midnight Fri.-Sat., 4-10 p.m. Sun.; Sun. brunch (mid-Sept.-mid-May), 10:30 a.m.-2:30 p.m. Closed Thanksgiving, Christmas, New Year's Day, Fourth of July and Sun. and Mon. of Labor Day weekend.

Nonsmoking: 60 percent.

Full bar.   Major credit cards.

Moderate.

Boodles is "Cheers" with a pastry cart. And a pastry chef, I might add. Yvette Deane has been here for years, turning out fresh breads and desserts to tempt the clientele.

So, despite its neighborhood bar persona, Bruno Ferguson and Timothy Kowalec's restaurant just off the freeway has definite ambitions.

The menu includes a lot of fancy-restaurant dishes you might have thought had disappeared. There's the very popular steak Diane, cooked at table side; crepes Suzette, and appetizers like Boursin cheese wrapped in filo in an especially pretty presentation.

More casual dishes are available, too, giving patrons a wide choice. Sunday brunch, during the fall, winter and early spring months, has become a draw, perhaps because of the fajitas bar, the made-to-order omelets and eggs Benedict, as well as the pastry chef's fresh desserts.

Because of its strategic, easily accessible location, Boodles is known as the place where "east meets west."

Brandy's

The younger generation has taken over at the restaurant established by Fred Gracyzyk after he sold the Vineyards in Southfield. When Fred's wife, Diane, persuaded him to retire to Florida, son Nick was ready in the wings. Nick, who worked with his dad for several years, is now the proprietor of this low-key spot that hides its dusky charm behind an anonymous exterior.

☆ ☆ 1/2

1727 S. Telegraph Road, Bloomfield Hills. (810) 338-4300.

Hours: 11 a.m.-10 p.m. Mon.-Thu., 11 a.m.-11 p.m. Fri., 4-11 p.m. Sat. Closed Sun. and major holidays.

Nonsmoking: 50 percent.

Full bar.   Major credit cards.

Moderate.

And since everything old seems to be new again, the menu these days spotlights steak. In fact, whole strip loins are brought to table side, and cut and trimmed right there to the diners' specifications. Steak is sold by the ounce, at $1.25 per, and says the younger Gracyzyk, "We're a steak house now!" Who would have thought it?

A choice of mixed green salad with the house ranch poppyseed dressing or a Caesar accompanies entrees, as do soup and potato, and there's a small list of simple, housemade desserts.

One Gracyzyk tradition that continues is the availability of a certain red wine. It's Chateau Greysac, a Bordeaux, which is available by the glass or bottle.

Fred Gracyzyk learned about the wine more than 22 years ago. Detroit restaurateur Joe Beyer came into the Vineyards after a trip to France and told him he'd found a "chateau that has your name on it." The wine has been served ever since, first at the late, lamented Vineyards, now at Brandy's.

Brighton Bar & Grill

☆ ☆ 1/2

400 W. Main Street, Brighton.
(810) 229-4115.

Hours: 11 a.m.-10 p.m. Mon.-Thu., 11 a.m.-11 p.m. Fri.-Sat., noon-9 p.m. Sun. Closed Thanksgiving and Christmas.

Nonsmoking: 75 percent.

Full bar.   Major credit cards.

Reasonable.

The town of Brighton welcomed this cheerfully casual restaurant from the very start in 1990. And the ever-changing menu that ranges from fresh fish to signature steaks continues to pack them in.

Steaks are especially hot these days, as the pendulum swings once again and people go back to the basics. Two especially popular ones are the Sante Fe porterhouse, rubbed in a dry Southwestern spice marinade and seared on the griddle, and the top sirloin called the Aussie, with a bow in the direction of the flourishing Outback Steakhouses in the area.

Things have been busy enough in Brighton to inspire proprietors Craig and Renee Heath to open their second restaurant in the town. Called Genoa, it's a casual Italian spot with a wood-burning oven and a rustic menu of pizzas and pastas.

Britt's Cafe

☆ ☆ ☆

151 W. Fort, Detroit.
(313) 963-4866.

Hours: Lunch, 11 a.m.-3 p.m. weekdays. Closed Sat., Sun. and major holidays.

Nonsmoking: 100 percent.

Soft drinks only.   No credit cards.

Reasonable.

Cafeteria menus are rarely as imaginative as this one, which offers an array of made-to-order sandwiches, two hot main dishes and two hot soups each day. Side dishes include fresh fruit, pasta salad and mixed greens. Homey desserts are another plus.

There's an ensemble feeling to the place, which is fostered by chef/proprietor Jim Britt. He cares about his staff as well as his customers.

Though the amenities are few — throwaways are the order of the day, and everyone knows to bus his or her own table — the quality of the food is recognized by knowledgeable diners. These include Detroit Mayor Dennis Archer, a number of judges and attorneys. When the same faces reappear in the line day after day, that says something about a place.

Broadstreet

The creative approach of chef/proprietor Luis Fernandes is what powers this small-town restaurant with big-city aspirations. The 1985 graduate of Michigan State University has an interesting multi-ethnic background, and he puts it into play. From the island of Macao near Hong Kong, and with a Portuguese/Chinese heritage, he loves a lively spice level.

Recently, Fernandes has been experimenting with what he calls "mountain cuisine" — Colorado beef, buffalo and lamb served with roasted garlic and sauteed mushrooms, or Denver barbecue sauce, Cantonese barbecue sauce, and whole grain mustard.

The accompanying fries are made of sweet potato, one of his favorite vegetables. He also offers a choice of wild mushroom-mashed potatoes or grilled potato cakes with the mountain fare. And it's a winner.

From the regular menu, diners may choose from a wide array of hot appetizers from chicken tempura and oyster fritters to Louisiana crab cakes, and such entrees as five-spice crispy duck, fricassee of whitefish and grilled pork loin. These give an idea of the versatility of this interesting spot.

103-107 E. Broad Street, Linden. (810) 735-5844.

Hours: 11 a.m.-10 p.m. Tue.-Thu., 11 a.m.-11 p.m. Fri.-Sat., noon-9 p.m. Sun. Closed Mon., major holidays and the first week in January.

Nonsmoking: 75 percent.

Full bar. AE, MC and Visa.

Moderate.

Bruschetta Cafe

What a surprise to find a cozy little Italian restaurant in one of the biggest malls in Michigan.

There are no brick-paved streets here. No white-aproned proprietor with a broom. But once inside the warm and inviting space that houses Bruschetta (pronounced brew-SKET-ta), you seem to leave the mall behind. The setting is in keeping with the fare: bright and festive, with seating for 82 in church pew booths, at tables, at the marble-topped bar and at a perch overlooking the kitchen. Every

Oakland Mall, 14 Mile Road at I-75, Troy. (810) 589-2900.

Hours: 11 a.m.-10 p.m. Mon.-Thu., 11 a.m.-11 p.m. Fri.-Sat., noon-8 p.m. Sun. Closed Thanksgiving and Christmas Day.

Nonsmoking: 70 percent.

Full bar. Major credit cards.

Reasonable.

part of the restaurant is open to view, including the stainless steel kitchen.

Sunset-pink walls are set off by dark wood, the gleam of solid copper, the glow of Italian pottery, and splashes of color from a huge bouquet of sunflowers.

The premise is fresh, light dishes. You'll find mostly pastas, salads and sandwiches, plus a few classics like eggplant Parmesan. It's a menu that absolutely zeroes in on what the kitchen can do quickly and well.

There are half a dozen variations on the bruschetta theme, from tomatoes, basil, olive oil, Parmesan and garlic atop the thick slices of grilled bread to toppings of grilled eggplant, sweet peppers, olives and herbs.

Inside Oakland Mall's gargantuan 1.4 million square feet, this interesting, cozy spot of only 2,400 square feet offers a much-needed oasis of fresh food.

Buddy's Pizza

Six Mile and Conant, Detroit.
(313) 892-9001.

31646 Northwestern Hwy.,
Farmington Hills. (810) 855-4600.

22148 Michigan Avenue, Dearborn.
(313) 562-5900.

33605 Plymouth Road, Livonia.
(313) 261-3550.

8100 Old 13 Mile Road, Warren.
(810) 574-9200.

4370 Highland Road, Waterford.
(810) 683-3636.

Hours: 11 a.m.-11 p.m. Mon.-Thu., 11 a.m.-midnight Fri.-Sat., noon-10 p.m. Sun. Closed Thanksgiving and Christmas Day.

Nonsmoking: 75 percent.

Full bar.   Major credit cards.

Reasonable.

Quintessential Detroit pizzas have been turned out since the '40s by this local chain, which retains a family-restaurant appeal even after spreading far and wide. Friendly service and unpretentious settings are the hallmark of Buddy's, though in recent times, some of the suburban locations have been given more visual appeal.

The menu includes a number of solid Italian-American dishes (or should that be American-Italian?). But the soups, sandwiches, pastas and salads take a back seat to the thick square pizzas, which remain a favorite.

These are full-service restaurants. The chain also includes a few carry-out cafes with just a few seats.

Cadieux Cafe

Very much a neighborhood bar in atmosphere and ambitions, this 35-year-old spot draws a diverse crowd for its brief menu headed by steamed mussels as well as for its sports activities: feather bowling and English darts.

The big, main dining room has long rows of tables that look as if they expect parties of 10 and 12, and often get them. Presiding is an old-fashioned back-bar, the room's focal point.

Buckets of steamed mussels and spinach mashed potatoes uphold the Belgian food tradition, as does the Sunday special, roast rabbit. Other dishes have found their way onto the menu, including hamburgers, big Greek salads and Cajun chicken salad.

**4300 Cadieux Road, Detroit.
(313) 882-8560.**

Hours: 4-11 p.m. Mon.-Wed., 11 a.m.-11 p.m. Thu., 11 a.m.-midnight Fri.-Sat., 4-10 p.m. Sun. Closed major holidays except Labor Day.

Nonsmoking: 20 percent.

Full bar.   Major credit cards.

Reasonable.

Cafe Appareil

Proprietors Joseph Stetson and Rosemary Purtell met at the Culinary Institute of America in Hyde Park, N.Y., and quickly became cooking partners. The couple — she from Michigan, he from Florida — are still at it, in their offbeat cafe which by day is a modest Coney Island called Caris' Red Lion.

When they bought the venerable place a couple of years after their CIA graduation, the two decided the Coney Island should be preserved. It had been a popular Bay City spot for many years. So, they've kept the place intact during the day, and added linens, soft lights and more elaborate cooking in the evening.

At 6 p.m., the Coney Islands are nowhere to be seen and the place becomes Cafe Appareil — the French word for "mixture" or "combination." They believe it describes their culinary style nicely, which integrates many influences from French and Asian to Midwestern. The common denominator is freshness and quality.

The menu changes every night. It begins with a few appetizers, possibly fresh

**201 Center Avenue, Bay City.
(517) 893-7105.**

Hours: Dinner only, 6-10 p.m. Mon.-Sat. Closed Sun. and major holidays.

Nonsmoking: 80 percent.

Full bar.   MC and Visa.

Moderate.

buffalo mozzarella, Roma tomatoes and herb oil, or grilled soy-ginger marinated chicken with pickled green papaya.

Main dishes might be marinated leg of lamb with dried fruit compote, sauteed whitefish with a crispy cayenne potato pancake, or medallions of veal.

Lovely salads come with the entrees, and there are two or three fresh desserts. One special favorite is apple pie with fresh caramel sauce. Bay City is lucky to have this interesting, two-sided restaurant in the heart of town.

Cafe Bon Homme

844 Penniman, Plymouth.
(313) 453-6260.

Hours: Lunch, 11:30 a.m.-3 p.m. weekdays; dinner, 5-9 p.m. Mon.-Thu., 5-10 p.m. Fri.-Sat. Closed Sun. and major holidays.

Nonsmoking: 100 percent.

Full bar.   AE, MC and Visa.

Expensive.

Greg Goodman's fine little spot, which shares space in the heart of town with an antique shop, may look a bit like a tea room, but there's nothing wimpy about the cuisine. Goodman calls it modern European.

Each dish is a specialty on the correctly brief menu. Choices include beautifully garnished roast pork loin, Lake Superior whitefish, pan-seared salmon and rack of lamb.

The single-page menu, simplicity itself, lists in straightforward fashion a half dozen appetizers and soups, a pair of salads and seven main courses. No inflated descriptions, no hyperbolic overstatements.

Vegetables and garnishes are distinctive to each plate. No mounds of green beans or zucchini piled indiscriminately beside the meat or fish here. The setting in soft rose and gray, with chamber music and jazz on the sound system, is soothing.

While the price structure at dinner is far from inexpensive, those who appreciate attention to detail and quality won't find the fare overpriced. The dinner entrees range from $18.95 to $27.95, including a choice of soup or salad.

House salads, like house wines, can be less than memorable. Not so here. You need to be a mathematician to count the different lacy greens, from curly endive to arugula, in the salad that comes with entrees. There's a choice of two house dressings: raspberry or mustard vinaigrette.

The cozy yet ambitious cafe is exactly what you hope to find in a nostalgia-wreathed town like Plymouth.

Cafe Edward

Chef Michael Tuma and his brother Todd prepare lovely, three-course dinners at this somewhat out-of-the-way spot. In a more accessible area, they'd be beating people away with a stick.

5010 Bay City Road, Midland.
(517) 496-3012.

Hours: Dinner only, 5-9 p.m. Mon.-Thu., 5-10 p.m. Fri. and Sat. Closed Sun. except Mother's Day, Father's Day and Easter. Closed Thanksgiving, Christmas Eve and Christmas Day.

Nonsmoking: 85 percent.

Full bar.   Visa and MC.

Moderate.

Their food is exceptionally good and exceptionally well-priced given the quality. The Tuma family has a long restaurant tradition and it continues, even though their elaborate Justine restaurant, which for some years offered five-course dinners under the same roof, could not be maintained.

Several times each year, however, the brothers revive the Justine menu for a special feast. Call, and they'll put you on the mailing list to let you know when the dinners are scheduled.

It certainly wasn't for lack of quality that Justine failed, and a stop for dinner at Cafe Edward bears that out.

The price of the entree ($11-$21) determines the price of the complete meal, including appetizer course and dessert.

A typical array might include cream of corn soup or an appetizer pizza topped with eggplant, spinach and black olives to start, followed by grilled salmon with mustard sauce or shrimp tempura, and old-fashioned chocolate layer cake for dessert.

Calabrisella Ristorante

☆ ☆ ☆

614 Erie Street East, Windsor,
Ontario. (519) 977-7306.

Hours: 11 a.m.-11 p.m. Mon.-Thu., 11 a.m.-midnight Fri.-Sat. Closed Sun., Christmas and New Year's Day.

Nonsmoking: 50 percent.

Full bar.   Major credit cards.

Reasonable.

One of many inviting, unpretentious trattorias in the heart of Windsor's Italian section, this one is especially warm because of its friendly young proprietors, Toni and Biagio Spadafora.

The sound of spoken Italian is as pervasive as the aroma of roasting peppers and veal searing in the pans. The cooking style is robust, simple and very satisfying. Pastas and veals are attractively served. The room itself has been enhanced by wallpaper in a brick pattern that has the effect of making what is basically a boxy room into something much cozier.

Among the recommended entrees are veal Calabrisella (Biagio is from Calabrisa in Italy), a dish that combines capers, mushrooms and white wine; housemade penne with wild mushrooms and tomato sauce, and spaghetti carbonara.

Carl's Chop House

☆ ☆ 1/2

3020 Grand River, Detroit.
(313) 833-0700.

Hours: 11:30 a.m.-11 p.m. Mon.-Thu., 11 a.m.-midnight Fri.-Sat.; brunch, 10:30-2:30 p.m. Sun.; dinner, 2:30-11 p.m. Sun. Closed Christmas.

Nonsmoking: 50 percent.

Full bar.   Major credit cards.

Moderate.

When the staff at the city's venerable emporium of red meat starts talking about making the dining room completely nonsmoking, you know the trend has really taken hold. And that was the discussion in early '95. Otherwise, this is a place that seems to have changed very little over the years. Founder Carl Rosenfield was still on duty well into his 90s. When the family sold the big restaurant to Frank Passalacqua in 1990, he vowed to keep the place pretty much as it was.

And he has. The classic relish tray complete with creamed herring, cottage cheese and pickled watermelon rind still comes to the table at dinner. Steaks are as humongous and earthy as ever. Though we might look nostalgically at the price structure when Rosenfield opened the place in the '30s — sirloin steak dinners were $1 — the current price of $19.50 for 16 ounces of sirloin doesn't seem out of line.

While beef is king, seafood is also spotlighted. Dover sole is perennially popular. A recent addition to the menu is a nightly pasta selection.

Carl's doesn't take its clientele for granted. For instance, its shuttle service doesn't just go to Joe Louis Arena — numerous hockey fans dine at Carl's and have for years — but to any downtown venue whatsoever, even a private meeting room.

That's probably one reason why the place is still around after all these years.

Casa Bianca

The rooms of an Edwardian house in the heart of downtown Windsor make an appropriate setting for the Italian specialties served at tableside by chef Aldo Cundari. His kitchen-bound partner Settimio (Sam) Naccarato does the behind-the-scenes work.

Cundari is well known — especially to the music-loving crowd that shares his affection for opera — as the man with the saute pans. He prepares veal piccata, shrimp provencale and spaghetti Neapolitan as diners watch.

 1/2

345 Victoria Avenue, Windsor, Ontario. (519) 253-5218.

Hours: Lunch, 11:30 a.m.-3 p.m. weekdays; dinner, 5-10 p.m. Mon.-Sat., noon-10 p.m. Sun. Closed Sun., Jan.-March; Dec. 24-26; New Year's Day and Good Friday.

Nonsmoking: 50 percent.

Full bar.   Major credit cards.

Reasonable.

It's real artistry, and he makes it look easy. Back in the kitchen, Naccarato's specialties include filet mignon and rack of lamb.

This is not the gutsy style of Windsor's Little Italy on Erie Street East, but quiet, Old World dining that is becoming harder and harder to find.

Casa de Espana

☆ ☆ 1/2

6138 Michigan Avenue, east of
Livernois, Detroit. (313) 895-4040.

Hours: Lunch, 11:30 a.m.-2 p.m. Tue.-Sat.;
dinner, 6-11 p.m. Tue.-Sat. Closed Sun.,
Mon., Thanksgiving, Christmas and New
Year's Day.

Nonsmoking: 25 percent.

Soft drinks only.   No credit cards.

Moderate.

Spanish fare is a rarity in the metropolitan area. In fact, aside from a few places that occasionally offer *tapas* (appetizers or "little plates"), Case de Espana is the only Spanish restaurant around.

Very much of a family affair is this collaboration of Juan and Eva Llobell, who hail from Valencia. The Llobells and their children live upstairs in the converted 1895 firehouse that Juan remodeled himself, even to constructing a map of Spain in blue and brown ceramic tile which is the backdrop to the stage where flamenco performers appear.

The menu is small, yet interesting. At lunch, Spanish sandwiches called bocadillos are served with a choice of sides. They include soup, salad or tapas, perhaps garlicky potatoes, garlicky shrimp or grilled fresh mushrooms.

The dinner menu is more extensive but still pared-down. Those who want lobster paella may have it if they call a day ahead. There's also duck cooked with prunes, orange juice and carrots; marinated quail; lamb shanks, and rainbow trout. Salad or soup — including garlic soup — are included with dinner. Soup is the better choice. On Friday and Saturday evenings, live music adds to the atmosphere.

Caucus Club

☆ ☆ ☆

150 W. Congress, Detroit.
(313) 965-4970.

Hours: 11 a.m.-8:30 p.m. Mon.-Thu., 11
a.m.-10 p.m. Fri. Closed Sat., Sun. and
major holidays.

Nonsmoking: 40 percent.

Full bar.   Major credit cards.

Expensive.

The intimate, dimly lit restaurant replete with gleaming copper and brass decorative pieces hangs on, hoping for more life in downtown Detroit. If that happens, its shortened hours will expand to what they were when this was a late-night spot.

The classic American menu is still being served, dishes that include baby back ribs, Dover sole, London broil and, seldom-encountered in the '90's, that old war horse steak tartare, prepared at tableside.

Chef Arthur Calloway has been in charge of the kitchen for years, and he knows how to handle this hallowed menu — right down to the Gold Brick sundae dessert.

The wine list is extensive. At holiday time every year, the bar serves another vintage item — Tom and Jerrys, which are the perfect warmup in blustery weather.

Charley's Crab

Stylish seafood items as well as traditional ones emerge from chef Peter Ashcraft's kitchen from a big, ever-changing menu that reflects seasonal availability.

In other words, don't ask for shad roe or Nantucket cape scallops in December. Whatever is fresh stars on the menu, and that includes what the restaurant calls "under-utilized" fish, such as skate wings and wolf fish.

This flagship of the C.A. Muer restaurant corporation has a setting that successfully combines baronial hall with seafood tavern. The crowd is a diverse one, from high-powered business types to big families, and the kitchen takes that into consideration.

5498 Crooks Road, Troy.
(810) 879-2060.

Hours: Lunch, 11:30 a.m.-5 p.m. weekdays; dinner, 5-10 p.m. Mon.-Thu., 5-11 p.m. Fri.-Sat., 2-9 p.m. Sun. Closed Christmas and New Year's Day.

Nonsmoking: 50 percent.

Full bar.   Major credit cards.

Moderate to expensive.

Cedar-plank cooking is one way to go — salmon is especially popular when prepared this way — and never fear, Charley's Bucket, a combination of lobster, crab, mussels, clams, corn on the cob and potatoes, a dish founder Chuck Muer came up with at the Pine Lake predecessor to this restaurant, will probably always be on the menu.

Pianist Bob Seeley, one of the world's foremost practitioners of vintage piano styles from ragtime and stride to boogie-woogie, is on hand Tuesday through Saturday in the bar.

Cheers on the Channel

☆ ☆ ☆

**6211 Pte. Tremble Road,
Pearl Beach. (810) 794-9017.**

Hours: 2-10 p.m. Sun.-Thu., 2-11 p.m. Fri.-Sat. Closed Thanksgiving, Christmas Eve, Christmas Day and Easter.

Nonsmoking: 35 percent.

Full bar.　　　　Major credit cards.

Moderate.

Anyone who delights in surprises certainly will find a pleasant one behind the modest exterior at this out-of-the-way spot.

Where you might expect to encounter burgers and fried fish, there's an ambitious menu in the hands of proprietors Ray and Paula Randall and chef Mark Clark.

A good deal of the upscale appeal comes from such dishes as roasted mandarin duck with sesame-pink peppercorn sauce, herb-rubbed filet mignon topped with Gorgonzola and port wine butter, and veal scallopini with angelhair pasta. The wine list is recognized by the Wine Spectator.

The chef isn't afraid to serve offbeat things, like sauteed mustard greens, wild mushrooms and game dishes. From November through March, he offers special culinary evenings on the first Monday of the month, each featuring a different theme.

Freshly made desserts from an ever-changing list top off the menu. Two rooms for overnight guests are upstairs at the cozy place. It's not a bed-and-breakfast, say the Randalls, but a bed-and-dinner.

Cherry Blossom

☆ ☆ ☆ ☆

West Oaks II strip mall, 43588 West Oaks Drive at Novi Road, Novi. (810) 380-9160.

Hours: Lunch, 11:30 a.m.-2 p.m. Mon.-Sat.; dinner, 5:30-10:30 p.m. Mon.-Thu., 5:30-11 p.m. Fri.-Sat., 4-10 p.m. Sun. Closed major holidays.

Nonsmoking: 50 percent.

Full bar.　　　　Major credit cards.

Moderate to expensive.

Just about anything a Japanese food fancier might desire has been thought of in these honey-beige and plum-colored rooms, typical of the clean Japanese design approach.

The three restaurateurs who put it together — chefs Seiji Ueno, a master of the art of sushi; Masahiro Ohkawa and front-of-the-house person Shigeru Yamada — have years of experience, and it shows.

No less than four menus are presented at dinner, reflecting selections from the sushi bar, the specials of the night, the yakitori selections (an array of meats and vegetables brushed with sauce and cooked on skewers on a special grill), and the big list of tempuras, teriyakis and noodle dishes.

An element of beauty infuses everything from the California roll to the slices of superb beef teriyaki and the green tea ice cream. Plates, bowls and platters in soft blues, greens and browns in a variety of shapes and sizes are all part of the harmony of the meal.

Chez Pierre Orleans

The sunny N'awlins feeling in mood and menu lingers, even though the chef that brought it here, Louie Finnan, stayed only a short time. The spirit survives at this bigger, livelier version of the original, tiny Chez Pierre that opened in '91.

☆ ☆ ☆

543 N. Main, Rochester.
(810) 650-1390.

Hours: Dinner only, 5:30-10 p.m. Mon.-Thu., 5:30-11 p.m. Fri.-Sat. Closed Sun. and major holidays.

Nonsmoking: 70 percent.

Full bar.   Major credit cards.

Expensive.

Now both classic French dishes and Creole ones share the menu, and it's in the hands of two young chefs who trained with Finnan, Rob Beebee and Sean Hartwell. In fact, chef Beebee is the fiance of Traci Finnan, Louie's daughter. That ought to keep the Southern flavor alive.

Appetizers include, in addition to snails in garlic butter, Creole offerings like baked oysters and crawfish Alexander. Barbecue shrimp, another appetizer, is one of the more delectable dishes for those who like a peppery kick. On the list of entrees, an odd couple: blackened redfish and lobster thermidor, dishes that illustrate vividly the two sides of the menu.

This is a very pretty restaurant, especially the original pink-and-white dining room with its fireplace on one side and view of Paint Creek on the other.

Chianti

☆ ☆ ☆

28565 Northwestern Highway,
Southfield. (810) 350-0130.

Hours: Lunch, 11:30 a.m.-3 p.m. weekdays;
dinner, 5-10 p.m. Mon.-Thu., 5-11 p.m. Fri.-
Sat., 4-8 p.m. Sun. Closed major holidays.

Nonsmoking: 90 percent.

Full bar.   Major credit cards.

Moderate.

The Jimmy Schmidt reworking of the former southwestern-style Cocina del Sol bears the name of the robust red wine that is, of course, the house pour. Since opening in '94, the sunny Italian trattoria has attracted diners in droves.

With some new partners, notably Germano Minin, a 27-year-old chef only a couple of years out of his native Italy, Schmidt has turned the adobe hacienda with its cactuses and Day of the Dead figures into a Hollywood version of a Tuscan villa.

An intricate, multicolored exterior paint job, including a trompe l'oeil effect that makes the facade look like not just one but three structures, has given the place a new appearance. The look complements the fresh Italian fare.

Within, the sponge-painted walls range from the warm sunset color of the cozy bar to patches of faux brick and a bright blue and green spectrum in the two main dining areas. One high-ceilinged, the other low, they flow into one another. Murals copied from wine labels and epigrams in Italian add a friendly, informal tone to the setting.

The premise here: Bring a group. You'll enjoying choosing from antipasti, like the terrific grilled eggplant stuffed with ricotta cheese and sun-dried tomatoes; equally appealing fluffy salads of arugula, radicchio, olives and goat cheese, and an array of pastas, veal and chicken. All of these come in portions to share, although Chianti does not offer literally family-style service.

This is one restaurant where that table for two has to feel like they're missing out when they look around at bigger parties passing and dipping into platters of colorful food.

Bring at least three others with you — and if you are splitting the check, you'll get a happy surprise at the end of the meal. Three dishes are plenty for four. If you stay away from the $15.95 items on the menu, you can do very nicely for about $10 to $12 apiece, excluding wine or cocktails.

Chia Shiang

When the Golden Chef vegetarian restaurant changed its name, the proprietors didn't go for the typical fanciful title. Not Jade Princess. Nor Empress Garden. Not even close.

Their choice was Chia Shiang. And though most of us have to ask for an interpretation on that one, it becomes crystal clear as soon as we do. Chia Shiang (pronounced *Ja Shung*) simply means "hometown."

That friendly hometown feeling truly permeates the place despite the fact that not everyone in the Sih family from Taipei, Taiwan, is comfortable speaking English.

☆ ☆ ☆

2016 Packard Road, Ann Arbor. (313) 741-0778.

Hours: 11:30 a.m.-9:30 p.m. Mon.-Thu., 11:30 a.m.-10:30 p.m. Fri.-Sat., noon-9 p.m. Sun. Taiwanese dim sum served noon-3 p.m. Sat.-Sun. Closed Thanksgiving, Christmas Day and Dec. 26.

Nonsmoking: 80 percent.

Soft drinks only.   AE, MC and Visa.

Reasonable.

An interesting menu of both spicy and mild dishes, including a healthy helping of vegetarian and seafood and meat choices, also make Chia Shiang more than routine.

The menu has been tripled, and now attracts a wider audience for such dishes as Hunan pork, rose scallops and sesame chicken, as well as for vegetarian soups, appetizers and 21 vegetarian main dishes.

Some vegetarians might fear that since the total veggie approach has been left behind, the purity of their favorite dishes will be diluted. It's not so. Chef Shui-min Sih, better known as Tom, and his wife, Show-lam, better known as Mimi, use all-vegetable stocks.

For the miso soup, for instance, the chef uses mushroom stock, Japanese soybean paste, tofu and scallions. Yet you'd swear the broth was made with chicken.

There's a nice pan-Asian spin to the menu, as the miso soup attests. Lunch specials are served in a compartmented lacquered box called a bento, most often seen in Japanese restaurants but something that spans many Asian countries.

The bento contains the chosen main dish, which could be anything from Hunan shrimp or chicken to something called "tasty wheat gluten stick," along with fresh melon, orange and a wedge of skin-on banana, a heap of rice and a fortune cookie.

On weekends, dim sum is served at midday. The brunch array of small dishes ordered from a special menu gets more of a Taiwanese spin. Only a couple of the typical Cantonese bite-sized dumplings presented in steamers are on the list, which changes every weekend.

Taiwanese dim sum is typified by home-style beef stew noodle soup, and squid ball (think meatball) in a soup similar to hot and sour, sometimes with rice noodles added.

In three visits to Chia Shiang, I've been impressed not only with the ginger-and-garlic-infused sauces and the jewel-like vegetables, the resonant spicing and the array of choices, but with the friendliness and efficiency.

China Ruby

☆ ☆ 1/2

157 W. Nine Mile Road, Ferndale.
(810) 546-8876.

Hours: 11 a.m.-9 p.m. Mon.-Thu., 11 a.m.-10 p.m. Fri.-Sat. Closed Sun. and major holidays.

Nonsmoking: 75 percent.

Soft drinks only.   AE, MC and Visa.

Reasonable.

Tina Luu runs the front of the house while her husband Cong presides over the galley kitchen that is almost part of the dining room itself. This is a tiny place with just a handful of tables and counter seats.

The Luus are Vietnamese, but their experience is with Chinese fare, so that's what they've chosen to serve. Hunan scallops, Kung Pao chicken, Peking shrimp and many other dishes are offered, about equally divided between spicy and bland. There are a number of vegetarian dishes, too, including curried vegetables and Hunan broccoli.

The modest spot shows vestiges of the American lunch counter it once was, but over the years has developed a loyal clientele that passes by many more elaborate spots to dine here. A very modest price structure is part of the appeal.

Chung's

☆ ☆ 1/2

4187 Highland Road, Waterford.
(810) 681-3200.

3177 Cass, Detroit. (313) 831-1100.

Hours: 11 a.m.-10:30 p.m. Mon.-Thu., 11 a.m.-midnight Fri.-Sat., noon-10 p.m. Sun. Closed Thanksgiving.

Nonsmoking: 70 percent in Waterford; 50 percent in Detroit.

Soft drinks only.   Major credit cards.

Reasonable.

Philip Chung vividly remembers his introduction to the family business at age 13. It was his duty to get up at 2 in the morning on Friday and run downstairs to his parents' restaurant, then on Third Avenue south of Michigan. "The bars closed at 2:30, and at 2:25 there'd be nobody in the place. At 2:35, the place would be filled up," recalls Chung.

That pre-dawn duty in the early '50s was tough, but didn't dissuade Chung from continuing in the business his mother and dad, Shee Chin and Harry Chung, established in 1940.

Philip Chung and his cousin, Allen Chin, now collaborate in running Chung's, which moved to Cass Avenue at Peterboro some 33 years ago and manages to hang in there. Dinner business hardly resembles what it once was, but lunch and a flourishing carry-out business keep the old Chung's going.

The second Chung's has brought a new audience for the famous egg roll and warr dip harr (a perennially popular dish of shrimp wrapped in bacon atop onions in a sweet red sauce.)

The Cass Avenue restaurant's basic Cantonese menu offers all the old war-horses, from chow mein, sweet-and-sour pork and almond chicken to breaded fried shrimp. The menu is most appealing to non-Chinese, but has some Asian fans, too.

In Waterford, the bill of fare has been greatly expanded to include some of the trendier dishes from the Hunan and Sichuan areas of China. Among them are General Tso's chicken, stir-fried scallops, Mongolian beef and Singapore noodles.

About that crowd-pleasing Chung's egg roll: the eggroll wrapper is made in-house from water chestnut flour, and the filling is a blend of cabbage, shrimp, pork and just a touch of bean sprouts. It is lighter and more delicate than the traditional egg roll. Chung's serves it with plum sauce dappled with mustard sauce on a small china dish.

City Grill

The former Machus Sly Fox hasn't just been freshened up, it's been rejuvenated. The upbeat approach includes lots of white woodwork, walls painted the color of golden raisins, contemporary furnishings and light fixtures in the dining room. The bar has its own look, with wood, mirrors and intriguing murals of faces for whom the viewer can supply the identity.

725 S. Hunter, Birmingham. (810) 642-6900.

Hours: Lunch, 11 a.m.-3 p.m. Mon.-Sat.; light fare, 3-5 p.m. Mon.-Sat.; dinner, 5-10 p.m. Mon.-Thu., 5-11 p.m. Fri.-Sat., 4-9 p.m. Sun. Closed major holidays.

Nonsmoking: 60 percent.

Full bar. Major credit cards.

Moderate.

All of this happened in '94, when the Machus family snagged chef Ed Janos and decided to take a drastic turn away from the tried-and-true in both setting and menu.

The fare offers a varied and imaginative range of dishes with a wide ethnic background, from Asian egg rolls to Russian caviar. Many dishes are available in half portions and a hamburger is always a possibility. An impeccable hamburger, of course.

The eclectic selection typifies upscale American restaurants these days:

everything from pastas and risotto to wood-roasted swordfish, grilled yellowfin tuna, grilled venison medallions, steaks and even a four-course spa dinner. Janos has pared down the menu at lunch to a few main course salads, sandwiches and such entrees as chicken pot pie, quiche and baked whitefish, prepared in an open kitchen.

Despite the sound of all this, the menu is not too lengthy. There's a reasonable number of choices in each category, starting with appetizers, typified by paper-thin, housemade air-dried beef tenderloin with arugula and nuggets of fresh mozzarella; mushroom gratin atop angelhair pasta; housemade egg rolls filled with Oriental vegetables.

Tables are left uncovered, which is just fine considering that they are inlaid with bird's-eye maple surrounded by a rim of black lacquer. Great-looking Stickley-esque chairs in hickory wood with black accents seem to have been chosen with the same care as the menu.

Just about the only vestige of the Sly Fox is the Machus salad, the blue-cheese-and-red-onion-dappled salad beloved by veteran Machus diners. It is on the lunch menu — "but with different lettuces," as the proprietors put it.

The fresh culinary style has given this restaurant a new lease on life.

Clawson Steak House

 1/2

56 S. Rochester Road at 14 Mile Road, Clawson. (810) 588-5788.

Hours: Lunch, 11 a.m.-4 p.m. Mon.-Sat.; dinner, 4-11 p.m. Mon.-Thu., 4 p.m.-midnight Fri.-Sat. Closed Sun. and major holidays (except Mother's Day).

Nonsmoking: 50 percent.

Full bar.   Major credit cards.

Reasonable.

Dining and dancing survives here, at least on Wednesday through Saturday evenings when there's live music and live bodies showing off what they learned at the dance studio.

People love it.

While it's far from elegant, Clawson Steak House has a lot to offer: friendly service, an unpretentious atmosphere and much better than routine fare from the kitchen headed by John Alexopoulos. He uses quality raw materials from choice beef to fresh fish. Prime rib is a specialty, and at $11.95 it's a very good deal. Prices have held the line here.

When the lights dim, the beef is especially tender and the band hits all the notes, this is a pleasant place indeed.

Cloverleaf Bar and Restaurant

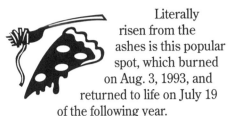

Literally risen from the ashes is this popular spot, which burned on Aug. 3, 1993, and returned to life on July 19 of the following year.

Gus Guerra's kids, Jack, Frank and Marie, run the place founded by their late dad in '53 after selling Buddy's.

He founded the original Buddy's as a bar in '43. The pizza came three years later when his late wife, Anna, persuaded him to add it to the menu. The rest is Detroit history.

☆ ☆ 1/2

24443 Gratiot, Eastpointe.
(810) 777-5391.

Hours: 11 a.m.-midnight Mon.-Thu., 11 a.m.-1:30 a.m. Fri.-Sat., 1-10 p.m. Sun. Closed major holidays.

Nonsmoking: 50 percent.

Full bar. Major credit cards.

Reasonable.

The claim to fame at Cloverleaf is, of course, the square pizza, which comes in two sizes: big and small. Also noteworthy is the antipasto salad, which is just the right accompaniment to the sturdy pie.

The rooms have been done up in appropriately nostalgic fashion with the help of Birmingham design firm Peterhansrea, which loves to hang old family photos on the wall. There was no shortage of old photos in the Guerra scrapbooks.

It's quite obvious that people are happy to have this venerable pizza emporium back again and, in turn, the Guerras are ecstatic to be running full-steam again.

An outdoor patio adds 52 to the 190 available seats from Memorial Day to the end of September.

Common Grill

Proprietor Craig Common is the source of the name for this sprightly cafe, which was a major hit practically from the day it opened in '91 inside a vintage storefront. The property is owned by partner Bob Daniels, whose actor son Jeff put the town on the map with his Purple Rose Theater.

☆ ☆ ☆

112 S. Main Street, Chelsea.
(313) 475-0470.

Hours: 11 a.m.-10 p.m. Tue.-Wed., 11 a.m.-10:30 p.m. Thu., 11 a.m.-11 p.m. Fri-Sat., 11 a.m. 10 p.m. Sun. Closed Mon. and major holidays.

Nonsmoking: 70 percent.

Full bar. AE, MC and Visa.

Moderate.

The restaurant's brick walls are brightened with Edward Hopper-style murals by Barney Judge, who also did the artwork at the Common Market across the street. The upscale grocery store took over space that for 80 years had housed the Schneider Grocery. The market opened in '94 at 125 S. Main.

You might say the Daniels/Common connection has really made people notice this town, where the milling company continues to churn out box after box of Jiffy Mix.

Fresh fish and seafood, grilled lamb and chicken, pasta dishes and imaginative treatments of vegetables and garnishes give the restaurant its personality.

The only problem is getting a table. To shorten the waiting time, patrons may phone starting at 3:30 p.m. each day to be put on the list for the evening. It's not exactly a reservation, but does cut the waiting time to about 20 minutes, promises proprietor Common.

I tried hard not to go for the obvious, but it's tough to avoid saying that the Common Grill offers an uncommon treat.

Cook's Shop/Pasta Shop

**683 Ouellette, Windsor, Ontario.
(519) 254-3377 or (519) 254-1300.**

Hours: Dinner only, 5-10 p.m. Sun. and Tue.-Thu., 5 p.m.-midnight Fri.-Sat. Closed Mon. and Dec. 24-26, Canadian holidays and one week in August. Pasta Shop only closed Sun.

Nonsmoking: By request.

Full bar.   AE, MC and Visa.

Reasonable.

It would be easy to bypass the self-effacing facade: just an awning marks the spot. But those who forge ahead will find a warren of rooms where a flaming open hearth glows behind a lighted glass butcher case.

The sauces for fresh pastas are put together at tableside, and some desserts are created there, too. The menu offers a choice of eight pastas, as well as a number of dishes cooked on the grill: a fish of the day brushed with oil, garlic and herbs; rosemary-grilled lamb; brochettes of beef liver, sausages, beef cubes and chicken.

Each of the small rooms is romantically lit, and the feeling is one of an intimate hideaway. Reservations are pretty much a must.

Upstairs at the 50-seat Pasta Shop, it's just a little more casual. The menu has been expanded beyond pastas, however.

Cosmic Cafe

A typical campus vegetarian cafe in every respect, this Wayne State University spot is as plain as a college lunchroom despite the startling acid green paint job on the outside of the building.

Inside, the color scheme may be drab by comparison, but the completely meatless fare has a lively spice level that makes all those veggies and sprouts very palatable.

☆ ☆ 1/2

87 W. Palmer, Detroit.
(313) 832-0001.

Hours: 8 a.m.-8 p.m. weekdays, 11 a.m.-4 p.m. Sat. Closed Sun., major holidays, week between Christmas and New Year's, and week of July 4.

Nonsmoking: 100 percent.

Soft drinks only.　　　　　　No credit cards.

Reasonable.

On my last visit, I ordered a Monster and a Fountain of Youth — and how many times is it possible to say that? They were a plate of sauteed potatoes, mushrooms, peppers and tofu with Cajun spices and salsa, and a vegetable drink combining all manner of juices from carrot and cucumber to celery, one of a number of freshly prepared drinks. With its earthy brown hue, the drink wasn't very pretty, but its distinct aura of "good for you" made up for it.

There are daily soups and specials chalked on blackboards around the room, which is furnished modestly with posters, plastic cloths and padded green chairs from some forgotten era — possibly the '70s, the decade from which the cafe seems to have sprung.

Anyone in the market for a healthy meal in the WSU area can do a lot worse than to stop here.

Costanzo's Victorian Room

 ☆ ☆ 1/2

3601 E. 12 Mile west of Ryan Road, Warren. (810) 751-6880.

Hours: Lunch, 11 a.m.-4 p.m. weekdays; dinner, 4-9 p.m. Tue.-Thu., 4-10 p.m. Fri.-Sat. Closed Sun., Mon. evenings and major holidays.

Nonsmoking: 50 percent.

Full bar.   AE, MC and Visa.

Reasonable.

Consistency is an admirable quality of the Costanzo family's restaurant, which is a collaboration between Antonio and Ofelia Costanzo and their son and daughter-in-law, Francesco and Lori Costanzo.

The highly traditional Italian-American menu stays the same except for daily specials. It offers a solid list of veal treatments from piccante to Tosca, and pastas including most of the traditional favorites from linguine and spaghetti with a variety of sauces, to fettuccine Alfredo.

Dinner includes soup, salad, potato or vegetable, and a side dish of spaghetti in the hallowed traditions of the full-course meal.

Ofelia Costanzo's freshly made desserts are notable. They, too, follow a traditional pattern, from zuppa Inglese to tiramisu.

The setting of high-backed banquettes has an appropriate Victorian twist with lots of deep red, globe lights, and a gladiola print wallpaper that is something to see. The year 1995 marks 10 years in business for the hard-working family. They obviously enjoy what they do, and their close family feeling gives this place something special.

Country Epicure

 ☆ ☆ 1/2

42050 Grand River, Novi. (810) 349-7770.

Hours: 11 a.m.-10 p.m. Mon.-Thu., 11 a.m.-11 p.m. Fri., 5-11 p.m. Sat. Closed Sun. and holidays except Mother's Day and Easter.

Nonsmoking: 80 percent.

Full bar.   Major credit cards.

Moderate.

Very popular with its clientele from Novi, Farmington and other western and northern suburbs, the friendly spot run by Karen Angelosante just keeps humming along, managing to fulfill both parts of its name.

It offers a free-wheeling menu of favorite American dishes that run the gamut from veal chop and salmon to pastas, sandwiches and burgers.

Desserts have become so popular that the restaurant added a bakery to the premises. Bakers work behind a big, uncovered window in view of the patrons, who may stop by for coffee and pastry or carry out elaborate concoctions like those served in the restaurant.

There's live piano music in the bar nearly every night, and outdoor seating during appropriate weather.

Courthouse Brasserie

Ravi Dhanjal's 10-table restaurant is a true hideaway in the heart of the city. From the exterior, few would guess what a civilized restaurant is inside. The name is a misnomer — this is anything but a noisy, lively brasserie.

Classical music wafts through the room with its ivory walls, dark woodwork, and antique chandeliers and furnishings. This surely is the most soothing setting in downtown Detroit.

Dhanjal became his own chef after Darryl Graham, who had been with him for years, died tragically young. In the hospital, Graham gave his recipes to Dhanjal. He now has made them his own.

They include calves' liver Madagascar, marinated lamb rack, a gingery grilled chicken breast and poached salmon. The subtle sauces are what patrons remember.

On the last Sunday evening of each month, Dhanjal puts aside the regular menu and prepares an array of Indian home-style dishes.

1436 Brush, Detroit.
(313) 963-8887.

Hours: Lunch, 11 a.m.-3 p.m. weekdays; dinner, 5-10 p.m. Tue.-Thu., 5-11 p.m. Fri.-Sat., 5-8:30 p.m. Sun. Closed Mon. evenings, major holidays and Sun. during July and August.

Nonsmoking: 100 percent.

Full bar.   Major credit cards.

Moderate.

Cousins Heritage Inn

☆ ☆ ☆ ☆

7954 Ann Arbor Street, Dexter.
(313) 426-3020.

Hours: Lunch, 11 a.m.-2 p.m. weekdays; dinner, 6-9 p.m. Tue.-Sat. Closed Mon. evenings, every Sun. except Mother's Day, and major holidays except Thanksgiving.

Nonsmoking: 90 percent.

Full bar.   Major credit cards.

Moderate to expensive.

Proprietors Paul and Patricia Cousins are always on hand to see that things run smoothly in the small-town house that's grown from a seating capacity of 45 to nearly twice that. Eighty diners now may be accommodated in a woodsy setting of dark green and butterscotch since a porch was enclosed to add more space.

The expansion included the kitchen, which is, of course, the heart of the matter. Everything is made in-house, from four house dressings for the multi-lettuce house salads to the raspberry tarts that crown the meal.

When chef Greg Upshur made the move to Novi's Too Chez, Jim Johnson took over, and his game dishes are especially popular. They range from medallions of venison and antelope to roasted and sliced elk and wild boar. There's always a fish or seafood selection, roast Amish chicken, and perhaps a rabbit dish.

Unless you plan ahead, you won't get a reservation around the time of the University of Michigan graduation in the first week in May. This spot is very popular with the Ann Arbor crowd.

Cyprus Taverna

☆ ☆ ☆

579 Monroe Street, Detroit.
(313) 961-1550.

Hours: 11 a.m.-2 a.m. Mon.-Thu.; 11 a.m.-4 a.m. Fri.-Sun. Closed Thanksgiving and Christmas.

Nonsmoking: 50 percent.

Full bar.   Major credit cards.

Reasonable.

There's not much doubt that Greektown restaurants have gotten complacent over the years. It's somewhat understandable. The block of Monroe between Beaubien and St. Antoine has been one of Detroit's major tourist attractions for years, always able to draw a crowd.

But somewhere along the line, pretty uninspired food and bored recitations of "Opa!" crept in. They've been the standard for too long. This spot proves it's possible to take the old dishes and make them new again.

At Cyprus Taverna, the level of cooking is more refined, more careful, and presentation is very nice indeed. This food doesn't look as if it comes from a commissary, as is so often the case in Greektown.

For starters, order the avgolemono (egg-lemon soup). The soup has a natural broth containing discernible pieces of white meat chicken, the juices from the bird, lots of rice, egg and lemon. It doesn't resemble the glutinous concoction that sometimes goes by the name.

And if you are tired of the flaming cheese routine, try haloumi. It's a Cypriot cheese served as an appetizer, not aflame, but delivered warm to the table. Another appetizer from Cyprus is koupes (spiced minced meat in a bulgur casing).

An interesting Cypriot main dish is seftalies (pronounced chef-tal-YES): four sausage-like rolls of mixed pork and lamb blended with onion, garlic, parsley and spices. Another is afelia (aff-FELL-ya), which is pork braised with red wine and spiced with coriander.

The Cypriot influence comes from the proprietors, Vassos Avgoustis, Yiannis Papaionnou and Tony Christou. They all hail from the island republic of Cyprus, a lovely spot of sandy beaches and vistas off the Turkish coast. Food there has Greek and Turkish influences. Eleni Avgoustis, also one of the proprietors, is of Greek heritage.

The Greek influence is in the appetizer platter, definitely meant for sharing: tzatziki (a blend of yogurt, cucumber and lots of garlic), more garlic in the scordalia dip, fried eggplant, artichoke hearts and stuffed grape leaves. A notable main dish is the Greek trio. Their rendition of the standards — spinach pie, moussaka (baked eggplant with ground meat and white sauce) and pastitsio (a similar dish using macaroni instead of eggplant) — demonstrates why these dishes are on so many menus.

All the principals here have lots of Greektown experience. After 20 years of working for other people, Vassos Avgoustis says he and his partners were more than ready to go out on their own. They have created their soothing setting in soft shades of off-white, gray and blue, sparked with well-chosen framed needlework from Cyprus and reproductions of busts, vases and platters.

Da Edoardo

☆ ☆ ☆

19767 Mack, Grosse Pointe Woods. (313) 881-8540.

Hours: Pasta/pizza rooms, lunch 11:30 a.m.-4 p.m. Mon.-Sat., dinner 4-10 p.m. Mon.-Thu., 4-11 p.m. Fri.-Sat., 5-9 p.m. Sun.; dinner only in the formal dining room 5-9 p.m. Tue.-Thu., 5-11 p.m. Fri.-Sat. Pasta/pizza rooms closed on major holidays. Formal dining room closed Sun., Mon. and on major holidays.

Nonsmoking: 50 percent.

Full bar.   AE, MC and Visa.

Moderate.

Once known only for fine dining, the trend toward casual settings and menus has taken over here, too.

Though the formal room still has its fans, the pasta/pizza rooms are the real favorites, especially with the families in the area.

Dishes including lasagna, Italian sausage, spinach pasta filled with ricotta cheese, thin-crusted pizzas and Caesar salads hold sway. Those who want the subtle wine and cream sauces and more elaborate veal and seafood dishes that the Barbieri family is noted for may still have them, but at dinner only, in a much quieter, dimly lit setting.

You might call it the no-children section.

Dakota Inn Rathskellar

☆ ☆ 1/2

17324 John R, Detroit. (313) 867-9722.

Hours: Lunch, 11 a.m.-2 p.m. Tue.-Fri.; dinner, 5-10 p.m. Thu., 5-11 p.m. Fri.-Sat. Closed Sun.; Mon.-Wed. evenings and major holidays.

Nonsmoking: 50 percent.

Full bar.   Major credit cards.

Reasonable.

It's even happened at Detroit's bastion of knackwurst, bratwurst, sauerkraut and German potato salad. Chicken has been added to the menu.

Aside from that, however, the amazingly well-preserved German bar and restaurant hasn't changed much since 1933. You can check that out by looking at the vintage photos on the wall.

Special events during the year include a pig roast, a chili cook-off and, of course, a month-long Oktoberfest. Still a tradition on a weekly basis, though, are the sing-alongs on Thursday through Saturday nights. The words to the old drinking song "Schnitzelbank" have been sung by generations of Detroiters whenever the bell clangs and the lights flash.

Members of the founding Kurz family still run the place. A true Detroit tradition lives on.

Da Luciano Ristorante/Pizzeria

Early in 1995, Luciano Verardi closed his casual Erie Street pizzeria and combined its offerings with his more elaborate restaurant. The two are now under the same roof, allowing patrons to order the wood-roasted pizzas or to have the more elaborate Italian dishes Verardi is known for — pastas, sole Piedmontese style, steaks and quail, accompanied by fresh salads and roasted potatoes.

☆ ☆ ☆

1317 Hall Road, off Ottawa Street, Windsor, Ontario. (519) 977-5677.

Hours: Lunch, 11:30 a.m.-2:30 p.m. Mon.-Sat.; dinner, 4:30-10 p.m. Mon.-Thu., 4:30-11 p.m. Fri.-Sat. Closed Sun. and major holidays.

Nonsmoking: 40 percent.

Full bar.   Major credit cards.

Reasonable.

In any case, Italian is the language most likely to be heard wafting through the air, as it is in so many spots on the east side of Windsor. Da Luciano is a little bit away from the cluster of *trattorias* that give Erie Street so much charm, but the same feeling is apparent here in the softly lit dining room. Its cove ceilings and creamy plaster walls are set off by dark wood accents and black-and-white photographs of Italy.

The Verardi family is from Cosenza in southern Italy. Luciano's three brothers now work with him in the enterprise.

Daniel's

☆ ☆ ☆

**209 W. Sixth St., Royal Oak.
(810) 541-8050.**

Hours: 5-10 p.m. Mon.-Thu., 5-11 p.m.
Fri.-Sat., 4-9 p.m. Sun. Closed Christmas Eve
and Christmas Day.

Nonsmoking: 85 percent.

Full bar.   Major credit cards.

Moderate to expensive.

Daniel's adds something different to Royal Oak, a city teeming with casual restaurants. This one is a departure from the informal, drop-in style of so many of them.

It offers Daniel Kozak's European style of cooking in a traditional setting of paintings, sparkling crystal and fresh flowers. The look is reminiscent of his late, lamented Royal Eagle restaurant in the Parkstone Apartments in Detroit.

This time around he's branched out beyond his former Polish ethnic approach, offering dishes from a wider spectrum. They include stuffed saddle of rabbit with carmelized onions and chicken with escargot sauce.

I like people who march to a different drummer. And Kozak certainly does. In this case, it means fancy food in a fancy decor.

Doesn't he know that the Doc Martens-pierced eyebrow set is flocking into casual spots like the Mongolian Barbeque and Monterrey, not ones that waft Vivaldi into lace-curtained rooms where service is on fine china plates?

Of course he does, but he is committed to the style he knows best.

"In most Royal Oak spots, everybody's 22. At Daniel's, everybody's 42," pointed out a diner with some validity. "They are casually dressed but they have a little more money to spend." It's good they do. The food is not only rich at Daniel's, but the price structure tends that way, too. Entrees, with the exception of the vegetarian stuffed cabbage, are all in the $14-$23 range.

The two dining rooms at Daniel's include the Viennese room in a vivid scarlet and the smaller Florentine room in deep green. The soft light level is another plus. Each table is set with service plates in a different pattern from Kozak's collection of literally hundreds of Sevres, Bavarian and Bohemian china plates.

Kozak has added a number of dishes to his Polish portfolio, including salmon with a fine herb sauce, and whitefish broiled and unadorned or with a sauce of tomatoes, onions and herbs.

Dinner is a la carte except for the addition of a house salad, a mix of greens with a refreshing slice of melon and a choice of several house dressings.

At Daniel's to say "rich and creamy" is to be redundant. That's the theme. Plates are nicely garnished with fresh vegetables, and potatoes get lots of attention from the chef. His potato knishes are notable.

Daniel's is an oasis of courtesy and Old World charm.

D. Dennison's Seafood Tavern

Fresh fish, pastas and chicken are the backbone of the menu at these upbeat spots, brought to us by the Mainstreet Ventures people who also run Gratzi, Palio, Maude's and the Real Seafood Company in Ann Arbor. Staffers are generally cheerful and casual, like the places themselves. Nothing particularly outstanding about them, and rather clone-like in feeling, these are, nonetheless, a cut above the usual chain operations.

12 Mile and Orchard Lake Road, Farmington Hills. (810) 553-7000.

Laurel Park Place, 37716 Six Mile Road, Livonia. (313) 464-9030.

Hours: 11 a.m.-10 p.m. Mon.-Thu., 11 a.m.-midnight Fri.-Sat., noon-9 p.m. Sun. (3-9 p.m. in Farmington Hills.) Closed Thanksgiving, Christmas Day and New Year's Day.

Nonsmoking: 85 percent.

Full bar.   Major credit cards.

Reasonable.

Deacon Brodie's Tavern

There could hardly be a less politically correct bill of fare than the one at Deacon Brodie's Tavern. There's steak and kidney pie. Roast beef. Scotch eggs (hard-boiled eggs wrapped in pork sausage and deep-fried). Bangers and mash (sausages and mashed potatoes). Chicken wings, fried cheese sticks and fried potato skins. Haggis 'n' chips, and haggis served atop potato skins.

Yes, Deacon Brodie's offers haggis, the notorious Scottish pudding made of oatmeal and onions, lamb and liver that was originally boiled inside an animal's stomach lining, but now is simply inside a sausage casing. It's available along with those other items that might put low-fat fanatics into shock. This may be the only menu in the metro area that doesn't mention pasta. Not even once.

75 Macomb Place, Mt. Clemens. (810) 954-3202.

2650 S. Rochester Road, just north of Auburn Road, Rochester Hills. (810) 299-3890.

Hours: 11 a.m.-10 p.m. Mon.-Sat., 4-10 p.m. Sun.

Nonsmoking: 30 percent.

Full bar.   AE, MC and Visa.

Reasonable.

The Mt. Clemens tavern, namesake of the original in Edinburgh, Scotland, in nearly every respect reflects the heritage of proprietor Tom Plunkett, a man who hasn't lost a single lilt of his Scottish accent. Plunkett opened his second outpost early in '95 and like the original, this one is done up in authentic pieces brought from Great Britain.

Traditional British and Scottish dishes are what set Deacon Brodie's apart from the pack. British fare is pretty hard to come by in these parts and it's a refreshing change. Choices include the shepherd's pie (minced beef with onions and carrots topped with a crust of cheese and mashed potatoes); Scotch meat pie (ground beef encased in pie pastry and looking something like a pillbox hat with its flat top), and fish and chips (an "all ye can eat" item, as the menu phrases it).

Fish and chips, served in a basket atop waxed paper printed like an old newspaper, is the most popular item. The ale-based batter is light and fluffy, and so is the fish, North Atlantic pollack.

Forget what you've heard about haggis: We tried it atop potato skins that had about an inch of potato left, and dolloped with a bit of melted cheese, and it was delicious.

Entrees come with soup or salad, potato, vegetable, and rolls and butter. Some of the accompaniments — the routine iceberg lettuce salads, too liberally doused with dressing, for instance — are less than wonderful. Coleslaw is a better bet. And forget the uninspired vegetables, aside from the chips and baked beans.

On the plus side, Deacon Brodie's offers a choice among 22 draft beers, as well as many bottled brews. The taps feature such offbeat selections as Fullers London Pride, Watneys Red Barrel, John Courage, Double Diamond and Youngs Oatmeal Stout and McEwens Export Ale from Scotland.

Detroit Beach Restaurant

☆ ☆

2630 N. Dixie Hwy.
(off Exit 15 of I-75), Detroit Beach.
(313) 289-9865.

Hours: 11:30 a.m.-1 a.m. Tue.-Thu. and Sun., 11:30 a.m.-3 a.m. Fri.-Sat. Closed Mon., Thanksgiving, Christmas Day and Easter.

Nonsmoking: 55 percent.

Beer and wine.   No credit cards.

Reasonable.

A family restaurant in the best sense of that phrase, this obscure pizzeria/Italian spot is run by the Contes, Peter and Rita, sons Silverio and Joseph and daughter Suzette — five out of the seven Contes, as Joseph puts it. One brother and one sister have moved on to other enterprises.

In June of '95, they celebrate the 30th anniversary of the place, which hasn't changed much over the years. The Contes talk a lot about making some changes, but they move slowly.

In addition to the pizzas, the most popular dish is one they put on the menu in

'64 called mostaccioli in casserole. It is still the No. 1 dish.

Down-to-earth and unpretentious, this is a good spot to remember when heading south on I-75. It has warmth and tradition, and modest as it is, it beats the chains by a country mile.

Diamond Jim Brady's Bistro

For more than just a few years, a primo burger and a bowl of chili were enough for Jim Brady and his loyal customers at the original Diamond Jim's in Detroit. And both are still available at the bar, pardon me, bistro, run by Brady's son Tom and his wife Mary, with help from Tom Jr.

26053 Town Center, Novi.
(810) 380-8460.

Hours: 11:30 a.m.-10 p.m. Mon.-Thu., 11:30 a.m.-11 p.m. Fri.-Sat., 4-8 p.m. Sun. Closed Thanksgiving, Christmas Eve and Christmas Day.

Nonsmoking: 50 percent.

Full bar.   Major credit cards.

Moderate.

But those simple items have been joined by a creative list of dishes from the repertoire of Mary Brady, a certified chef with all manner of culinary credentials.

She's added such choices as Creole calamari spiced with cumin and tarragon and served with aioli (garlic mayonnaise); quesadillas filled with grilled chicken or house-cured salmon; and fettucini Alfredo embellished with shrimp — these on the appetizer or "small plates" list.

House specialties, served with Caesar salad, include chicken pot pie, barbecued baby back ribs, mustard and herb-crusted salmon and Mary's version of beef Wellington.

I can't help but wonder what the late founding father would think about all this "fancy food," which is what he would have called it. The setting, however, would win his approval. It's still very reminiscent of the classic bar and grill.

Dos Pesos

☆ ☆ 1/2

11800 Belleville Road, ¼ mile south of I-94, Belleville. (313) 697-5777.

Hours: 11 a.m.-9:30 p.m. Mon.-Thu., 11 a.m.-10:30 p.m. Fri., 3-10:30 p.m. Sat., noon-9 p.m. Sun. Closed major holidays.

Nonsmoking: 70 percent.

Full bar.   MC and Visa.

Reasonable.

If you need a restaurant in fairly close proximity to Metropolitan Airport, this is a good one to keep in mind. Just 10 minutes west of the terminals is this cheerful Mexican restaurant that takes routine dishes and makes something out of them.

It's a family collaboration of Hope and Jesse Perez and their son Daniel. Their dishes from tacos and enchiladas to fajitas, and shrimp sauteed with garlic atop rice, are all nicely garnished and look fresh and appealing.

Even the inevitable tortilla chips and sauce are above average.

Ducks on the Roof

☆ ☆ 1/2

1430 Front Road S. (Hwy. 18), two miles west of Amherstburg, Ontario. (519) 736-6555; Detroit number: (313) 961-3228.

Hours: Dinner only, 5-8:30 p.m. Tue.-Sat., 2-6:30 p.m. Sun. Closed Mon. and Christmas Day.

Nonsmoking: 25 percent.

Full bar.   MC and Visa.

Moderate.

Primitive pine tables and chairs, a fireplace blazing away in the clubby bar and a collection of 117 hand-carved duck decoys all combine to give a one-of-a-kind personality to this idiosyncratic place.

Under one regime or another, it's been a favorite of Detroiters for generations. Currently run by Brian Lucop and John Tersigni, the place has had its ups and downs but seems to be on an up lately.

The menu is a rather formal one, with such dishes as herbed rack of lamb, chicken breast in Calvados (apple brandy) and boneless breast of pheasant in brandied cream sauce, and oh, yes, duck with apricot or honey-garlic sauce.

I'd like to see them loosen up a bit and have some fun with the menu, because this is truly a unique setting.

Dunleavy'z

A classic bar and grill menu is served in two adjoining vintage buildings, which retain their character though they've been updated by partners Jack Dunleavy and Paul Zosel.

The saloon feeling is the primary one at this hangout for sports fans. They like the lively bar action as well as the burgers, steaks, ribs and seafood with accompaniments of steak fries, onion rings and coleslaw.

Irish coffee is a house specialty.

267 Jos. Campau at Franklin, Detroit. (313) 259-0909.

Hours: 11 a.m.-10 p.m. Mon.-Thu., 11 a.m.-11 p.m. Fri., 5-11 p.m. Sat. Closed Sun. (except when there is Red Wings hockey) and major holidays.

Nonsmoking: 20 percent.

Full bar.   Major credit cards.

Moderate.

Dusty's Wine Bar and Pub

☆ ☆ ☆ ☆

1839 Grand River, Okemos.
(517) 349-8680.

Hours: 11 a.m.-10 p.m. Mon.-Thu., 11 a.m.-11 p.m. Fri.-Sat.; brunch, 11 a.m.-3 p.m. Sun. Closed Sun. evenings and major holidays, including New Year's Eve.

Nonsmoking: 75 percent.

Full bar.   Discover, MC and Visa.

Moderate.

Respect for the best and freshest ingredients and a lot of creative imagination are hallmarks of this surprising spot that shares space with a gourmet food and wine shop.

Chef Eric Villegas uses Michigan and Midwestern products as much as humanly possible. During the summer months, farmer Dennis Greenman grows herbs, corn, purple Peruvian potatoes, fingerlings and lettuces for the restaurant at his farm in Holt. The produce comes from seeds he and Villegas choose each fall.

Villegas' menu stays the same all day, and features such dishes as venison meat loaf with grilled tomatoes and oyster mushrooms; a dish he calls Midwest choucroute using wild game sausage; gumbo made with andouille sausage, tasso ham, chicken and wild rice, and Great Lakes smelt with sage and garlic.

Don't look for all of those dishes on the same day, of course. But certain standards include torta rustica (brioche dough stuffed with smoked turkey, spinach, artichoke hearts, capers, sweet peppers and cheese), grilled or smoked whitefish (Villegas does his own smoking of pheasant, chicken and fish), an upscale version of macaroni and cheese, and, because he's not the least bit of a snob, a notable burger.

Lately, desserts have had a bistro theme typified by pot de creme and creme caramel.

Other attributes: a wine list with 20-some wines by the glass, a 50-item beer list with brews listed by fermentation method as well as type, and a pleasant, unpretentious setting with bare-topped tables made of French wine crates and a mishmash of chairs.

The Earle

Pressing on toward its 20th anniversary is this dimly lit spot that offers a well-stocked wine bar and a bill of fare with a European country flavor. Light jazz is offered most evenings.

Chef Shelley Adams has been in charge of the kitchen for a good number of years now, adding to the consistency of fare that relies on fresh, seasonal ingredients.

Adams tries to change the menu every eight weeks, but admits it doesn't always work out that way. She usually offers a duck, beef, veal, fresh fish and pasta dish along with fresh salads, at least two soups, and housemade desserts that include wonderful ice cream.

Dishes typifying her sturdy style include pork, duck and veal *pate,* medallions of lamb with fresh herbs and garlic, and duck breast sauteed with garlic, shallots and mushrooms.

121 W. Washington at Ashley, Ann Arbor. (313) 994-0211.

Hours: 5:30-10 p.m. Mon.-Thu., 5:30 p.m.-midnight Fri., 6 p.m.-midnight Sat., 5-9 p.m. Sun. Closed Sun. from Memorial Day through Labor Day and major holidays.

Nonsmoking: 90 percent, 100 percent on Saturdays.

Full bar.   Major credit cards.

Moderate.

East Franklin

What is it about the hulking warehouses and dumpy brick structures of another century that makes them so ideal as this century's entertainment spots and restaurants?

It's true in Toronto, it's true in Baltimore, it's true in New Orleans, among other cities. And while Detroit's warehouse district, now known as Rivertown, has yet to reach full potential, its narrow streets and other-era buildings definitely have that old-time charm.

East Franklin is part of it, but offers something quite different from most of the other spots in the neighborhood that focus on cocktails or music.

Solid, Southern-style home cooking — soul food, though its proprietor doesn't call it that — is the premise here. The dining room's 170 seats are under a soaring ceiling on the first floor of an eye-catching, three-story building that

1440 Franklin, Detroit. (313) 393-0018.

Hours: 11 a.m.-9 p.m. Tue.-Thu., 11 a.m.-10 p.m. Fri., noon-10 p.m. Sat., noon-9 p.m. Sun. Closed Mon. and major holidays, including Thanksgiving, Christmas Day and New Year's Day.

Nonsmoking: 60 percent.

Soft drinks only.   Major credit cards.

Reasonable.

has been nicely rehabbed. The setting of bare wooden beams, brick walls and spinning fans seems just right.

Doing the cooking and managing at East Franklin is 30-year-old John Thompson. He's another member of the big family that helped brother Joseph Thompson get his Edmund Place restaurant going in Detroit's historic Brush Park area shortly before this one opened.

East Franklin has a menu that zeroes in on what John Thompson feels is his kitchen's strength. At both lunch and dinner, the bill of fare includes such basic American dishes as meat loaf, country-fried steak, roasted or fried chicken, baby back ribs, and the classic sides: corn bread dressing, macaroni and cheese, green beans, yams and collard greens, among others.

The fresh food is definitely the draw here, in addition to the setting and the reasonable price structure. Among dishes I've sampled, standouts include the baby back ribs, oven-roasted chicken, moist and crumbly meat loaf — ask for the gravy on the side — and the crispy, Southern-fried chicken.

Dessert includes two delicious cobblers, peach and apple.

East Franklin offers the essence of comfort food, and if the leisurely pace of service could be kicked up a notch, it would make this interesting spot even better.

Edmund Place

☆ ☆ 1/2

69 Edmund Street, Detroit. (313) 831-5757.

Hours: 11 a.m.-3 p.m. Mon., 11 a.m.-9 p.m. Tue.-Thu., 11 a.m.-11 p.m. Fri., 1-11 p.m. Sat., noon-9 p.m. Sun. Closed Mon. evenings, Thanksgiving, Christmas Day and New Year's Day.

Nonsmoking: 90 percent.

Full bar.   Major credit cards.

Reasonable.

The roof had fallen in. Not so much as a shard of glass rested in a window frame, and the staircase was missing when Joseph Thompson first saw the brick and stone house in the historic Brush Park section of Detroit.

Undeterred, he bought the circa-1882 house anyway. "Everybody thought I was crazy," says Thompson. Everyone included Thompson's own father, who felt his son must be losing his mind to pay $1,000 to the city for what was — at best — the ghost of a Victorian house surrounded by mostly vacant, abandoned and burned-out houses.

The younger Thompson, however, saw beyond the ruin. He saw plum-colored walls and big mirrors and rosy tapestry draperies looped over tall windows, and people dining at linen-covered tables under brass and glass wall sconces.

And it became a reality.

The menu offers made-from-scratch dishes produced by home-style cooks. Choices include chicken and dumplings, barbecued ribs, meat loaf, smothered pork chops and short ribs, and classic sides of candied yams, corn, macaroni and cheese, and corn bread dressing. Fruit cobblers are for dessert.

Additions to the menu lately include a changing variety of pan-fried fish, some pasta dishes, soups and salads.

Sundays after church are the busiest times for this down-home spot in the city.

E.G. Nick's

This lively, popular spot features familiar, crowd-pleasing dishes. Pizzas topped with roasted garlic and chicken, Greek salads, baby back ribs and barbecued chicken are all served in a bright setting.

Lately, certain dishes have come to the fore. Oak-planked whitefish served with Duchess potatoes is the biggest seller in the house. Pastas including linguine with white or red clam sauce are strong, and pasta-encrusted salmon, a fairly new dish, ought to be a contender. For the latter dish, multi-colored angelhair pasta is chopped and added to a herb and oil-treated salmon.

☆ ☆ 1/2

6066 Maple Road, West Bloomfield. (810) 851-0805.

Hours: 11 a.m.-11 p.m. Mon.-Thu., 11 a.m.-midnight Fri.-Sat., 4-10 p.m. Sun. Closed Thanksgiving, Christmas Day and New Year's Day.

Nonsmoking: 90 percent.

Full bar.   Major credit cards.

Moderate.

There's really nothing complicated about the cooking or the friendly, informal atmosphere, which are two reasons why this place continues year after year. Of course, its strategic location is another plus.

The Nicholas family, which runs this restaurant, also has others: E.G. Nick's outposts in Brighton and Lapeer, the Tomato Brothers in Howell, and Highland House in Highland.

899 Pillette

☆ ☆ 1/2

899 Pillette, Windsor, Ontario.
(519) 948-1959.

Hours: Lunch, 11:30 a.m.-2:30 p.m. week-days; dinner, 5-10 p.m. Tue.-Sat. Closed Mon. evenings and major holidays.

Nonsmoking: Arranged by request.

Full bar.   MC and Visa.

Reasonable.

Just 22 seats are available in Donna and Roy Morykot's miniature storefront that once housed an Italian grocery store. A small Italian grocery store.

Opened in the late '80s by the couple after Donna's graduation from culinary school, the menu at first was fairly elaborate. Now chef Donna Morykot has taken a turn toward the casual, and her menu is predominantly pastas. The setting has been lightened, too: the place is now done in a spectrum of cream, green and salmon shades.

My favorite dishes include a spicy Thai pasta made with chicken, shrimp or vegetables, and Creole pasta with shrimp, crabmeat, tomatoes and peppers. Half orders are available.

For those who like tiny, offbeat restaurants, this one is a find.

El Comal

☆ ☆

1414 Junction, Detroit.
(313) 841-7753.

Hours: 11 a.m.-10 p.m. Tue.-Thu. and Sun., 11 a.m.-midnight Fri.-Sat. Closed Mon. and major holidays.

Nonsmoking: 20 percent.

Full bar.   No credit cards.

Reasonable.

Guatamalans Elda and Rafael Castellanos and their family have decorated their simple room with woven shawls and colorful artwork from their country. It's not solely a Mexican restaurant, for Elda's kitchen turns out a few Guatamalan and Salvadoran dishes.

These more unusual dishes are, of course, the things to order. They include Guatamalan tamales wrapped in a banana leaf, and pupusas (flour tortillas filled with beans, cheese or fried pork, or a mixture of the three).

There are just seven Guatamalan dishes on the menu, which is fleshed out with tacos and other familiar Mexican dishes.

The restaurant is named for the clay pan used to cook tortillas.

Elizabeth Street Cafe

Unpretentious, comfortable, with food quality that outpaces the setting, this sunny spot could be transplanted to a college town with ease. A low-key, almost intellectual feeling imbues the high-ceilinged room. Maybe it's all those people quietly reading as they sip coffee or have a sandwich.

☆ ☆ 1/2

2100 John R, Detroit.
(313) 964-0461.

Hours: 11 a.m.-4 p.m. weekdays. Closed Sat., Sun. and major holidays.

Nonsmoking: 100 percent.

Soft drinks only.　　　　　　No credit cards.

Reasonable.

Step up to the counter and order, and the staff will tote the food to your table. The soups, salads and sandwiches are fresh and there's always a vegetarian dish in the array. It's simple fare ranging from club sandwiches, tuna melt, grilled chicken and curried chicken salad to egg salad and French dip.

Freshly baked muffins, cookies and brownies add the finishing touches.

Elwood Bar & Grill

The problem with this revamped Art Deco spot, aside from its high decibel level, has been its inconsistency over the years. It seemingly can't decide what it wants to be. The menu has flip-flopped a number of times.

Lately, the Elwood's gone back to the basics, concluding that it is, indeed, a bar and grill.

☆ ☆

2100 Woodward at Elizabeth, Detroit. (313) 961-7486.

Hours: 11:30 a.m.-4 p.m. Mon., 11:30 a.m.-11 p.m. Tue.-Thu., 11 a.m.-midnight Fri., noon-1 a.m. Sat., noon-7 p.m. Sun. Closed major holidays.

Nonsmoking: 40 percent.

Full bar.　　　　　　AE, MC and Visa.

Reasonable.

The menu includes the kinds of dishes most people expect in that setting. Burgers, ribs, sandwiches and soups are served casually.

The exterior of the blue-and-cream gem has been restored to its original state. Inside, completely redone in three-toned maple, mahogany and birch, it harks back to the days of the '50s lunch counter.

El Zocalo

☆ ☆ 1/2

3400 Bagley, Detroit.
(810) 841-3700.

Hours: 11 a.m.-2 a.m. Sun.-Thu., 11 a.m.-2:30 a.m. Fri.-Sat. Closed Thanksgiving, Christmas Day and New Year's Day.

Nonsmoking: 65 percent.

Full bar.   Major credit cards.

Reasonable.

Victor Hugo Cordoba's colorful restaurant does the Mexican standards as well as anybody along Bagley. And after a number of years of churning out the familiar dishes from enchiladas to tostados, he's added a selection of more formal Mexico City-style fare to the menu.

He first tried out the new dishes on a range of customers from native Mexicans and other Hispanics to mainstream Americans to see how they were accepted.

And while he found that the mainstreamers, as might be expected, were less accepting of highly spiced dishes, he's been able to tone down the spice level for individual orders.

Some of the esoteric items include a number of seafood and fish selections and regional soups, like caldo jardinero (red snapper stock with fresh vegetables), that aren't often seen in Mexican restaurants in this city.

Emily's

☆ ☆ ☆ ☆

505 N. Center, Northville.
(810) 349-0505.

Hours: Dinner only, 5:30-10 p.m. Tue.-Thu., 5:30-11 p.m. Fri.-Sat., 4-9 Sun. Closed Mon., major holidays and first week in Aug.

Nonsmoking: 100 percent.

Full bar.   Major credit cards.

Expensive.

For some reason, people in the metro area seem to resist the fixed-price, multi-course menu. Undeterred, Rick Halberg decided to go that way when he opened his dream restaurant in '94 in a Victorian house in Northville.

And — surprise — it's worked out well.

He offers an ever-changing list of dishes with a Mediterranean spin and well-thought-out flavor combinations. Halberg does not go for oddball combinations to assert his creative skill. He's on very solid ground with dishes that span the area from Spain and Morocco to France and Italy.

The price of the entree ($29-$40) includes an hors d'oeuvre, an appetizer, and a salad. The latter includes mixed greens — and reds such as radicchio — with pressed ricotta cheese, pine nuts and garlic croutons in balsamic vinaigrette. It's obvious Halberg has made an effort not to trot out just another boring salad.

Dishes I love have included a fennel-cured salmon appetizer combining paper-thin Atlantic salmon and a delicate filling of cucumber, dill cream, onion and a hint of horseradish — he also does this dish with creme fraiche and herb oil — roasted butternut squash soup accented with Moroccan spices, and sea scallops with a sauce made of pink grapefruit and red wine.

Other dishes typifying his style include veal chop, sometimes served with truffle butter; porcini mushrooms and fettuccine; red snapper in a paprika-cumin marinade, and balsamic-roasted duck with port-wine duck essence.

Only desserts, including a trio of mousses, are a la carte.

Halberg prepares each dinner, with the help of sous-chef Donna Brown. Pastry chef Jeanne Bartlett comes in to do the baking.

This Mediterranean menu is made for red wine. And the list of reds includes a selection of Bordeaux that will have connoisseurs raving. It includes most of the great chateaus (in a price range of $48-$150), and maitre d' Michael Korn is proud to show off his cellar. There are, of course, lesser wines for us ordinary mortals, as modest as $18-$24 a bottle.

Every detail of the meal, right down to the French rolls, is important in this house (circa 1850-1870), which looks gingerbready from the outside but has been stripped of frou-frou within.

The bright sunflower-yellow walls with French blue accents on the ceiling and the tiled fireplace in the main dining room give the place a much more contemporary feeling than is the usual style in Northville. Tables are admirably well-spaced.

Note that this is not a place to bring small children.

Empress Garden II

For years people on this side of the river have flocked to Windsor's Asian restaurants in search of more authentic fare than they can find in their own neighborhoods. That's had a beneficial effect on our Chinese restaurants. Many on these shores have taken the cue and now serve much more than the routine Americanized fare that was once the norm.

☆ ☆ ☆

3032 Dougall Avenue, Windsor, Ontario. (519) 969-9723.

Hours: 11 a.m.-11 p.m. Mon.-Thu., 11 a.m.-midnight Fri., 11:30 a.m.-midnight Sat., noon-10 p.m. Sun. Closed Christmas Eve and Christmas Day.

Nonsmoking: 75 percent.

Full bar.   Major credit cards.

Moderate.

But there's no doubt that Windsor is still a popular destination, and one of the spots people head for is Teresa Yau and

Tony Chaw's showcase for authentic, Hong Kong-style fare. It offers one of the prettiest settings in Windsor, done up in a slick, subdued, contemporary look that would do credit to the most sophisticated restaurant.

Rather than just reprise the typical tassel-and-lantern Chinese restaurant style, they've made Empress Garden II an oasis of deep gray, black and jade. Stained-glass windows are in rich tones of rose, garnet and aquamarine, with carved-glass interior panels.

The menu includes an incredible 18 soups, everything from the familiar won ton to minced chicken with sweet corn, shark's fin, and melon with crabmeat. There's an equally dazzling choice among the main dishes. Vegetable and noodle dishes are there. So are hot pots, several variations on fried rice, and an especially extensive list of seafood options, featuring shrimp, lobster, abalone, pickerel, oysters, clams and scallops.

Somewhat smaller selections of chicken and duck are featured, with pork and beef dishes bringing up the rear. It's all part of the trend in Hong Kong toward a lighter approach, with dishes emphasizing fruit and vegetable flavors and scaling back from heavier sauces.

The style of presentation is in keeping with the ambitions of the kitchen. Everything is served on white china platters and plates, with matching accessories including the tea pots. There are no clattery metal compotes. The food looks as good as it tastes.

Soups are served in tureens in large, medium and small sizes, or they may be ordered by the bowl. Two I can recommend are the classic hot and sour, and meat with crackling rice. From the seafood list: sauteed Sichuan shrimp prettily served atop curly lettuce leaves with a scattering of green peas, and sauteed pickerel with black bean sauce. Our table loved the sauteed sliced chicken with hot chili sauce and lots of carefully cut vegetables — and when the menu indicates hot, you may trust it. It's hot.

Enzo's Warren Cafe

☆ ☆ 1/2

32747 Mound Road, south of 14 Mile Road, Warren. (810) 939-7800.

Hours: 10:30 a.m.-9 p.m. Mon.-Thu., 10:30 a.m.-10 p.m. Fri., 2-10 p.m. Sat., 2-8 p.m. Sun.

Nonsmoking: 60 percent

Full bar.   Major credit cards.

Reasonable.

Lodzia Winarski spoke only a few halting words of English when she arrived from Poland. For that reason, she almost didn't get hired as a cook at Enzo's. Then-proprietor Vince Marzolo wondered if she would get the orders straight. Would she understand whether patrons wanted pepperoni or anchovies on their pizzas?

Coming to Winarski's aid was staff

member Luba Bujan, whose own family had come to this country from Russia just a few years earlier. Bujan persuaded Marzolo to give Winarski a chance.

Today, Winarski is not only cook and baker but also proprietor of the cafe, along with partner John DiLauro, whom she met in an English class at Macomb Community College.

Welcome to America. And to Enzo's, an offbeat spot where the menu has two faces: Polish and Italian. You can try potato dill soup — known here as dill pickle soup — or an excellent minestrone; cabbage rolls or linguine with clam sauce; pierogi or chicken cacciatore.

American selections also are offered, including London broil and liver and onions that turn up as daily specials.

Enzo's has many niceties not often seen in this modest price range. And its kitchen staff has experience. In addition to Winarski and a couple of other women who help with the ethnic dishes, the cafe boasts the talents of chef James Glees. His professional spin is evident in such things as cream of asparagus soup, Caesar salad, roasted duck, prime rib, pan-fried rainbow trout, and in the garlic-accented sauteed spinach, which is one of a number of interesting side dishes.

Service is kind and caring. A tiny bar in the front room offers a very nice little selection of wines.

The two rooms are pleasant, if conventional. Cozy booths in the nonsmoking room make it the nicer of the two.

Ernesto's, An Italian Country Inn

 About all that's left to remind diners of the old Hillside Inn that preceded Ernesto's in this rambling space are the six fireplaces. A major renovation by designer Joy Walker has given it a fresh look, from the Italian villa exterior to the series of dining rooms, each with its own personality.

The less formal trattoria, which serves pastas and pizzas in a Roman garden setting, and the piano bar offer other seating options to the series of main dining rooms. This is a big restaurant, with gutsy fare by chef Ernie DeMichelle. His signature dishes include sauteed chicken breast with mushrooms and artichoke hearts in white wine sauce; sauteed salmon and scallops with roasted red peppers, grilled red onions and herb-shrimp cream sauce over linguine, and baked fresh pickerel with lemon sauce.

Of the pasta dishes, his most requested is a meatless mix of penne with fresh

41661 Plymouth Road, Plymouth.
(313) 453-2002.

Hours: Lunch, 11 a.m.-3 p.m. Mon.-Sat.; dinner, 5-10 p.m. Mon.-Thu., 5-11 p.m. Fri.-Sat., 1-9 p.m. Sun. Closed major holidays except Thanksgiving and Easter.

Nonsmoking: 75 percent.

Full bar.   Major credit cards.

Moderate.

tomatoes, olive oil and basil. It's a dish he calls Ernie's Peasant Pasta.

DeMichelle has been in the restaurant business all over the Detroit area since 1945, when he started a little place called Triangle Lunch on Grand River at Lawton. Among the stripes on his *toque blanche* (if he wore one) would be such names as Mario's, Ginopolis, Picano's, Como's, Carmelo's and Famous Pizza, one of the city's first pizzerias.

Evie's Tamales

☆ ☆ 1/2

3454 Bagley, Detroit.
(313) 843-5056.

Hours: 8 a.m.-6 p.m. Mon.-Sat., 8 a.m.-3 p.m. Sun. Closed Thanksgiving, Christmas Day and New Year's Day.

Nonsmoking: 60 percent.

Soft drinks only.   No credit cards.

Reasonable.

The modest, 75-seat restaurant in the heart of Mexican Town's tourist strip retains a simple, friendly neighborhood spirit. Evie's bridges the gap between the tourist-oriented places that attract crowds and the neighbors-only haunts.

The specialty, of course, is tamales. The corn husk-wrapped, steamed bundles of shredded, seasoned pork coated with corn flour dough emit a tantalizingly earthy aroma when unwrapped. With sides of rice and refried beans, they make a solid meal at $3.50. Tamales are also available by the dozen to take home, and many smart people pick up a few dozen to serve at parties.

There are a few other things on the menu, including caldo de res (short rib and vegetable soup) and menudo (tripe and hominy), as well as tacos, enchiladas and tostadas. But the tamales are the draw.

Excalibur

A bit of the late, lamented London Chop House, Detroit's most famous restaurant, lives on in this strategically located suburban spot. It's visible in the upscale setting that has a nightclubby feeling to it. It's in the sophisticated American menu that offers traditional, upper-crust dishes like lobster and scallop bisque; the hors d'oeuvre platter of ribs, shrimp, scallops and steak bits; beefsteak tomatoes with hearts of palm; chilled asparagus with vinaigrette, and 24-ounce porterhouse steak.

☆ ☆ ☆

28875 Franklin Road at Northwestern Hwy., Southfield. (810) 358-3355.

Hours: Lunch, 11 a.m.-5 p.m. weekdays; dinner, 5-11 p.m. Mon.-Thu., 5 p.m.-midnight Fri., 6 p.m.-midnight Sat. Closed Sun. and major holidays.

Nonsmoking: 30 percent.

Full bar.   Major credit cards.

Expensive.

Chef/proprietor Marty Wilk spent six years at the Chop House when he was just starting out as a teenage kitchen helper, and he retains a lot of the influence.

His restaurant has built its reputation since 1978 on doing whatever it takes to please its well-dressed guests. "If they want it and we can get it, we will prepare it for them," says Wilk.

I've never forgotten what one Excalibur regular told me a few years ago. "If you ask for your lobster served in a gym shoe, they'll simply inquire, 'Do you want a Ked or a Reebok?' "

The Farm

☆ ☆ 1/2

699 Port Crescent Rd., Port Austin.
(517) 874-5700.

Hours: 5-10 p.m. Tue.-Sat., noon-8 p.m. Sun. from Memorial Day to Labor Day. Open Mother's Day and weekends until the season starts on Memorial Day. After Labor Day, weekend hours continue through November. Closed Dec. through mid-May.

Nonsmoking: 95 percent.

Soft drinks only.   Discover, MC and Visa.

Moderate.

Cornfields and farmland stretch on all sides. A silo pokes into the open sky, a high-rise country style. Two-lane roads replaced freeways many miles back.

In the midst of this prairie-like setting in Huron County, almost at the tip of the Thumb, is a sign of life: a gaggle of cars pulling up and parking in the yard of an old house painted a grainy-mustard shade.

This must be the place. There's nothing else for miles. How did master chef Jeff Gabriel and his wife, Pamela, a pastry chef in her own right, ever find this in the first place?

The two still have that big-city look, in their crisp white professional chefs' coats, but they say they are in the country to stay. They bought the house and the five acres around it where they grow corn, carrots, peapods, squash and tomatoes, as well as flowers for the tables. The couple did it without partners, opening the seasonal restaurant in May '94.

This is not a country estate by any means. It's a simple house, with sagging floorboards and a cluttered look. Improvements are being made, however.

For now, there is no liquor license, though it is in the works. When a waiter asks, "Do you wish a beverage other than water?" it must be soft drinks, tea or coffee, which is not really conducive to a leisurely dining experience.

What is just fine about the place is the food, a blend of country-style dishes such as chicken and dumplings, fried green tomatoes and corn plucked from the garden, along with more sophisticated stuff. Gravlax, for example, beautiful morsels of bright pink house-cured salmon handsomely arranged on a plate, is a dish that looks as upscale as anything served in the city.

Perhaps surprisingly, the menu prominently features fish — pesto-grilled yellowfin tuna, sauteed pickerel with a hazelnut crust and seared rainbow trout — along with grilled New York sirloin and Swiss steak, farmer style. Of course.

Some dishes are meant to be shared. Each table is centered with a lazy Susan for the black skillets holding such dishes as broccoli and mushroom gratin with farmer mashed potatoes or seasonal vegetables.

Soups include a delicious sweet corn and clam chowder. The dark, thick, five-grain bread is housemade. The salad bar tempts quite a number of the guests and there's a more elegant romaine and tomato salad for those who prefer to be served.

Desserts, by Pamela, are exactly what you would hope to have in this setting

— warm plum cobbler, bread pudding, and pecan pie with caramel sauce.

Certainly, the food needs no improvement. It's an imaginative menu, and the mix of down-home dishes with sophisticated stuff allows guests lots of leeway in ordering.

Fishbone's Rhythm Kitchen Cafe

Set into the first floor of the International Center, a restored 1881 brick warehouse, this New Orleans wannabe has succeeded mightily with its crowd-pleasing elements. It has a setting that captures the Crescent City atmosphere in grillwork, wooden shutters, open kitchen and Dixieland background music. The bill of fare offers spicy seafood, ribs and chicken dishes in Creole/Cajun style.

It's the kind of place where you can't always pinpoint why you are enjoying yourself. You don't know whether to attribute it to the seafood — or to the atmosphere that pulses with the beat of vintage Dixieland music.

☆ ☆ 1/2

400 Monroe at Brush, Detroit. (313) 965-4600.

Hours: Breakfast, 6-10 a.m. Mon.-Sat.; lunch, 11 a.m.-4 p.m. Mon.-Sat.; dinner, 4 p.m.-midnight Mon.-Thu., 4 p.m.-2 a.m. Fri.-Sat.; Sun. brunch, 10:30 a.m.-2:30 p.m. and dinner, 3 p.m.-midnight. Closed Christmas Day.

Nonsmoking: 50 percent.

Full bar.   Major credit cards.

Moderate.

The carefully contrived setting, which can fool you into thinking you're on Decatur Street, and the crowd of diners — the typically eclectic mix you hope to find in a big city — also contribute to the good feeling.

Fishbone's, which is busy most of the time, does have a problem with inconsistency. One time the oysters Bienville or the gumbo or the shrimp Creole will be excellent, another time, pretty lackluster. Because it serves so many people, is open such long hours, and has the usual problems with staff turnover, it's difficult to keep the kitchen as quality-conscious as it might be.

Still, there's no denying the popularity of this Greektown area spot.

Fonte D'Amore

32030 Plymouth Road, west of Merriman, Livonia. (313) 422-0770.

Hours: Lunch, 11 a.m.-4 p.m. weekdays; dinner, 4-10 p.m. Mon.-Thu., 4-11 p.m. Fri.-Sat.

Nonsmoking: 75 percent.

Full bar.   Major credit cards.

Moderate.

One of the interesting aspects of this Italian restaurant on a strip of Italian restaurants is that patrons may phone chef/proprietor Luciano Del Signore, and with just 24 hours' notice, he will prepare a menu just for their party of four or more.

Del Signore, whose father established the restaurant in 1971, offers 10 specials every day. They range from housemade pastas to such dishes as filet Marino (pan-roasted filet seasoned with shallots, onions, mushrooms, sherry and cream) and mahimahi encrusted in peppercorns and flavored with liqueur.

The wine list, with more than 200 bottles, is completely Italian to go along with the cuisine.

Franco's Cafe

3614 Rochester Road, north of Big Beaver, Troy. (810) 528-0153.

Hours: 11 a.m.-9 p.m. Mon.-Thu., 11 a.m.-10 p.m. Fri., 4-10 p.m. Sat., 4-8 p.m. Sun. Closed Thanksgiving, Christmas Day and Fourth of July.

Nonsmoking: 80 percent.

Full bar.   Major credit cards.

Reasonable to moderate.

It takes only a glance at the soup of the day, perhaps sorrel or a resonant clam chowder made with olive oil, garlic and anchovies, and then a peek into the fresh bread basket, to know that this is not just another strip mall eatery.

Virtually everything on the menu shows a personal touch, reflecting the Sicilian heritage of Franco Giorlando and his wife, Anna Maria. It's not that the dishes are necessarily unusual — all the Italian standards are there — but the execution is out of the ordinary.

Pastas are housemade — and the most popular these days is angelhair with a sauce of olive oil, garlic, diced tomatoes and spinach. Franco calls angelhair "the pasta of the '90s." There are specials every day, in addition to the regular listing of veal, beef, fish and chicken dishes. Dinner includes soup, salad, vegetable and pasta. Suffice it to say that first timers are usually surprised by what they find behind the modest exterior of Franco's Cafe. And that includes its fine wine list.

Franklin Street B.C.

The low-slung, 100-year-old brick foundry building marked by a huge hand clutching a glass of beer is a paragon of industrial chic. Looking around the sand-blasted exposed wood and brick setting brightened by huge murals, skylights and ingenious indirect lighting, you could be in Toronto or Chicago.

Franklin Street B.C. (for brewing company) was originally intended to be a brew-pub where beer was produced in-house. Because such places were not legal at the time of the opening in '91, owners Mark Vincent, his sister Ginny Vincent, Greg Sebel and Gary Danis had their beer brewed and labeled at Frankenmuth Brewery. It worked out so well, they decided to keep it that way, even though the law has since been changed.

And the food, served at galvanized steel- and copper-topped tables covered with brown butcher paper, is surprisingly good. This is not, as some might expect, a hamburger joint — though there is indeed a burger on the menu, in fact, two. One is completely vegetarian.

Other offerings from chef John Wesenberg's kitchen include interesting shrimp, crab and thin-crusted pizza appetizers; creative soups, typified by tomato, basil and Asiago cheese soup, and such entrees as house-smoked duck breast with wild mushroom and cognac sauce, blue crabcakes, baked bourbon shrimp and a number of pastas.

After 9 o'clock on Friday and Saturday nights, it does get noisy here, with deejays and high decibel music. Those who prefer dining on the quiet side should be sure to claim tables earlier in the evening.

☆ ☆ 1/2

1560 Franklin Street at Orleans, Detroit. (313) 568-0391.

Hours: Lunch, 11:30 a.m.-5 p.m. weekdays; dinner, 5-10 p.m. weeknights, 5-10 p.m. Sat.; late-night menu, 10 p.m.-midnight Fri.-Sat. Closed Sun. and major holidays.

Nonsmoking: 50 percent.

Full bar. Major credit cards.

Moderate.

Fran O'Brien's Maryland Crabhouse

☆ ☆ 1/2

621 S. Opdyke Road, Auburn Hills.
(810) 332-7744.

Hours: 11 a.m.-11 p.m. weekdays, 3-11 p.m. Sat., 3-9:30 p.m. Sun. Closed Thanksgiving, Christmas Day and New Year's Day.

Nonsmoking: 30 percent.

Full bar.   AE, MC and Visa.

Moderate to expensive.

Seafood taverns hit a lot of the right buttons these days, and this one offers more than just the expected dishes. True to its name, crab stars on the menu. When Maryland blue crabs are in season, during the months of April through October, guests are offered the opportunity literally to attack their food.

The spiced, hard-shelled crabs make quite a game out of dinner. At tables spread with brown paper, diners are given mallets and crackers and usually a little guidance on the best way to get at the meat inside those tough shells.

When the hard-shells are unobtainable, Florida's wonderful stone crab claws offer an alternate experience. Neither dish is inexpensive. Maryland crabs can reach the $36.95 region per dozen. Stone crab claws are $28.95. These prices include the trimmings, however.

With the hard-shelled crabs, accompaniments include redskins, cole slaw or salad, and a vegetable. The claws come with mustard sauce, sweet potato French fries, salad and bread.

The menu also includes sandwiches, burgers, and barbecued ribs and chicken in a much lower price range.

Gandy Dancer

Like many other C.A. Muer restaurants, this one is housed in a historic building. The circa-1886 Michigan Central Depot was purchased and restored in 1969, and in 1986, the massive granite and brick structure was refurbished again, just in time for its centennial.

I've always appreciated restaurants with daily-changing menus, and this is one of them. The day's date appears at the top of each menu. That's reassuring. Seasonal, fresh-catch items are served broiled, grilled, poached, blackened or sauteed.

Then there are the featured entrees that have a little more embellishment, including sauteed petrale sole, potato-topped whitefish, and shrimp, scallop and mussel jambalaya.

Maine lobster, rack of lamb and New York strip or filet mignon are pretty regularly available.

A secondary specialty for years has been the pasta, including such dishes as Cajun seafood pasta and seared tuna fettuccine.

This is still among Ann Arbor's most popular restaurants.

☆ ☆ ☆

**401 Depot Road, Ann Arbor.
(313) 769-0592.**

Hours: Lunch, 11:30 a.m.-4 p.m. Mon.-Thu.; dinner, 5-10 p.m. Mon.-Thu., 5-11 p.m. Fri.-Sat.; Sun. brunch, 10 a.m.-2 p.m. and dinner, 3:30-9 p.m. Closed Christmas Day, Memorial Day and Labor Day.

Nonsmoking: 80 percent.

Full bar.   Major credit cards.

Expensive.

Genitti's Hole in the Wall

Toni and John Genitti have come a long way from their little dining room in the back of a country store. They've expanded into quite a production, with a cocktail bar where the store once was, additional rooms for dining, and a 132-seat theater where guests may choose to go for interactive theater productions after dinner.

The meal, however, has pretty much stayed the same. The family dishes up

☆ ☆ 1/2

**108 E. Main Street, Northville.
(810) 349-0522.**

Hours: Lunch, 11 a.m.-2 p.m. weekdays, 11 a.m.-3 p.m. Sat.; family style dinner, 7 p.m. Fri., 6 p.m. Sat.; Mon.-Thu. evenings available for private parties of 30 or more. Closed Sun., except Thankgiving through New Year's Eve, and major holidays.

Nonsmoking: 100 percent.

Full bar.   AE, MC and Visa.

Moderate.

seven courses of sturdy Italian fare from soup and pasta to breaded steak, chicken, peppers and onions, with cannolis for dessert.

It's not an intimate scene, but one reminiscent of an Italian wedding, with tables seating eight, 10 and 12. If you want a cozy table for two, go down the street to Mackinnon's.

You might think you're too sophisticated for this sort of thing, but don't sell the Genittis short. Their expansive personalities just might win you over.

The price of $37.10 includes dinner, theater, tax and tip — everything except alcoholic beverages. Dinner only is $26.45, also all-inclusive.

Ginopolis on the Grill

 ☆ ☆ 1/2

27815 Middlebelt at 12 Mile Road, Farmington Hills. (810) 851-8222.

Hours: 11 a.m.-11 p.m. Mon.-Thu., 11 a.m.-midnight Fri.-Sat., 2-9 p.m. Sun. during the winter months, 4-10 p.m. in the summer. Closed Christmas Day.

Nonsmoking: 50 percent.

Full bar.   Major credit cards.

Moderate.

It's big, bustling, and a cross between a restaurant and a sports bar — basketball, baseball, you name it, are abiding interests of the Ginopolis brothers, John and Pete. They offer a reliable stop for solid American fare with a Greek twist.

Ribs cooked in a sweet and spicy sauce are a specialty. They are the ribs served at the Montgomery Inn in Cincinnati, and they're of the falling-off-the-bone variety.

The big menu also includes a number of fresh fish from lake perch and whitefish to swordfish, and lamb chops, big Greek salads and pastas. The setting is colorful and informal.

Giovanni's Ristorante

This off-the-beaten-track Italian restaurant exudes friendliness and warmth. Proprietor Fran Cannarsa Truant, upbeat and effusive, greets many of her patrons by name and all of them with enthusiasm. The waitstaff reflects the same spirit.

330 S. Oakwood Blvd., west of Fort, Detroit. (313) 841-0122.

Hours: 11 a.m.-9 p.m. Tue.-Thu., 11 a.m.-10 p.m. Fri., 4-10 p.m. Sat. Closed Sun., Mon. and major holidays.

Nonsmoking: 50 percent.

Full bar.   Major credit cards.

Moderate.

The dining room is decorated with dozens of family photographs and some nice antiques, creating a cozy, intimate feeling. While the menu includes many Italian classics, the skill of preparation takes them out of the ordinary. Chefs Joseph Bushnell and Anthony Polito have the little kitchen running as smoothly as the Marsala sauce swirled around the veal.

Pastas are wonderful here — and anyone who has never found gnocchi a memorable dish is advised to try this version. The dumplings of potato and spinach in a delicate cheese sauce are outstanding.

Accompanying the pasta dishes is peperonata, a mixture of sweet peppers, tomatoes, onions and garlic, as well as garlic bread and a choice of soup or salad. The more elaborate entrees, including veal, chicken and seafood dishes, come with all of the above and a side dish of pasta.

Desserts change daily, and the chefs always come up with interesting special entrees on weekends. The crowning touch is an outstanding Italian wine list.

Truant's mother, Rosa Cannarsa, is still active in the business she started as a little pizza carry-out in 1970. It's named for Rosa's late husband.

Golden Mushroom

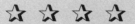

★ ★ ★ ★

18100 W. 10 Mile Road at
Southfield Road, Southfield.
(810) 559-4230.

Hours: Lunch, 11:30 a.m.-4 p.m. weekdays
in the main dining room and in the
Mushroom Cellar; dinner, 5-11 p.m. Mon.-
Thu., 5 p.m.-midnight Fri., 5:30 p.m.-mid-
night Sat. Closed Sun. and major holidays.

Nonsmoking: 50 percent.

Full bar.   Major credit cards.

Expensive.

A big-city atmosphere combines with intricate and elegant fare at the long-standing Southfield spot. Its ambitions belie the unprepossessing location next door to a gas station.

To sum up the aspirations of this restaurant, it is one where luxury is evident from the Russian caviar and foie gras terrine on the appetizer list to the dessert souffles that end the meal.

Even amidst this upper-crust approach, however, those who shy from heavy cream and butter may find choices from a nutritionally conservative list. Such dishes as poached salmon, grilled swordfish and roasted eggplant ratatouille are options to the lobster bisque, roast duckling with wild rice, double lamb chops and seafood fettuccine.

Naturally, mushrooms are spotlighted throughout the menu, from the Golden Mushroom soup to the wild mushrooms in puff pastry and the grilled shiitakes and wild mushroom sautes on the list of side dishes.

Perennially popular main courses include Dover sole, either half or whole, grilled veal chop, and tournedos with foie gras, Madeira sauce and fettuccine with truffles.

Lunch is a relative bargain, with some entrees under $10. At both lunch and dinner, accompaniments include a choice of Caesar salad or the house version, which combines Boston lettuce, dried cherries, red onions, walnuts and blue cheese in red wine vinaigrette.

While the fare is indeed opulent, I like the menu style: straightforward and succinct, without high-flown descriptions. Tables are impeccably set with china and crystal.

Chef Steven Allen is in charge of a kitchen staff that starts from the ground up, learning the classic techniques in the European tradition of master chef Milos Cihelka. Cihelka, semi-retired, still stops by to see how things are going.

Goulash King

In a cookie-cutter world, it's a pleasure to stumble upon a restaurant like Goulash King. This highly personal restaurant, seating just 32 on benches at trestle tables covered in red-and-white gingham, is truly an oasis for the solid dishes and homespun folk art of Hungary.

The antithesis of the sophisticated restaurant, its very innocence is refreshing. The white eyelet embroidery around the red-and-white gingham trappings, the dolls and deerskins and decorative plates all around the room give the place a peasanty look that is very appealing.

☆ ☆ ☆

470 Ouellette Avenue, Windsor, Ontario. (519) 252-4011.

Hours: Noon-8 p.m. Tue.-Thu. and Sun. (until 10 p.m. during summer); noon-10 p.m. Fri.-Sat. Closed Mon. and last week of December and first week in January.

Nonsmoking: Ashtrays only by request.

Soft drinks only.   AE and MC.

Reasonable.

Just about everything in the room was brought from Hungary.

Proprietor Steve Balogh and his teenage son Adam and daughter Eva came to Windsor just a couple of years ago, persuaded to make the big move from the old country by friends in Windsor who told him that opportunity beckoned.

The menu lists only specialties. What a novel approach! Imagine serving only dishes you do very well. Restaurateurs everywhere would do well to emulate Balogh in this.

There is a soup of the day, perhaps chicken or beef noodle, bean or leek. And always goulash soup, a richly flavored mix of tender beef, carrots and tomatoes with tiny dumplings.

Main courses, lunch or dinner, are limited to just eight. Each dish is handsomely served, garnished with potatoes or the tiny dumplings, perhaps a dollop of sour cream or some lettuce and tomato. And the correctly spelled words on the menu — words including lecso (a traditional vegetable mix) and kolozsvari (a type of bacon) — show that Balogh is as precise with language as he is with his cooking.

Delicate and delicious chicken paprikas is served with tender dumplings. Other notable dishes: cabbage rolls filled with sauerkraut, pork and rice and served with freshly sauteed potatoes; pork chops with lecso, which blends green peppers, onions and tomatoes into a savory relish that is a harmonious counterpoint to the crisp pork, and beef goulash with dumplings.

Dessert is part of any Hungarian meal. Displayed in a glass case is a beautiful array of tortes, including the classic Dobos.

Service is very much in keeping with the family orientation of the place. The young servers are courteous, soft-spoken and anxious to please.

Still back in Gyor, Hungary, an industrial city between Budapest and Vienna, is

Balogh's wife, Elizabeth. She runs another family business, the Viennese Coffeehouse.

Govinda's at the Fisher Mansion

☆ ☆ 1/2

383 Lenox Avenue, Detroit.
(313) 331-6740.

Hours: noon-9 p.m. Fri. and Sat.; noon-7 p.m. Sun. Closed Mon.-Thu.

Nonsmoking: 100 percent.

Soft drinks only.   Major credit cards.

Reasonable.

Vegetarian through-and-through, this restaurant — its name means "pleaser of the senses" in Sanskrit — has an eye-popping setting that is a mix of vintage Hollywood and Italian Renaissance. The house is a 1927 extravaganza lavished with tile, carvings and ornate furnishings.

The fare includes sandwiches and salads, but many people opt for the Indian assortment. This features such dishes as basmati rice with pine nuts, vegetables and spices, lentil or split pea soup, and cucumber and yogurt salad.

Service is calm and gentle, as befits the Krishna Consciousness group that runs the place.

Gratzi

☆ ☆ ☆

326 S. Main, Ann Arbor.
(313) 663-5555.

Hours: 11:30 a.m.-10 p.m. Mon.-Thu., 11:30 a.m.-11:30 p.m. Fri.-Sat., 4-9 p.m. Sun. Closed Thanksgiving, Christmas Day and New Year's Day.

Nonsmoking: 90 percent.

Full bar.   Major credit cards.

Moderate.

The bold, balconied space boasting an eye-catching mural is a made-to-order setting for Gratzi's colorful regional Italian fare. There's an air of excitement about the multi-level room. It was the Orpheum Theatre before the Mainstreet Ventures people took over in '89 (with a bow toward Chicago's Scoozi!) and made it into what has become their most successful restaurant.

The place seats 180 at paper-covered tables. Seats in the balcony offer a view of the main floor, where tables are tucked into banquettes along the walls or next to the front windows.

Chef Susan Jo Carter's gutsy menu offers thin-crusted pizzas, linguines, raviolis, leafy salads, and fish, veal, chicken and quail from the grill and saute pans.

Popular dishes include *polenta* with Italian sausage, goat cheese and tomato sauce; tortelloni with two cheeses, fresh rosemary and garlic, and shrimp in garlic, butter, lemon and white wine sauce.

Many dishes are available in two portion sizes — *piccola* or *grande*. Reading the menu is a short course in the Italian language, with subtitles provided.

Great Lakes Inn

In an area where the informal burger and beer approach is typical of dining options, this gracious Georgian-style inn will be a welcome surprise to those who like quiet, candle-lit dining. You might be somewhere in the Virginia countryside as you look around the seven acres that surround this interesting spot. The French doors, multi-paned windows and brass sconces, the white-covered tables and sparkling glassware impart a soothing, vintage quality.

9334 N. River Road, Algonac.
(810) 794-0900.

Hours: Lunch, 11:30 a.m.-2:30 p.m. Tue.-Sat.; dinner, 5:30-9:30 p.m. Tue.-Sat., noon-7 p.m. Sun. Closed Mon., Christmas Day and New Year's Day.

Nonsmoking: 50 percent.

Full bar.   Major credit cards.

Moderate.

Holding fast to this approach since its opening in 1989, the very civilized dining room offers a traditional menu including filet mignon, sea scallops, whitefish and pickerel. These are accompanied by vegetable or potato and an upgraded house salad that has a mix of greens with sweet and sour dressing.

Desserts include that American classic, the parfait.

The inn has eight handsome suites for overnight guests.

Haab's

☆ ☆ 1/2

18 W. Michigan, Ypsilanti.
(313) 483-8200.

Hours: 11 a.m.-9 p.m. Mon.-Thu., 11 a.m.-10 p.m. Fri.-Sat., 11 a.m.-9 p.m. Sun. Closed Christmas.

Nonsmoking: 80 percent.

Full bar.   Major credit cards.

Reasonable.

American dining as our grandparents knew it still exists here in a series of country-style dining rooms. Solid American dishes are served to people who love the old-time feeling of the place as much as they do the straightforward menu.

"It's like being home again," patrons tell proprietor Mike Kabat over and over again.

Haab's opened in 1934, and still serves chicken in the rough. A vintage dish on the menu since the beginning, it is batter-dipped and pan-fried chicken cooked in a patented contraption. This, of course, is not an especially popular dish in the '90s. More likely to be ordered is one of the fresh fish and seafood items.

Entrees are served with a choice of soup or salad, potato and bread. And what would you have for dessert in a flowered-wallpaper place like this but pie?

Interestingly enough, about 75 percent of the diners pulling up captain's chairs to the wooden tables are from somewhere outside of Washtenaw County. Haab's is a destination restaurant for those in the western and northern suburbs of Detroit.

Harlequin Cafe

☆ ☆ 1/2

8047 Agnes, Detroit.
(313) 331-0922.

Hours: Lunch, 11:30 a.m.-3 p.m. Tue.-Fri.; dinner, 4:30-10 p.m. Tue.-Thu., 4:30-11 p.m. Fri.-Sat.; Sun. brunch, 11 a.m.-3 p.m., and dinner, 3-9 p.m. Closed Mon. and major holidays.

Nonsmoking: 50 percent.

Full bar.   Major credit cards.

Moderate.

The epitome of the civilized urban cafe, atmosphere simply oozes from the vintage contours of what was once an old-fashioned drug store, complete with the still-present marble soda fountain and wooden apothecary cabinets.

For some dozen years the cafe has waxed and waned, sometimes thriving, sometimes barely hanging on. For the past two, it's been in the hands of Sherman and Ceferina Sharpe, and they have emphasized its French direction. From time to time, they've added such dishes as oysters *a l'orange,* escargots, and scallops Florentine, while still preserving a bit of the East Indian flavor that came with the previous owners.

In fact, the chef is Paramjit Batra, brother of former proprietor Ajinder Singh.

Dinner includes soup or house salad along with the nicely garnished main course. Courteous service is emphasized. And it's important that people be willing to sit back and relax and enjoy the leisurely pace of the meal. This is not a place to rush in and out of.

The Sharpes added lunch to the proceedings and also spotlight piano music every evening. There's classical on Tuesday evening and more jazz and pop-oriented piano stylings on other evenings. Marty Balog, an irresistible Tin Pan Alley-style pianist, plays at Sunday brunch, which is a leisurely, sit-down affair.

Hattie's

If some film theaters can call themselves art theaters, surely Jim Milliman rates an art designation for his fine restaurant in the postcard-pretty town of Suttons Bay on the Leelanau Peninsula.

His food is certainly artistic. And it's enhanced by the changing array of works on display by Michigan artists. There's a new exhibit each month in the restaurant. This is not the output of the local high schoolers, but professional works by noted artists from throughout the state.

☆ ☆ ☆ ☆

111 St. Joseph, Suttons Bay.
(616) 271-6222.

Hours: Dinner only, 5:30-9:30 p.m. Tue.-Sat. (Labor Day to Memorial Day); 5:30-10:30 p.m. daily (Memorial Day to Labor Day). Closed Sun. and Mon. in winter and major holidays.

Nonsmoking: 90 percent.

Full bar.   Major credit cards.

Moderate.

Certainly, the fresh ingredients and creative combinations of Milliman's kitchen are art-quality. On a monthly changing menu, the chef offers such dishes as roasted red peppers filled with puffy cheese souffle, poached salmon with white bean stew, and the obligatory whitefish brightened with sesame breading and orange-ginger relish. In the summer, house salads are made with local greens in lemon dressing.

He likes to use broths to add flavor without fat, and fennel broth is one of his favorites. After a trip to North Carolina, Milliman came back inspired by, of all things, grits, and created a dish of shrimp with grits cooked with white wine, garlic and cheeses. The staff laughed at first, but not after they tried it.

Some dishes are offered in half portions. All of those mentioned above can be ordered that way. By the time you get to Hattie's, Milliman will have undoubtedly come up with other variations on his fresh, seasonal theme.

The chef got his start at the Rowe Inn in Ellsworth, another outstanding up-north art house.

Haymakers

☆ ☆

2375 Joslyn Court, Lake Orion.
(810) 391-4800.

Hours: 11 a.m.-10 p.m. Mon.-Thu., 11 a.m.-
midnight Fri.-Sat., 11 a.m.-10 p.m. Sun.
Closed Christmas Day and New Year's Day.

Nonsmoking: 60 percent.

Full bar.   Major credit cards.

Reasonable.

Feel free to walk in and say "What a barn!" It really is — a vintage dairy barn that has housed restaurants of one kind or another for years. At one time, it specialized, appropriately enough, in beef.

You can still get a burger, but the menu has become more of a middle-of-the-road American one, with items that have the fresh twist people want these days. Dishes like pecan-encrusted turkey, catfish and rainbow trout, a number of pastas, and salads dressed in raspberry vinaigrette.

Haymakers is adjacent to Olde World Canterbury Village, a series of 12 shops that plans to add a restaurant, cider mill and brewery in 1995.

Heinzman's Heidelberg

☆ ☆ 1/2

43785 Gratiot, south of Hall Road,
Clinton Twp. (810) 469-0440.

Hours: 11 a.m.-10 p.m. Tue.-Thu., 11 a.m.-
11 p.m. Fri., 3-11 p.m.-Sat.; Sun. brunch,
11 a.m.-3 p.m. and dinner, 3-9 p.m. Closed
Mon. and Christmas Day.

Nonsmoking: 50 percent.

Full bar.   Major credit cards.

Reasonable to moderate.

There isn't much middle ground about German restaurants. People either like or loathe the lederhosen and sometimes leaden fare of the Rhineland. If you are on the positive side of that equation, the resurrected Heidelberg restaurant, now known as Heinzman's Heidelberg, is a treat.

You may dine on German lentil soup, potato pancakes and spaetzle in what appear to be the rooms of an old castle. It's centered by a working, copper-hooded fireplace that houses a roaring, cherry wood fire when the weather is cold.

It's a pretty irresistible setting. On a dark night, you half expect Dracula to drop by the table. This place is a return to the days when restaurants wrapped diners in an atmosphere that took them completely away from the mundane.

Vintage details ornament the rough-plastered rooms with their dark woodwork and massive chandeliers, bottle-glass windows and arched doorways. In a brick-walled wine room, a cast-iron chess set (a replica of one found in a sunken ship) stands on a brass base. One tiny, circular room, its own vaulted ceiling painted to look like a summer sky, seats just six at a round wooden table put together with wood pegs. Such details fill the place, which was acquired three years ago by Jeff and Victoria Heinzman after a number of regimes dating back to 1909.

German specialties like Wiener schnitzel, rouladen, veal bratwurst and hasenpfeffer (braised young rabbit in a sauce of herbs and red wine) share the menu with some contemporary dishes. These include potato-crusted whitefish, a number of chicken treatments and prime ribs.

Hermann's European Cafe

Chef/proprietor Hermann Suhs presides over a vintage, small-town hotel; a cozy, old-fashioned bar and brick-walled dining room; a gourmet shop, and a butcher shop. The obviously energetic Suhs is an Austrian with an international background, and it shows up in a menu that ranges all over the map. He's as happy to dish up rack of lamb or lobster as he is the jaeger schnitzel of his heritage.

☆ ☆ ☆

214 N. Mitchell Street, Cadillac. (616) 775-9563.

Hours: 11 a.m.-9:30 p.m. Mon.-Thu., 11 a.m.-10 p.m. Fri.-Sat. Closed Sun., Thanksgiving, Christmas Day and New Year's Day.

Nonsmoking: 60 percent.

Full bar.   MC and Visa.

Moderate.

The clubby bar, with its daily specials chalked on a board, is my favorite place to dine, but there's also a formal dining room.

A glance at the pastry tray would reveal Suhs' heritage even if his accent didn't.

Himalaya

If you've shied away from Indian food, or have never tried it, you'll find that Himalaya makes the mysterious fare very accessible.

Jeff Nadasen, South African-born but Indian by heritage, is doing his best to bring the fare to a wider audience.

His premise: If he can entice people to try the Indian dishes on his lunchtime buffet served six days a week, perhaps

☆ ☆ 1/2

44282 Warren, Canton. (313) 416-0880.

Hours: 11:30 a.m.-2:30 p.m. and 5-10 p.m. Mon. and Wed.-Fri., 11:30 a.m.-10 p.m. Sat.-Sun. Closed Tue., Thanksgiving, Christmas Day and New Year's Day.

Nonsmoking: 80 percent.

Full bar.   Major credit cards.

Reasonable.

they'll come back in the evening to delve a little more deeply into the cuisine.

The buffet, offered every day except Tuesday, offers a cross-section of the menu. There are usually two meat dishes, perhaps tandoori chicken or chicken tikka masala (boneless breast cooked with fresh tomatoes, onions, peppers and coriander); four vegetarian selections; a hot bread such as naan; raita, the cooling yogurt and cucumber salad; rice, and dessert. A very good deal at just $5.95.

There are a few South African selections, too, including three that feature peri peri sauce. It's a blend of green peppers, tomatoes, onions and scallions that, frankly, tastes just about the way you might expect that combination to taste.

If you want it as hot as the South Africans eat it, ask and it can be spiced up with green chilies.

On the Indian side of the menu, there are a number of treats. They include samosas (pastries filled with potato, onions and fresh cilantro, or beef with those ingredients), the thin but resonant dall (a soup made with lentils or yellow split peas) and two wonderful vegetarian dishes, sag pan (spinach with little chunks of house-made cheese) and aloo gobi (cauliflower and potatoes with ginger, onions and spices).

Nadasen serves three Indian beers as well as a small selection of wines. Another choice is lassi, a yogurt-based drink in sweet or salty versions.

Hunan Hunan

☆ ☆ 1/2

4327 Allen Road, Allen Park.
(313) 389-0939.

Hours: 11 a.m.-9 p.m. Mon.-Thu., 11 a.m.-10 p.m. Fri.-Sat., noon-9 p.m. Sun. Closed Thanksgiving.

Nonsmoking: 50 percent.

Full bar. Major credit cards.

Reasonable.

Like so many Asian restaurants, this one is a family affair. The Wangs, including chefs Yen Shin Wang and Yen Heui Wang, are devoted to their restaurant and its Hunan, Mandarin and Cantonese fare.

Eight soups are on the extensive menu and even more appetizers, ranging from cold noodles with sesame sauce to fried dumplings. The 14 chefs' specials include sweet and sour fish and "hot plate" beef and scallops.

The Wangs squeezed out more room for tables by making the bar smaller, but a full array of cocktails is still available.

Hungarian Rhapsody

 Hungary is the theme in Steve and Darlene Szatmari's ingenuously done-up restaurant, bright with garlands of red peppers, colorful Herendi and Kalocsai porcelain plates and heavily embroidered tablecloths.

An alcove in the front is a mini-museum of Hungarian handicrafts, including an embroidered *szur*, the coat worn by shepherds, and a feather-bedecked hat, brought from the old country. Certainly they are a refreshing contrast to the slick designer decor seen elsewhere, and a reminder of the peasant roots most of us share regardless of our ethnic heritage.

☆ ☆ ☆

14315 Northline Road, Southgate. (313) 283-9622.

Hours: 11 a.m.-10 p.m. Tue.-Sat., 11:30 a.m.-8 p.m. Sun. Closed Mon. and Christmas Day.

Nonsmoking: 60 percent.

Full bar.   Major credit cards.

Reasonable.

Open up the big beige and black menu, and go right to the Hungarian specialties. They are the heart and soul of this restaurant. Chicken and veal paprikas, stuffed cabbage and goulash are, of course, mainstays of this cuisine.

Other Hungarian specialties include palacsinta, crepes served with both savory and sweet fillings, and house-made noodle dishes such as turos teszta (noodles with cottage cheese and bacon) and kaposztas teszta (sauteed cabbage with noodles).

Soups are interesting and earthy, ranging from chicken vegetable to potato, green bean and mushroom. There's an American side of the menu, too, but I always wonder what would possess a person to come to a restaurant like this and order dishes that can be found almost anywhere.

The food is all house-made by the Szatmaris — Darlene being the author of the wonderful Hungarian desserts — and executive chef Dan Moro.

Stuffed cabbage is among the dishes leaving a favorable impression. Lighter and more delicate than the Polish version, it has a filling of paprika-sparked veal, pork and rice. Accompanying, as a little extra, is a small wedge of the Hungarian sausage kolbas.

Other dishes that can be recommended are both the chicken and veal paprikas with tiny dumplings, cucumber salad with sour cream dressing, and various palacsinta. Beef goulash, tender little cubes of meat and vegetables, arrives in a bogracs, a miniature of the traditional kettles that hung over the open fires.

The pastry desserts are simply wonderful, especially kremes, the Hungarian version of the French Napoleon, its satin-smooth cream filling wrapped in a light, flaky pastry. Others include the dobos torte, a seven-layer concoction of sponge cake with chocolate rum cream and burnt sugar; walnut torte and fruit strudels.

Il Centro

☆ ☆ 1/2

670 Lothrop, Detroit.
(313) 872-5110.

Hours: 11 a.m.-3 p.m. Mon., 11 a.m.-9 p.m. Tue.-Thu., 11 a.m.-11:30 p.m. Fri., 4-11:30 p.m. Sat. Open 4-8 p.m. Sun. when there is a show at the Fisher Theatre.

Nonsmoking: 75 percent.

Full bar. Major credit cards.

Moderate.

An upbeat re-do a few years ago preserved the character of the '20s vintage house on Lothrop, while bringing its series of rooms up to date with paper, paint and fabric. Joe Beato is the latest of many proprietors at this New Center address. Through it all, the place strategically located behind the Fisher Building has stayed something of a neighborhood hangout.

Many a theatergoer has skipped out mid-act from a bad show at the Fisher to find a haven here. And when the show's good, it's even more of a pre- and post-theater destination.

Beato's menu of Italian pastas, veal and chicken dishes, and fresh salads is served at paper-covered tables. It's a crowd-pleasing bill of fare with a lighter spin than at more traditional Italian restaurants. Beato is very much into a heart-friendly approach from his years as a chef at Henry Ford Hospital.

Il Gabbiano

☆ ☆ 1/2

851 Erie Street East, Windsor, Ontario. (519) 256-9757.

Hours: Lunch, 11:30 a.m.-2 p.m. Tue.-Fri.; dinner, 5-11 p.m. Tue.-Sat., 4-10 p.m. Sun. Closed Mon., Christmas Day and Easter.

Nonsmoking: 80 percent.

Full bar. AE, MC and Visa.

Reasonable to moderate.

Joe Fallea and Nick Politi, first cousins in their early 20s, offer surprisingly refined and light interpretations of Italian dishes at this 12-table restaurant.

You'll find no cloying sauces here, no tomato paste-y masks. That's because the cousins enjoyed an Italian-Canadian childhood during which good food was important in the family. "Ninety-five percent of the time, our mothers were cooking," says Fallea.

The menu emphasizes seafood — fitting, since the restaurant's name means the "sea gull" and one of the walls has a romantic seascape mural.

Also offered are pastas, veal and chicken dishes, all presented on an attractive, non-fussy plate with the correct style of service. Everything is cooked to order, and both lunch and dinner proceed at a relaxing pace.

Just about all the appetizers revolve around seafood, from shrimp cocktails to the seafood antipasti platter, which includes grilled calamari and shrimp and a mix of cuttlefish, octopus, squid, mussels and baby shrimp that the house calls seafood salad. The herb-dappled dish, served for two, arrives with lots of fresh lemon and is the tip-off that the kitchen really does emphasize lightness.

The dinner menu offers a number of familiar dishes, including veal or chicken Marsala, and grilled veal or beef filet with sauteed mushrooms. There's also shrimp grilled with lemon garlic sauce, mussels steamed in white wine, and rainbow trout with lemon garlic or white wine sauce.

Innfield's

It was a family affair when Sam and Mona Saad and her brother and his wife, Sam and Jennie Morey, took over in '94 from the founding Licari family. They knew a good thing when they saw it.

The four didn't make drastic changes at Innfield's, deciding to keep up the standards for creative fare that the place was known for. Some typical dishes include turkey, almond and fresh grape salad; salmon atop baby spinach in raspberry vinaigrette; blackened swordfish, and very affordable Caesar salads.

☆ ☆ 1/2

**4075 W. 12 Mile Road, Berkley.
(810) 548-0288.**

Hours: 8 a.m.-10 p.m. Mon.-Thu., 8 a.m.-11 p.m. Fri.-Sat., 8 a.m.-10 p.m. Sun. Closed Thanksgiving and Christmas Day.

Nonsmoking: 75 percent.

Full bar.   Major credit cards.

Reasonable.

Affordable is a word that fits well here at this prime example of an unpretentious, yet solid neighborhood-style cafe, the kind of place where lots of people stop by for the Friday fish fry.

Inn Season

☆ ☆ ☆

500 E. Fourth Street, Royal Oak.
(810) 547-7916.

Hours: 11 a.m.-9 p.m. Tue.-Thu., 11 a.m.-10 p.m. Fri., noon-10 p.m. Sat.

Closed Sun., Mon. and major holidays.

Nonsmoking: 100 percent.

Soft drinks only.   Major credit cards.

Reasonable.

Vegetarian to the core, George Vutetakis' restaurant does make one small departure from greens and grains. Some fish is served along with the vegetable stir-fries, pastas, soups — including a good meatless chili — and pizzas with such toppings as garlic and roasted fennel, sauteed tofu, feta cheese and broccoli.

The seasoning level here is assertive — something that is especially important when dealing with vegetarian dishes. It does take a little something extra to liven up brown rice, whole wheat pita, sea vegetables and tempeh (bean) patties. Vutetakis, who took over several years ago from restaurant founder John Armstrong, certainly does knows how to dish up the spicy salsas and relishes.

Interestingly enough, Armstrong is back functioning as the restaurant manager. It adds to the consistency of this popular spot.

Izakaya Sanpei

☆ ☆ 1/2

43327 Joy Road at Morton Taylor, Canton. (313) 416-9605.

Hours: Lunch, 11:30 a.m.-2 p.m. weekdays; dinner, 5:30-10:30 p.m. Mon.-Thu., 5:30-11 p.m. Fri.-Sat., 5-10 p.m. Sun. Closed Christmas Day and New Year's Day.

Nonsmoking: 20 percent.

Full bar.   Major credit cards.

Moderate.

In its suburban strip mall location, a restaurant named Izakaya Sanpei (E-za-kai-ya SAN-pay) is a reminder that though the good old USA may have gotten a little homogenized, it is still multicultural.

Though the spot is completely authentic, it is more accessible to non-Asians than other Japanese restaurants in the area for a couple of reasons. One is the setting. Another is the well-organized menu.

There are no tatami rooms, just seats at sturdy, Formica-topped tables or at the tiny sushi bar and the slightly larger grill area that share space along a counter. There you may watch not only the sushi chef at work, but also the cooks as they prepare the hot food — more fun than karaoke, but Izakaya has that, too.

The pair of rooms is done up with blond wood and translucent white shoji screens, yet with accents of surprisingly bright colors all around. A glowing tangerine awning covers the little bar. Multicolored Japanese kites dangle above the dining room. This is not the usual understated Japanese style.

The restaurant was designed by George Nakashima, who says he came up with color to substitute for more elaborate decorative effects that simply weren't possible in the budget.

Proprietor Hidezo Fujiwara, whom everyone calls Fuji, admits that he thought all that color was a bit, well … American, until a Japanese visitor reminded him that Kabuki theater costumes are in similar vivid hues.

The other reason for the accessibility of Izakaya Sanpei is the easy-to-read menu. It doesn't go on and on, but restricts the offerings to a workable number with descriptions that are clear.

With such headings as broiled, deep-fried, hot pot, noodle, rice and salad, written in both English and elegant Japanese characters, it is relatively easy to zero in on a dish you want to try.

"Izakaya" restaurants are neighborhood pubs in Japan. They are casual places, where people order lots of appetizers with their big silver cans of Sapporo beer as they sit and chat with their friends. That theme is followed here. Diners may nibble sushi or sashimi to start. Ask the wait person for "beginner sushi" — items carefully chosen for American tastes — if you've never tried it. Or, you can go for such hot appetizers as gyoza, house-made dumplings virtually identical to Chinese pot stickers, served with a dipping sauce of sesame seed oil, soy sauce and hot pepper oil; or yakitori, marinated chicken grilled on wooden skewers.

Jack's Waterfront Restaurant

☆ ☆

24214 Jefferson, Emerald City
Harbor, St. Clair Shores.
(810) 445-8080.

Hours: 11 a.m.-11 p.m. Mon.-Thu., 11 a.m.-midnight Fri.-Sat., 9 a.m.-11 p.m. Sun.

Nonsmoking: 60 percent.

Full bar.   MC, Visa, Discover.

Reasonable to moderate.

There are just two seasons at waterfront spots like this one. The boating season — and that other one. The boating season — April 15 to October 15 — is, of course, prime time. But east siders seem to like this revamped Quonset hut all year round.

The main dining room is reminiscent of Sindbad's in Detroit, but has a better view. During the season, anyone with a latent case of boating fever can't help but be mesmerized by the parade of craft passing in review by the windows — everything from sleek cigarette boats to sailboats and stately yachts.

Since the revamped Quonset hut opened as a restaurant early in '94, the menu has been sensibly pared down from the too-long version. Wisely, many elaborate dishes have been axed for a straightforward approach that offers steaks, fish, shrimp, and frog's legs.

Lighter selections include the ground round, club and Reuben sandwiches, some salads and soups, chicken and pasta dishes.

Char-grilled salmon also comes in a sandwich version that is a nice twist on the burger. The salmon is plunked on a kaiser roll with romaine, tomato, onion and a dill mustard dressing.

The bottom line on Jack's? You won't get the best meal you ever had, but if you order wisely (hold the escargots) everything will turn out pretty well.

One friend says the place reminds him of Southwest Airlines — the peanuts-on-the-floor informality, the friendly staff, the comfort level. And that's pretty apt. The bright-eyed crew in the 175-seat dining room wears mechanics' jumpsuits, and provides the casual service you'd expect in a place like this.

There's also an outdoor bar, a pool and an adjoining indoor area where drinks are served in plastic cups and the atmosphere is even more basic. During the season, of course.

Jacoby's

Members of the Jacoby family have been running this friendly downtown saloon since 1904. And even a major fire a few years ago didn't stop them. They rebuilt the place, unfortunately losing some of the vintage feeling, and moved right along.

Ed Jacoby is behind the bar these days and the menu still features some of the solid German dishes — kassler rippchen (smoked pork chop), sauerbraten, knackwurst and sauerkraut — that have been around since the founders, Albert and Minnie Jacoby, were here. Recently added lighter dishes include a turkey pastrami Reuben on an onion roll and smoked turkey sandwiches.

The entire second floor dining room is now nonsmoking, and that represents as much of a departure from the old days as the low-fat dishes.

☆ ☆ 1/2

624 Brush, Detroit.
(313) 962-7067.

Hours: 11 a.m.-6 p.m. Mon.-Tue., 11 a.m.-9 p.m. Wed.-Fri. Closed Sat.-Sun. and major holidays.

Nonsmoking: 60 percent.

Full bar.   Major credit cards.

Reasonable.

Jennifer's Cafe

Celebrating the 10th anniversary of the cafe he named for his daughter, hands-on chef and proprietor Jack Suidan continues to run a remarkably consistent little restaurant that spotlights fresh fare. That's somewhat of a cliche these days, but not at this well-run cafe. He still boils 150 pounds of chicken every morning for his stocks, sandwiches and salads. "There's just no substitute for it," he says simply — and he's simply right.

Sandwiches wrapped in lavash-style pita bread are among his specialties, and the Maurice salad is his signature salad. The menu stays the same all day, and offers the option of full entrees, including lamb chops (reflecting his Middle Eastern heritage), or lighter selections.

If only more modest cafes had the standards of this place.

☆ ☆ ☆

4052 Haggerty Road at Richardson Road, Walled Lake. (810) 360-0190.

Hours: 11 a.m.-9 p.m. Mon.-Thu., 11 a.m.-10 p.m. Fri.-Sat., 11 a.m.-9 p.m. Sun. Closed major holidays.

Nonsmoking: 65 percent.

Soft drinks only.   MC and Visa.

Reasonable.

Joe Bologna's Trattoria

☆ ☆ 1/2

2135 17 Mile Road at Dequindre, Sterling Heights. (810) 939-5700.

Hours: 11 a.m.-10 p.m. Mon.-Thu., 11 a.m.-11 p.m. Fri.-Sat., 11 a.m.-9 p.m. Sun. Closed Christmas Day.

Nonsmoking: 75 percent.

Full bar.   Major credit cards.

Reasonable.

When I first saw this restaurant's name, I assumed it had to be made-up. The real Joe Bologna, however, quickly relieved me of this misapprehension. He's the son of Ambrose Bologna, who ran an east side grocery store in the '50s, and those are real family photos on the wall.

Joe runs the place with a lot of enthusiasm. He's brought it along from its fairly modest pizza/pasta beginnings to a full-scale restaurant with a sit-down bar and one entirely smoke-free dining room.

Diners may still order the familiar Italian dishes like pizza, lasagna or fettuccine with chicken and they may still watch the dough being tossed behind a glass wall. But now there are more elaborate dishes, too, typified by salmon with lemon-caper sauce. Plate presentation has taken a step toward the more artistic.

After opening and closing a small satellite operation, Bologna says he's decided one restaurant is plenty for him. His customers applaud that decision.

Joe's Bar & Grill

☆ ☆ 1/2

30855 Southfield Road, south of 13 Mile Road, Southfield. (810) 644-5330.

Hours: Lunch, 11:30 a.m.-3 p.m. weekdays; dinner, 5-10 p.m. Mon.-Thu., 5-11 p.m. Fri.-Sat. Closed Sun. and major holidays.

Nonsmoking: 70 percent.

Full bar.   Major credit cards.

Moderate.

Trying to change an established image is pretty tough. Sometimes impossible. Just ask Joe Muer.

He is so closely identified with the traditional seafood house in Detroit that bears his name — and his father's and grandfather's — that he can't escape it.

When Muer and partner Chick Taylor opened this Southfield spot called Joe's Bar & Grill in March '94, everyone expected it to be Joe Muer's North, despite the fact that Muer himself professed that it was not intended to be. Joe's was to be a contemporary spot, with a menu to match. No white linens. No deferent black-suited waiters. No creamed spinach and stewed tomatoes.

And no customers, either, when people discovered he was serious, and the place definitely was not a clone of Joe Muer's.

So, in customer-is-always-right fashion, a new menu was introduced. Now it looks a whole lot more like Joe Muer's. The white bean salad and cottage cheese, staples at the downtown restaurant, are on the a la carte appetizer list. So is Boston clam chowder and the time-honored wedge of head lettuce with Russian dressing. Meat selections have shrunk and seafood items increased. Maine lobster has been added Tuesday through Saturday. Finnan haddie is there, too, along with Lake Superior whitefish and soft-shell crabs. And those un-Muerlike items from the original menu — house-made duck sausage, grilled veggie pizzas and baby back ribs — are among the missing.

Will the changes be enough to entice crowds again? Or are they holding out for white tablecloths, framed seascapes and stewed tomatoes?

Jumbo Buffet

Since hitting Windsor, Ontario, like a fire-breathing dragon, the all-you-can-eat Chinese buffet has made the move across the border. One could be coming to your neighborhood, too, with its array of Chinese dishes from won ton soup and Mongolian beef to mussels in black bean sauce and pepper steak.

Of the several around town, Jumbo Buffet is the most elaborate. Its 100 dishes offer diners a chance to stuff themselves for amazingly reasonable prices — around $6 for lunch and $11 for dinner.

 ☆ ☆ 1/2

1555 E. Maple, east of Stephenson Highway, Troy. (810) 524-9228.

Hours: Buffet lunch, 11 a.m.-3 p.m. Mon.-Sat.; buffet dinner, 4:30-10 p.m. Mon.-Thu., 4:30-11 p.m. Fri. and Sat., noon-10 p.m. Sun.

Nonsmoking: 60 percent.

Full bar.   Major credit cards.

Reasonable.

This is just the beginning. The Jumbo people — who have three buffets in Montreal — have their eye on space in a new strip mall near Lakeside in Sterling Heights.

Chinese buffets are geared to a volume audience. They are not really for those with a deep interest in the intricacies of Asian food. The array of dishes ranges from the mundane — almond boneless chicken and egg rolls — to the fairly exotic — eggplant in garlic sauce and Singapore noodles.

They do introduce people to Chinese fare in a very painless way. By allowing people to sample whatever they wish from such a wide choice, the end result should be a clientele that wants to move on to more challenging menus.

Some American food is offered in addition to the Chinese fare. Jumbo has an especially nice salad bar as well as an array of desserts, including dip-your-own ice cream, little pastries and fresh fruit.

Seafood dishes are featured at dinner and, not surprisingly, a lot of people zero in on the crab legs, shrimp, mussels and squid.

Though there certainly are deep-fried items, there are fewer than I expected. Spice levels are pretty gentle, however, and even the items marked "spicy" are only slightly so.

The down side is that, naturally, presentation is lacking. You can't really make big pans of food look very good when they are under attack on all sides by hungry diners.

In addition to the affordable price structure, the time-saving quality of the buffet is a major factor. You can be in and out as quickly as you wish.

My best advice: Arrive early, when the food is freshest and most plentiful. Even though the food is replenished regularly, when it gets close to closing time, the dishes tend to run out, and they start looking tired.

Kana Family Restaurant

Byung Dok and Kun Hi Ko established their restaurant in small quarters on East Huron Street a number of years ago. In 1995, they were able to move into a more accessible location in downtown Ann Arbor.

That's good news for anyone who has yet to try their carefully prepared Korean dishes. The Kos have a wonderful philosophy: they take great joy in serving people and introducing them to their native fare. Some of it is enticingly hot and spicy, but those who prefer a gentler level may find it here, too.

The Kos are happy to explain the dishes, though menu descriptions should be enough. Each dish is pretty completely translated.

For instance, yook ke chang, a soup, is spelled out as "a rich, hot and spicy beef soup with bean sprouts, green onion, cabbage and noodles." About the only thing the menu leaves to the imagination are the ingredients of the sauce simply called "Kana's sauce." It turns up on vegetarian selections, such as stir-fried rice cakes, and deep-fried shrimp with ginger and pineapple chunks, among others.

Hot ginger tea is a popular drink and very satisfying with the well-textured fare. While influenced by China and Japan, Korean food has a character of its own.

☆ ☆ ☆

110 Liberty, Ann Arbor. (313) 662-9303.

Hours: 11 a.m.-9 p.m. weekdays, 5-9 p.m. Sat. Closed Sun. and Thanksgiving, Christmas Day and New Year's Day.

Nonsmoking: 100 percent.

Soft drinks only.　　　　MC and Visa.

Reasonable.

Karpinski's

Since the days of the Model T — 1924 to be exact — there's been a restaurant run by the Karpinski family in this sturdy building in an industrial area not far from Hamtramck. Currently, it's Rob and Mike Karpinski, grandsons of the late Alex, who are carrying on the family tradition.

At one time, this was an almost totally male bastion, and the place still has that look with its brown, brown and more brown color scheme. But more and more

☆ ☆

7740 Chrysler Service Drive at Clay Street, Detroit. (313) 871-7766.

Hours: 11 a.m.-8 p.m. weekdays. Closed Sat., Sun. and major holidays.

Nonsmoking: 40 percent.

Full bar.　　　　AE, MC and Visa.

Reasonable to moderate.

women are among the diners, especially at lunchtime.

The menu is a straightforward American one, with simple side dishes like coleslaw, sliced tomatoes and cottage cheese. New York sirloin and filet mignon are featured steaks at a reasonable $11.95 and $12.95, respectively. Some lighter dishes have crept onto the menu: char-grilled chicken breast, broiled salmon and chicken Caesar salad.

Friday's perch is still a favorite, and so is Wednesday's fish and chips.

The place has a Joe-sent-me aura, especially since you enter from a doorway in the back, past a courtyard garden.

Key Largo

☆ ☆ ☆

142 Walled Lake Drive, Walled Lake. (810) 669-1441.

Hours: Lunch, 11 a.m.-4 p.m. Mon.-Sat.; dinner, 4-10 p.m. (11 p.m. in the summer) Mon.-Thu., 4-11 p.m. Fri.-Sat. (year-round), 3-9 p.m. Sun. Also, Sun. brunch, 11 a.m.-3 p.m. May through September.

Nonsmoking: 85 percent.

Full bar.   Major credit cards.

Reasonable to moderate.

With the addition of executive chef Patrick Dunn, and sous-chefs Matt Kind and John Schofer, the Key Largo of today is a very different place from its beginning, when the kitchen did not back up the setting.

That's not to say it hasn't been popular all along. Since 1987, it's been a summer hangout for people who love the open-air deck, the steel bands, the pink drinks and the lure of the lake. And all of that is still part of the sprawling spot overlooking Walled Lake.

What's changed for the better is the food and style of presentation. All three top chefs are culinary school graduates, and they collaborate on a menu of dishes that reflect the tropical flavor of the 275-seat restaurant.

"Sun cuisine" is what they call it, and it is creative and interesting. Especially appealing on gray, cloudy days, these items, like the place itself, recall blue water and cloudless skies. They're dishes like Cuban black bean soup and conch chowder bisque — a Bahamian blend of conch, scallops, sherry, an infusion of rosemary, garnished with gremolata (minced parsley, lemon peel and garlic). I knew things had changed at Key Largo the minute I spotted the word "gremolata" on the menu.

Such dishes as bayou prawns, she-crab cakes, Tahiti stir fry and Bermuda-spiced pork chops follow the same tropical theme.

Suffice it to say that the menu is not just a clone of dozens of others. It has a real personality, with offbeat items like Bridgetown mashed potatoes — potatoes mixed with plantains, garlic, herbs and olive oil — and seafood etouffee "hobo style" — shrimp, scallops, swordfish, tuna, baked in a foil sack and garnished with dirty rice (basmati rice, chicken stock and duck livers).

A signature item is barbecued swordfish bones. The rib portion of swordfish is served with bourbon barbecue sauce, rice and corn. The fresh catch might include such items as skate wings with noisette butter and yellow-fin tuna.

Dinner entrees include a choice of coleslaw or the tossed salad with sweet-and-sour celery seed dressing.

And how else to end the meal but with classic key lime pie?

The waterfront location calls for a casual setting, and this has it, with lots of mounted fish trophies, flags and strings of lights, hibiscus-patterned tablecloths and island music in the background. Big containers of sea salt and an array of bottled hot sauces are on each table.

Kruse and Muer; Kruse and Muer on Main

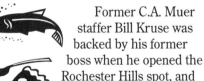

Former C.A. Muer staffer Bill Kruse was backed by his former boss when he opened the Rochester Hills spot, and then the slightly more formal entity in Rochester.

The menus and casual settings are absolutely crowd-pleasing. Staffers are upbeat and cheerful. That's always been the Muer way, and Kruse is nothing if not a devotee of the style.

The restaurants have irresistible hot bread made from the same dough as the pizza crust, a changing lineup of fresh fish served char-grilled, blackened or broiled, ribs and chicken and an array of pastas.

The Rochester Hills restaurant is in Meadowbrook Mall and is more casual than the downtown Rochester spot. The latter has linens and a slightly more upscale setting.

Fresh salads and vegetables, especially when Michigan produce is in season, are notable at both places.

Kruse and Muer ☆ ☆ 1/2

Meadowbrook Mall, 64 N. Adams, Rochester Hills. (810) 375-2503.

Kruse and Muer on Main ☆ ☆ 1/2

327 N. Main, Rochester.
(810) 652-9400.

Hours: 11 a.m.-10 p.m. Mon.-Thu., 11 a.m.-11 p.m. Fri.-Sat. at both locations, 12:30-8:30 p.m. Sun. at N. Adams only. Closed Sun. at N. Main location, and major holidays at both, except open Easter at N. Main only.

Nonsmoking: 85 percent.

N. Adams: Beer and wine. AE, MC and Visa.

N. Main: Full bar.   AE, MC and Visa.

Reasonable.

La Becasse

 ☆ ☆ ☆

Glen Lake, corner of Burdickville Road (County Road 616) and S. Dunn's Farm Road (County Road 675), Burdickville. (616) 334-3944.

Hours: Dinner only, 5:45-9:15 p.m. Tue.-Sun. from May through Oct. 15 and week between Christmas Day and New Year's Day; 5:45-9:15 p.m. Fri.-Sat. Jan. through mid-March. Closed mid-March through mid-May and mid-Oct. through Dec. 25.

Nonsmoking: 100 percent.

Full bar.   Discover, MC and Visa.

Moderate to expensive.

John and Caroline Rentenbach have been the proprietors of this 45-seat country-French restaurant for seven years now, taking over the role originally filled by Mary Ann O'Neill. They've very much carried on in the same unpretentious and friendly spirit. Their weekly-changing menu offers simple yet elegant dishes, typified by whitefish with remoulade, and scallops of veal and beef tenderloin with red wine and roasted garlic sauce. There's usually a *pate*, always a lovely soup and chocolatey desserts. The price range for main courses is $15.75-$24.75.

Burdickville is a village about 25 miles west of Traverse City, little more than a Leelanau County crossroads.

La Contessa

 ☆ ☆ ☆

780 Erie Street E., Windsor, Ontario. (519) 252-2167.

Hours: 11 a.m.-10 p.m. Mon.-Thu., 11 a.m.-11 p.m. Fri.-Sat. Closed Sun. and Easter Monday, Labor Day, Christmas Day and New Year's Day.

Nonsmoking: 40 percent.

Full bar.   Major credit cards.

Reasonable.

Don't be misled by the somewhat glitzy setting that gives a more formal feeling to the formerly modest storefront. However out of sync to the down-to-earth street the spruced-up look may be, Angela Finazzo's cooking is the real thing.

She turns out soulful Sicilian fare, from an array of pastas to veals and seafood. The maraschino penne has a particularly light and delicate tomato cream sauce, the salad includes fresh fennel, the soups are fine. It's obvious there is a real cook in the kitchen.

Among dishes sampled on visits to Erie Street are rich Parmesan- and spinach-dappled egg drop soup (stracciatella) and antipasto alla Contessa. The latter is a handsomely arranged assortment of prosciutto-wrapped melon, fresh bocconchino and pecorino cheeses, small herb-dappled black olives and big green ones, artichokes, anchovies and paper-thin, high-quality salami.

The tomato- and garlic-topped grilled bread comes with little slices of panelle (boiled, dried and sliced chick-pea flour and parsley). It's a dish from the Palermo area of Italy, where Finazzo lived before coming to Canada in 1972.

There certainly are standard items on the menu. What isn't standard is the execution. Pastas are particularly notable, including pannette San Gionavella. It is penne prepared with a light tomato sauce, eggplant and tender veal meatballs smaller than marbles.

La Contessa is very much a family business. Helping out are her daughter Maria Burgio, her sons John and Paul, and husband and partner Vito lending moral support along with Maria's husband, Sam. Angela Finazzo has made a place that exudes the warmth that comes from a close-knit family.

La Cuisine

The second-floor bistro is the province of Francois Sully and his wife, Janet. In the evening, Sully prepares such dishes as bouillabaisse, fresh salmon in a number of treatments, and filet of pork with prunes and brandy sauce. All of it is done on the six burners of a big gas stove in an open kitchen.

At lunch, it is Janet's turn. Quieter and less showy than her husband, she makes quiches and salads.

French wines, of course, are emphasized, and nearly everyone here speaks French. Probably most of the French classes on both sides of the river have practiced their language skills here in this bastion of Gallic culture.

The Sullys go to France each year during the months of September and October. Their daughter Natasha lives in Paris with her husband, chef Laurent Duchene.

☆ ☆ 1/2

417 Pelissier Street, Windsor, Ontario. (519) 253-6432.

Hours: Lunch, 11:30 a.m.-2:30 p.m. Tue.-Fri., 11:30 a.m.-2 p.m. Sat.; dinner, 5-9:30 p.m. Tue.-Fri., 5-10 p.m. Sat. Closed Sun., Mon., Christmas Day, Dec. 26, New Year's Day and months of Sept. and Oct.

Nonsmoking: 33 percent.

Beer, wine and after-dinner drinks.

DC, MC and Visa.

Moderate.

La Fondue

☆ ☆ 1/2

111 S. Main Street, Royal Oak.
(810) 399-1440.

Hours: Dinner only, 5-10 p.m. Mon.-Thu., 5-11 p.m. Fri.-Sat., 4-9 p.m. Sun. Closed major holidays.

Nonsmoking: 50 percent.

Full bar.   AE, MC and Visa.

Moderate.

An all-fondue menu is the premise, so there should be no surprises here. The Swiss created the dish, naming it for the French word *fondre* (to melt). Legend has it that during the Reformation, when provisions were scarce, people got together what they could — milk, crumbled cheese and crusts of bread — and shared it. Thus, the story goes, was fondue born.

At this downtown Royal Oak spot, diners carry on the tradition by spearing chunks of bread on long-handled forks and dipping them into melted cheese in a communal pot. White wine is the appropriate drink with cheese fondue.

The fondue theme later was extended to cubes of beef, chicken and fish cooked in pots of bubbling oil. For dessert, a pot of melted chocolate is teamed with pieces of fruit or sponge cake, again on the long-handled fondue forks.

Though in a sense diners are required to cook their own dinner, they at least don't have to wash the dishes.

The fondue experience takes about two hours to appreciate fully.

Laikon

☆ ☆

569 Monroe Street, Detroit.
(313) 963-7058.

Hours: 11 a.m.-2 a.m. Sun., Mon., Wed., Thu.; 11 a.m.-4 a.m. Fri. and Sat. Closed Tue., Thanksgiving, Christmas Day and New Year's Day.

Nonsmoking: 45 percent.

Full bar.   Major credit cards.

Reasonable.

With its balconied setting and central bar tucked under the stairway, this is one of the most appealing restaurants on the Greektown block. Similar to the others in cuisine, its Greek menu ranges from avgolemono (egg, lemon and rice soup) to battered squid and roast lamb dishes.

It takes a refined palate indeed to distinguish much difference in the fare along Monroe. People tend to choose one Greektown spot over another because of the perceived comfort level at an individual place, or perhaps a favorite waiter. This one does have its fans.

Lai Lai

The name means "welcome," and Lai Lai certainly lives up to that in the view of knowledgeable Chinese food fanciers in the Ypsilanti-Ann Arbor area.

☆ ☆ 1/2

4023 Carpenter Road at Ellsworth, Ypsilanti. (313) 677-0790.

Hours: 11:30 a.m.-10 p.m. Sun.-Thu., 11:30 a.m.-11 p.m. Fri.-Sat. Dim sum served 11:30 a.m.-3 p.m. every day.

Nonsmoking: 50 percent.

Soft drinks only.   MC and Visa.

Reasonable.

The first thing that triggers good feelings is a color photo tucked under each of the transparent covers atop linens on the tables. Similar to the photos of sushi and sashimi standard at sushi bars, this one illustrates the various kinds of dim sum that may be ordered every day at lunchtime. These bite-sized or slightly larger dumplings, buns, noodles and other items are meant to be ordered in multiples.

Diners mark their choices on red-and-white sheets that list the items by name. Offerings range from stuffed crab claw and shrimp and rice roll to stuffed bean curd and pan-fried turnip cakes. And I can attest that what arrives at the table on a series of small white plates looks remarkably like the photo representations.

Of the two dozen choices ($1.90-$2.40 an item), I tried silver noodles, a plate of tiny, pasta-like noodles mixed with sliced barbecued pork, shrimp and julienned vegetables; baked pork bun, and shiu mie, a faintly sweet, thin-skinned dumpling filled with pork, Chinese mushrooms and shrimp. Another one, sweet rice with chicken wrapped in a lotus leaf, issued a puff of fragrant steam as it opened like a neatly wrapped little package.

Dim sum is just one of the options. The full menu presents a whole other story, with its impressive array of Sichuan, Mandarin and Cantonese dishes, as well as the inevitable chop suey and chow mein.

The well-organized menu lists dishes in an easy-to-follow fashion. Seafood entrees are all listed together, followed by poultry, pork, beef, vegetable and noodle specialties.

Also, note the "Eastern pot" dishes, boiled beef brisket and bean curd assortments cooked in a pot rather than a wok.

Peony beef is particularly outstanding. It, like most dishes, arrives on a simple white platter, with the cubes of beef in the center completely surrounded by perfectly-cooked fresh broccoli and topped with glistening egg white. The spice level of this dish (one of a number listed in red as hot and spicy) had a pungent resonance rather than a knockout punch. This is true also of the shrimp with spicy ginger and garlic sauce, another of the red-listed dishes.

Service is helpful and friendly, and the room is attractively decked out in Oriental art works, smoked mirrors and bright red carpeting.

L

La Luna Grancaffe

☆ ☆ 1/2

183 N. Woodward, Birmingham.
(810) 642-7070.

Hours: 11 a.m.-10 p.m. Sun.-Thu., 11 a.m.-11 p.m. Fri.-Sat. Closed Dec. 24 and major holidays.

Nonsmoking: 90 percent.

Soft drinks only.   AE, MC and Visa.

Reasonable to moderate.

A casual, spirited, drop-in cafe, this Italian deli is designed for nibblers and sharers. The pizzas are presented on top of outsized cans of tomatoes instead of the conventional metal bases, and dishes have names like penne from Heaven, a bowl of noodles tossed with chicken, broccoli, sun-dried tomatoes, garlic and a dash of hot pepper.

That's typical of the bright, accessible menu. A fresh salad and peasanty bread with olive oil come with main dishes at dinner. A number of non-alcoholic beverages is offered, from designer waters to espresso.

Among the desserts, panna cotta (cooked cream) is a dish that is every bit as heavenly as the penne. This is another of the Al Valente family enterprises.

Larco's

☆ ☆ ☆

645 Big Beaver Road, Troy.
(810) 680-0066.

Hours: Lunch, 11 a.m.-4 p.m. weekdays; dinner, 4-10 p.m. Mon.-Thu., 4-11 p.m. Fri., 5-11 p.m. Sat., 4-9 p.m. Sun. Closed Christmas Day.

Nonsmoking: 70 percent.

Full bar.   AE, MC and Visa.

Moderate.

Members of the Larco family have been serving solid Italian fare in the Detroit area since the early '50s. When Larco's moved to this location in '90, it took a while before old-time customers were comfortable with the somewhat glitzy suburban setting.

Recently, a redo gave the place a more classic look. White walls have replaced the mauve and shiny brass trimmings inherited from a previous regime. Black-and-white photographs of Italian gardens, by photographer Balthazar Korab, have added freshness to the big room.

What hasn't changed is the classic Italian-American bill of fare. It features some 15 pasta dishes ranging from spaghetti with meat sauce to fettuccine primavera, and a number of chicken, fish and veal dishes. Added recently is Dover sole fileted at tableside.

Accompaniments are simple salads in oil and vingegar, bread and breadsticks, and side dishes of spaghetti or Anna potatoes.

Mark and Sue Larco are the current family members on hand. They carry on the tradition established by Mike, Nick and Pete Larco, the gentlemen in the huge photo that dates to the '30s.

The Lark

Whenever someone asks me about the Lark, I have a stock answer. Those who appreciate fine food enough to pay high prices for it should forge ahead. Those who feel dinner checks well above $100 per person (with cocktails or wine) are out of line probably won't enjoy it.

It's as simple as that.

By the standards of major cities like New York and Los Angeles, the Lark is not all that stratospheric. By local standards, however, it's at the top of the heap price-wise.

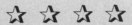

6430 Farmington Road, north of Maple, West Bloomfield. (810) 661-4466.

Hours: Dinner only, 6-8:30 p.m. Tue.-Thu., 6 or 9 p.m. Fri.-Sat. Closed Sun., Mon. (except for special theme dinners on last Mon. of each month), major holidays, first week in January and one week in summer.

Nonsmoking: 50 percent

Full bar.   Major credit cards.

Expensive.

First, an array of hors d'oeuvres is presented on a trolley, followed by a choice of soup, pasta or hot appetizer, main course and a salad served either before or after the chosen main dish. The price of dinner is determined by the choice of main course. Currently, that ranges from $47.50-$57.50, with specials higher. There is a minimum charge of $37.50 for those who wish to order a la carte. And, of course, beverages, dessert, tax and gratuity are not included.

Desserts are an extra $5-$7.50, tea and coffee are $2.75, with espresso and cappuccino $3 and $3.50 per cup.

Wines are $7.50-$10 by the glass.

Entree choices include rack of lamb ($55), honey-glazed duckling ($47.50), Dover sole ($55) and veal chop ($55).

Chef Marcus Haight has been with proprietors Mary and Jim Lark for several years now, and he and sous-chef Richard Ormsby certainly know their way around a kitchen.

The setting for all of this is an intimate room with just 12 tables. It is reminiscent of the Portuguese country inns that are favorites of the well-traveled Larks.

Service is, as would be expected, very courteous and attentive. Reservations are necessary.

La Shish, La Shish-West

La Shish ☆ ☆ ☆

12918 Michigan Avenue, Dearborn.
(313) 584-4477

Hours: 10 a.m.-midnight every day.

Nonsmoking: 75 percent.

Soft drinks only   Major credit cards.

Reasonable.

La Shish-West ☆ ☆ ☆

22039 Michigan Avenue, Dearborn.
(313) 562-7200.

Hours: 10 a.m.-11 p.m. Sun.-Wed., 10 a.m.-midnight Thu.-Sat.

Nonsmoking: 75 percent.

Full bar.   Major credit cards.

Reasonable.

Simply wonderful, fresh Middle Eastern fare from the Lebanese perspective of Talal Chahine has made the two Dearborn spots he named La Shish perennially attractive to a wide audience.

The older and smaller La Shish is much more basic and less dressed-up than La Shish-West, which has decorative tile and wood and a number of Middle Eastern artifacts and photographs. Nonetheless, the menus are the same and that's what counts to most of the diners.

The sampler plate offers a cross-section of available dishes. It includes tabbouleh, baba ganouge and hommus with pita bread to scoop them into, as well as meat and vegetarian stuffed grape leaves, chicken and lamb shawarma (marinated and grilled meats), spicy vegetarian patties called falafel, and herby green salads.

There is, of course, much, much more to try on the menus, from shish kebab and shish kafta (ground lamb) to baked or raw kibbee and an array of fresh fruit and vegetable juices.

Talal's, adjoining La Shish-West, opened in '93. It offers an even more fanciful setting and an elaborate menu that contains all the dishes found in the other two restaurants as well as seafood. It has a sit-down bar.

Le Metro

Tim Winterfield says his small restaurant "is growing up a little bit," and he's right. That doesn't mean it is getting more expensive. As Winterfield has grown in experience and confidence, he's just gotten more ambitious with the menu.

☆ ☆ ☆

29855 Northwestern Highway at Inkster, Southfield. (810) 353-2757.

Hours: Lunch, 11:30 a.m.-2:30 p.m. weekdays; dinner, 5-10 p.m. Mon.-Thu., 5-11 p.m. Fri.-Sat. Closed Sun. and major holidays.

Nonsmoking: 80 percent.

Full bar.   Major credit cards.

Reasonable to moderate.

You may still stop by for a simple bowl of black bean soup or spinach salad at the appealing spot in Applegate Square, a little shopping strip where even the eyeglass frames make a fashion statement.

Or, you may go for one of the game dishes that have been added of late, things like fresh venison or a pheasant/quail combination. Along with the game, pastas and fish are extremely popular, and interest in red meat in the minority. Winterfield's signature fish is whitefish stuffed with smoked salmon and coated with a crisp potato crust.

Many dishes may be ordered in half portions, something I especially like about this place. It has something of a bistro feel to it, with such items as French onion soup, crusty French bread, smoked salmon and chicken liver *pate*. You may catch live music by small jazz combos here, too, but only on Thursday nights.

Lepanto

☆ ☆ ☆

**316 S. Main Street, Royal Oak.
(810) 541-2228.**

Hours: Dinner, 5:30-9 p.m. Mon., 5:30-10 p.m. Tue.-Thu., 5:30-11 p.m. Fri.-Sat. Closed Sun. and major holidays.

Nonsmoking: 50 percent.

Full bar.   MC and Visa.

Reasonable to moderate.

So discreet it's almost invisible, even on busy Main Street, this tiny Italian restaurant has impressive numbers of loyal fans who swear by its colorful, contemporary dishes. They include upscale pizzas, focaccia, soups, salads and pastas.

Lately, fish is more prominent on the menu, and a notable dish is the salmon prepared with fresh oregano, capers, white wine and garlic. Heartier stuff, like lamb shanks, sometimes shows up as a special in the chic, not quite 50-seat restaurant.

Proprietors Chris and Laura Claire named the place for one of the Italian forebears on Chris' side of the family.

Lighthouse Inn

☆ ☆ 1/2

Lighthouse Cove, mouth of the Thames River at Lake St. Clair, Tilbury, Ontario. (519) 682-0600.

Hours: 11:30 a.m.-10 p.m. daily (until 11 p.m. from May 1 to mid-Oct.). Closed Dec. 24-26, New Year's Eve and New Year's Day.

Nonsmoking: 50 percent.

Full bar.   AE, MC and Visa.

Reasonable.

Perched on a piece of low-lying land that juts into Lake St. Clair, this friendly, casual boaters' hangout has that elusive characteristic: a great view. Despite our region's expanses of water, few restaurants take advantage of it. This one does.

The Sunset Grill on the second floor, in fact, is the perfect spot for those who appreciate the vista. The area is used for drinks and appetizers and accommodating the overflow that usually occurs on Saturdays on beautiful summer nights.

The menu started out as a very basic one, but has expanded to include more pastas and fish dishes served with herb sauces. That's in addition to the straightforward, lightly-battered perch and pickerel that have been staples for years. Boaters may call the Lighthouse Inn for transportation from one of the marinas in the area.

Lino's

Proprietor Lino Borracchio and chef Andy Toth are both transplanted Europeans who arrived here in the late '50s. Their years of restaurant experience culminated at this traditional Italian restaurant, which usually exudes a calm, everything's-under-control feeling.

Lino's, which opened in 1988, delivers quality at an affordable price. The menu holds no surprises. The pastas, veals and chicken dishes are typical of Italian restaurants in America. There's also linguine with red or white clam sauce. Veal Tosca and chicken cacciatore. T-bone Florentine. Veal chop with porcini mushrooms.

Seafood dishes have been added, including sauteed fresh perch, whitefish broiled or baked, and Dover sole amandine. Accompaniments include a worthy minestrone and tossed green salads with house-made dressings. One is a vinaigrette made with pine nuts and peanut butter. That may sound strange, but it works well, just like the Borracchio/Toth collaboration. Toth was for several years chef at another traditional restaurant, Joe Muer's in Detroit.

The restaurant was redecorated in 1994 and now has a much more stylish look.

☆ ☆ 1/2

50 W. Tienken Road, Rochester Hills. (810) 652-9002.

Hours: Dinner, 5-10 p.m. Mon.-Thu., 5-11 p.m. Fri.-Sat., 4-9 p.m. Sun. Closed major holidays.

Nonsmoking: 75 percent.

Full bar.   Major credit cards.

Moderate.

Little Bar

321 Chartier, Marine City.
(810) 765-9333.

Hours: 11:30 a.m.-10 p.m. Mon.-Thu., 11:30 a.m.-11 p.m. Fri.-Sat. Closed Sun. and major holidays.

Nonsmoking: 20 percent.

Full bar.   AE, MC and Visa.

Moderate.

For years people have loved this little spot for its hideaway quality and its solid meals of steak and fish.

Just eight tables are cozily jammed into a room paneled with redwood and replete with maps, charts, vintage photographs and marine memorabilia. Though it is not on the water, it is close enough to make it popular with boaters. They were the first to discover it some 33 years ago.

And nothing much has changed. Dinner includes a tossed salad, potato and vegetable and the small-town favorite, American pie, is the usual dessert. At lunch, sandwiches — including, of course, the steak sandwich — head the selections.

Little Italy

227 Hutton, Northville.
(810) 348-0575.

Hours: Lunch, 11:30 a.m.-2:30 p.m. weekdays; dinner, 5-10 p.m. Mon.-Thu., 5-11 p.m. Fri.-Sat. Closed Sun. and major holidays.

Nonsmoking: 55 percent.

Full bar.   AE, MC and Visa.

Moderate.

Small places have a certain charm that eludes the barnlike ones. This revived Victorian cottage with an Italian perspective has just 16 tables for pastas, veal, chicken and seafood dishes.

The restaurant is one of the Al Valente family spots, cozy places including Ristorante di Maria in West Bloomfield and La Luna Grancaffe in Birmingham. Yet another, Villa Maria, is scheduled to debut in late spring or summer of '95 at Haggerty and 15 Mile in West Bloomfield.

The Valentes have a solid Italian menu down pat. Popular dishes here include scallopine alla Maria (veal, shrimp and artichoke hearts in cream sauce), veal stuffed with prosciutto and mozzarella in wine sauce, scampi with garlic butter and such pastas as tortelloni in Gorgonzola cream sauce and linguine with red or white clam sauce. Nightly specials also are ordered by a strong percentage.

Dinners are accompanied by salad, and pasta or polenta, depending on the dish.

Loco Bar & Grill

The tin-ceilinged space that once housed Mykonos Supper Club was transformed a couple of years ago into a Texas bordertown-style saloon. Complete with cattle brands stamped onto the floor and metalwork cactus around the doors, it gives the Greektown area some much-needed diversification.

The area could use a few more options like this one. Loco, with its fake pony fabric on the booths, potted cactus and southwest memorabilia displayed under the glass-topped surface of the bar, is a haven for Tex-Mex cooking.

The theme is carried out with items like Frito pie (chips, chili, onions and cheese), quesadillas in a number of treatments, tamales, fajitas and chicken-fried steak.

As its name indicates, this is a casual, unpretentious spot. The tables are left uncovered under old-style spinning fans, and bottles of hot sauce rather than vases of flowers provide color.

My transplanted Texas friends swear by this place, and that's good enough for me.

☆ ☆ 1/2

454 E. Lafayette at Beaubien, Detroit. (313) 965-3737.

Hours: 11 a.m.-midnight Sun.-Thu., 11 a.m.-1:30 a.m. Fri.-Sat. Closed Christmas Day.

Nonsmoking: 40 percent.

Full bar. Major credit cards.

Reasonable.

Loon River Cafe

Field-and-stream prints and the repeated motif of Pewabic tiles set into wooden floors add to the earthy, north woods feeling of this lodge-like dining room.

The room's focal point is a huge fireplace. Its cobblestones may not be real, but there are real flames licking around real wood in winter.

Chef Ray Hollingsworth's creative approach parallels the decor theme beautifully. His menu doesn't just offer the products of Michigan's farmlands and streams, but goes farther to bring back some

34911 Van Dyke at 15 Mile Road, Sterling Heights. (810) 979-1400.

Hours: 6 a.m.-11 p.m. Mon.-Thu., 6 a.m.-midnight Fri., 7 a.m.-midnight Sat., 7 a.m.-9 p.m. Sun. Closed Christmas Day.

Nonsmoking: 50 percent.

Full bar. Major credit cards.

Reasonable.

hallowed dishes from farmhouse kitchens.

You can get an Upper Peninsula-style pasty, fresh walleye fried in butter, and such homey side dishes as mashed potatoes with pan gravy, stewed apples, spinach dip with black bread, and wonderful sweet potato fries in a basket.

The price of main dishes includes vegetable of the day and a choice of potato, wild rice or stewed apples, as well as either soup or salad.

Menu additions recently include venison burger, roast turkey sandwiches, turkey and white bean chili and hunter's goulash.

All the accompanying beers and wines are Michigan products. Or, you might want to try Loon River Lemonade, the house's answer to Long Island iced tea.

When this new approach was introduced in '93, the proprietors had no idea how successful it would be. They know now. People have responded well to the changeover. It gave new personality to a room that had had a dated look and was not in keeping with the talents of the chef.

Now they've got both: a competent kitchen and a snappy setting.

Lord Fox

☆ ☆ 1/2

5400 Plymouth Road, Dixboro.
(313) 662-1647.

Hours: Lunch, 11:30 a.m.-2 p.m. weekdays; dinner, 5-10 p.m. weeknights, 5-11 p.m. Sat., 3-9 p.m. Sun. Closed Christmas Day.

Nonsmoking: 80 percent.

Full bar.   Major credit cards.

Moderate.

Located just two miles east of U.S. 23 on Plymouth Road, this charming country inn has two personas, one for summer and one for winter. Those preferring to dine outdoors can choose the deck seating 70 above a flowing stream or a gazebo big enough for parties of eight or so.

When the weather turns cooler, it's very cozy inside. The rustic interior is a warm retreat with the flicker of candlelight on red-clothed tables. Hutches, English prints and old clocks provide a country setting.

The menu offers such dishes as pistachio-crusted ahi tuna, Canadian pickerel with chevre and red pepper puree, roasted duck, rack of lamb and grilled pork loin chops.

The wine cellar is a point of pride here, and visitors may browse among the racks.

Los Galanes

Three storefronts have been combined into an upbeat setting of sunny, southwestern colors and exposed brick, live cactus plants and bright murals.

☆ ☆ 1/2

3362 Bagley, Detroit.
(313) 554-4444.

Hours: 9 a.m.-midnight Sun.-Thu., 9 a.m.-3 a.m. Fri.-Sat. Closed Christmas Day.

Nonsmoking: 75 percent.

Full bar.   Major credit cards.

Reasonable.

The most attractive of the Mexican Town cantinas, this is not a carbon copy of other restaurants along the strip. For one thing, its row of big-paned windows facing Bagley is uncovered; so are the arched ones on 23rd Street. Only big pots of tall, spiky cactus plants block a diner's view of the street. That street scene is part of the decor, adding an element of vitality. It's interesting how appealing such an open look is, much more than the buttoned-up approach taken elsewhere on Bagley.

While popular Mexican tortilla dishes are certainly available here, more and more people are going for selections like roasted baby goat, swordfish fajitas and pork, beef or chicken stew.

Among the expected listings on the two-sided menus, I can recommend the beef enchiladas, served with rice, beans and a heap of shredded lettuce and chopped tomatoes; the pollo con nopalitos, stir-fried cactus with chicken pieces in a cilantro-tinged tomato sauce, and shrimp sauteed in garlic butter and oregano.

Big iceberg lettuce salads accompany many main courses, with a choice of creamy Italian, blue cheese or French dressings. Well, OK. As a friend who lived in Mexico attests, salad dressings are not big in Hispanic cuisine.

A simple yet satisying dish is caldo de res — beef short rib soup — with an array of fresh vegetables, including a small ear of corn, and some fresh lime and chopped fresh cilantro on the side.

Los Galanes is named for the Galan family, who runs the place.

Louie's on the River

★ ★ ☆

River Place Hotel, 1000 River Place, Detroit. (313) 259-2260.

Hours: 7 a.m.-11 p.m. Mon.-Wed., 7 a.m.-midnight Thu.-Sat.; New Orleans brunch, 11 a.m.-3 p.m. Sun. Closed Sun. evenings and Christmas Day.

Nonsmoking: 100 percent.

Full bar.   Major credit cards.

Expensive.

I've gone on record more than once as an admirer of the gutsy New Orleans cooking of chef Louie Finnan. During several stops he's made in kitchens in the metro area, he was always a notable talent.

Few would have expected him to turn up at this boutique hotel on the river, but that's exactly where Finnan landed, when the Grand Heritage hotel people decided to make the hotel seem more user-friendly. And what could be friendlier than this Southern-accented chef, a commanding figure in his whites, joshing with diners on his frequent trips out of the kitchen?

Finnan signed on to do the hotel food service and handle the restaurant and bar, which he quickly named the Mardi Gras Bar. One little problem is the clash of cultures between the luxury image of the hotel and a menu like Louie's. As much as I love the gumbo, the crayfish pies, the sauce-slathered spicy shrimp and the feather-light fried oysters that are his signatures, making that menu work in this particular location hasn't been easy.

The staid dining room begs for a redo, though the bar has a much more apt look with its Mardi Gras masks and New Orleans style artworks. Louie says changes in the dining room are coming. And that will help.

Certainly, the price structure is not likely to remind anyone of a little shrimp shack down on the Mississippi. Gumbo or bayou chowder are $4.50, a grilled shrimp appetizer, $11. Dinner entrees start at $14 and $15 (for pasta and chicken) and go up to $27. A fixed price dinner of hors d'oeuvre, salad and entree can be had for $30. While not astronomical, at those prices people expect expert service and a fair number of amenities, which is not always the case at the hotel.

But the food is the real thing. A lot of people around town want to see Finnan, and this historic hotel in the former Parke-Davis laboratory, make a go of it.

The patio, mere feet from the Detroit River, is a great place to sit for lunch or cocktails in the summer. It's one of the rare places in Detroit taking advantage of the waterfront setting. Louie comes into full flower in the summer heat.

There's just nowhere else in town dishing up New Orleans food like Louie's.

Mac & Ray's

Nearly floor-to-ceiling windows offer a sweeping view of Anchor Bay from this tri-level restaurant. Hands down, it is the most elaborate waterfront spot in the area. Seafood and fresh fish star on a menu that includes a range of meat and pasta dishes, from prime ribs of beef to wild mushroom fettuccine. Everything's well-prepared and served by a casually dressed staff.

☆ ☆ ☆

30675 N. River Road, Harrison Twp. (810) 463-9660.

Hours: April 1-Jan. 1: lunch, 11 a.m.-4 p.m. Mon.-Sat.; dinner, 4-10 p.m. Mon.-Thu., 4-11 p.m. Fri.-Sat.; Sun. brunch, 10:30 a.m.-3 p.m. and dinner, 3-9 p.m. Closed Mon. and Tue. from Jan. 1-April 1, Christmas Day and New Year's Day.

Nonsmoking: 65 percent.

Full bar.　　　　　　　　Major credit cards.

Moderate to expensive.

Of course, cozy it's not. Tri-level, 550-seat, 16,000-square-foot restaurants rarely qualify for that description. But when it comes to dramatic presence, Mac & Ray's certainly has an aura that matches its size.

This is a restaurant for people who like a helping of excitement along with lunch or dinner. It's for those who like to see and be seen, who thrive on the buzz in the air, and who like to make grand entrances — in this case, not *down* a wide staircase but *up*.

The restaurant is on the second floor, approached by a wide, colorfully carpeted staircase set off by a mural that recalls the golden days of lacquered wooden speedboats. And while it's certainly possible to order a burger, the big white plates with their bright vegetable garnishes are more likely to bear such things as hazelnut-crusted walleye, sauteed scallops or filet mignon. Chef Jeff Baldwin and his talented staff have come up with a winning combination.

The menu is fairly lengthy, but not so much so that it requires long study or casts doubt on the abilities of the kitchen to produce the fare.

I especially like the stainless steel-topped oyster bar, where just a handful of patrons may pull up stools to have the oyster bar chef serve them shrimp cocktail, stone crab claws, and casino or oysters Rockefeller.

Macaroni Grill

 ☆ ☆ 1/2

32729 Northwestern Highway,
Farmington Hills. (810) 851-3900.

39300 W. Seven Mile, Livonia.
(313) 462-6676.

Hours: 11 a.m.-10 p.m. Sun.-Thu., 11 a.m.-
11 p.m. Fri., noon-11 p.m.-Sat. (Farmington
Hills); 11 a.m.-10:15 p.m. Sun.-Thu., 11
a.m.-11:15 p.m. Fri.-Sat. (Livonia). Closed
Thanksgiving and Christmas Day.

Nonsmoking: 70 percent.

Full bar.   Major credit cards.

Reasonable.

You can just imagine the brainstorming session around the conference table in Dallas: "Let's put gallon jugs of red wine and tumblers on the tables and go for the honor system when it's time to pay.

"Put the kitchen out in full view, and have the cooks yell back and forth to each other as they dish up the pasta — and make sure they pull those white hats down over one ear. And, Charlie, crank up the corny accordion music."

Yes, these bright, friendly spots smack of corporate thinking all right, but that isn't necessarily the kiss of death. The concept arose out of an original in suburban San Antonio, and the updated mom-and-pop-at-the-spaghetti-pots theme has been fine-tuned.

With their open kitchens, red-white-and-green Italian flag color scheme and even strings of muted light bulbs that dangle over the scene, the Macaroni Grills offer an entertaining setting.

The menu includes thin-crusted pizzas topped with such things as tomatoes, basil and oregano, spinach and prosciutto, or grilled vegetables. The pizzas come from wood-burning ovens, including one in the bar to provide snacks for the cocktail crowd. Salads go beyond the expected tossed greens (which aren't there at all) to range from arugula and cheese to sauteed spinach and garlic. And who ever heard of a 95-cent Caesar? That's the price with entrees.

Diners choose among 15 sturdy pastas, many of which come in big white bowls to be plopped atop tables covered in shiny white paper. Crayons are provided. And so are big bottles of olive oil in which to dip the hot focaccia (herbed flatbread) that comes to the table gratis.

Breaded veal scallopini, chicken scallopini, grilled salmon, and grilled sausage with roasted peppers and onions are among the listings on big single-page menus.

I especially like Scampi al Romano, firm, grilled shrimp in garlic butter atop angelhair pasta (available in appetizer or main course portions), the grilled Portobello mushrooms with herb-dappled orzo, and the updated antipasto tray with its cheeses, meats and pickled vegetables.

Tables are small and crammed close together in the big rooms and it's certainly more fun to be seated in the area adjacent to the kitchen than back in the room's far reaches. Obviously, these restaurants operate on volume. Get 'em in, get 'em out is the philosophy, which is fine if you are pressed for time but not so good if a relaxing dinner is what you have in mind.

American

	Page	Rating	Price
Acadia, *Auburn Hills*	5	☆☆☆☆	Mod.
Alban's, *Birmingham*	7	☆☆	Rea.
America, *Royal Oak*	8	☆☆☆	Mod.
Ann Sayles Dining Room, *Royal Oak*	11	☆☆☆	Rea.
Appeteaser Cafe, *Milford*	13	☆☆☆	Rea.
The Bank 1884, *Port Austin*	21	☆☆☆	Mod.
Beverly Hills Grill, *Beverly Hills*	22	☆☆☆	Mod.
Bill's Duck Inn, *Marine City*	25	☆☆	Rea.
Brandy's, *Bloomfield Hills*	29	☆☆½	Mod.
Brighton Bar & Grill, *Brighton*	30	☆☆½	Rea.
Britt's Cafe, *Detroit*	30	☆☆☆	Rea.
Cafe Bon Homme, *Plymouth*	34	☆☆☆½	Exp.
Cheers on the Channel, *Pearl Beach*	40	☆☆☆	Mod.
City Grill, *Birmingham*	45	☆☆☆☆	Mod.
Common Grill, *Chelsea*	47	☆☆☆	Mod.
Country Epicure, *Novi*	50	☆☆½	Mod.
D. Dennison's Seafood Tavern, *Livonia, Farmington Hills*	57	☆☆	Rea.
Diamond Jim Brady's Bistro, *Novi*	59	☆☆☆	Mod.
Dunleavy'z, *Detroit*	61	☆☆	Mod.
E.G. Nick's, *West Bloomfield*	65	☆☆½	Mod.
Elizabeth Street Cafe, *Detroit*	67	☆☆½	Rea.
Elwood Bar & Grill, *Detroit*	67	☆☆	Rea.
The Farm, *Port Austin*	74	☆☆½	Mod.
Ginopolis on the Grill, *Farmington Hills*	80	☆☆½	Mod.
Haab's, *Ypsilanti*	86	☆☆½	Rea.
Hattie's, *Suttons Bay*	87	☆☆☆☆	Mod.
Haymakers, *Lake Orion*	88	☆☆	Rea.
Innfield's, *Berkley*	93	☆☆½	Rea.
Jack's Waterfront Restaurant, *St. Clair Shores*	96	☆☆	Rea./Mod.
Joe's Bar & Grill, *Southfield*	98	☆☆½	Mod.
Karpinski's, *Detroit*	101	☆☆	Rea./Mod.
Key Largo, *Walled Lake*	102	☆☆☆	Rea./Mod.
Le Metro, *Southfield*	111	☆☆☆	Rea./Mod.
Loon River Cafe, *Sterling Heights*	115	☆☆☆	Rea.
Lord Fox, *Dixboro*	116	☆☆½	Mod.
Mac & Ray's, *Harrison Township*	119	☆☆☆	Mod./Exp.

Belgian

	Page	Rating	Price
Cadieux Cafe, *Detroit*	33	☆☆	Rea.

Buffet

Jumbo Buffet, *Troy*	99	☆☆½	Rea.
Mongolian Barbeque, *Royal Oak, Ann Arbor*	151	☆☆½	Rea.

British

Deacon Brodie's Tavern, *Mt. Clemens, Rochester Hills*	57	☆☆☆	Rea.
Nisbet Inn, *Windsor*	162	☆☆½	Rea.

Cajun

Fishbone's Rhythm Kitchen Cafe, *Detroit*	75	☆☆½	Mod.
Louie's on the River, *Detroit*	118	☆☆☆	Exp.

Chinese

Ah Wok, *Novi*	6	☆☆☆	Mod.
Asian Garden, *Sterling Heights*	16	☆☆☆	Rea.
Bamboo Garden, *Midland*	18	☆☆☆	Mod.
Chia Shiang, *Ann Arbor*	43	☆☆☆	Rea.
China Ruby, *Ferndale*	44	☆☆½	Rea.
Chung's, *Detroit, Waterford*	44	☆☆½	Rea.
Empress Garden II, *Windsor*	69	☆☆☆	Mod.
Hunan Hunan, *Allen Park*	90	☆☆½	Rea.
Jumbo Buffet, *Troy*	99	☆☆½	Rea.
Lai Lai, *Ypsilanti*	107	☆☆½	Rea.
Mandarin House, *Windsor*	140	☆☆☆	Rea.
Mon Jin Lau, *Troy*	150	☆☆☆	Mod.
Oceania Inn, *Warren*	165	☆☆½	Rea.
Peking House, *Royal Oak*	176	☆☆½	Mod.
Rikshaw Inn, *West Bloomfield*	188	☆☆½	Mod.
Shin Shin, *Windsor*	205	☆☆☆	Rea.
Wah Court, *Windsor*	239	☆☆☆	Rea.
Yau Hing, *Windsor*	242	☆☆☆	Rea.

Deli

	Page	Rating	Price
Mati's Deli, *Dearborn*	144	☆☆½	Rea.
Russell Street Deli, *Detroit*	196	☆☆☆	Rea.
Stage & Company, *West Bloomfield*	210	☆☆☆	Mod.
Zingerman's Deli, *Ann Arbor*	243	☆☆☆☆	Mod.

Ethiopian

Blue Nile, *Detroit, Ann Arbor*	27	☆☆☆	Mod.

European

Cafe Bon Homme, *Plymouth*	34	☆☆☆½	Exp.
Daniel's, *Royal Oak*	56	☆☆☆	Mod./Exp.
Ducks on the Roof, *Amherstburg, Ont.*	60	☆☆½	Mod.
Hermann's European Cafe, *Cadillac*	89	☆☆☆	Mod.
Moveable Feast, *Ann Arbor*	156	☆☆☆	Mod./Exp.

Fondue (Swiss)

La Fondue, *Royal Oak*	106	☆☆½	Mod.

French

Chez Pierre Orleans, *Rochester*	41	☆☆☆	Exp.
La Becasse, *Burdickville*	104	☆☆☆	Mod./Exp.
La Cuisine, *Windsor*	105	☆☆½	Mod.
Vintage Bistro, *Grosse Pointe Farms*	237	☆☆☆	Mod./Exp.

German

Dakota Inn Rathskellar, *Detroit*	54	☆☆½	Rea.
Heinzman's Heidelberg, *Clinton Township*	88	☆☆½	Rea./Mod.
Jacoby's, *Detroit*	97	☆☆½	Rea.

Greek

Hungarian

Indian

Irish

Italian

Mideastern

Mixed Bag

Pizza & pasta

Polish

Russian

Seafood

Soul food

Southwestern & Tex-Mex

Spanish

Steak & chops

Thai

Turkish

Vegetarian

Vietnamese

Index

Dearborn

Bangkok Tiger. *Thai*
Big Fish. *Seafood*
La Shish, La Shish West. *Mideastern*
M & M Cafe. *Mideastern/American*
Mati's Deli. *Deli*
Peacock. *Indian*
Ritz-Carlton Grill Room. *Mixed bag*
Thai Palace. *Thai*

Detroit

America's Pizza Cafe. *Pizza & pasta*
Armando's. *Mexican*
Blue Nile. *Ethiopian*
Blue Pointe. *Seafood/Italian*
Britt's Cafe. *American*
Cadieux Cafe. *Belgian*
Carl's Chop House. *Steaks & chops*
Casa de Espana. *Spanish*
Caucus Club. *Mixed bag*
Cosmic Cafe. *Vegetarian*
Courthouse Brasserie. *Mixed bag*
Cyprus Taverna. *Greek*
Dakota Inn. *German*
Dunleavy'z. *American*
East Franklin. *Soul food*
Edmund Place. *Soul food*
El Comal. *Mexican*
Elizabeth Street Cafe. *American*
Elwood Bar & Grill. *American*
El Zocalo. *Mexican*
Evie's Tamales. *Mexican*
Fishbone's Rhythm Kitchen Cafe. *Cajun*
Franklin Street B.C. *Mixed bag*
Giovanni's Ristorante. *Italian*
Govinda's at the Fisher Mansion.
   Vegetarian/Indian
Harlequin Cafe. *Mixed bag*
Il Centro. *Italian*
Jacoby's. *German*
Karpinski's. *American*
Laikon. *Greek*
Loco Bar & Grill. *Tex-Mex*
Los Galanes. *Mexican*
Louie's on the River. *Cajun*
Majestic Cafe. *Mideastern/American*

Mario's. *Italian*
Money Tree. *Mixed bag*
Joe Muer's. *Seafood*
New Hellas. *Greek*
New Parthenon. *Greek*
O'Leary's Tea Room. *Irish*
Opus One. *Mixed bag*
Pegasus Taverna. *Greek*
Rattlesnake Club. *Mixed bag*
Risata. *Italian/American*
Roma Cafe. *Italian*
Russell Street Deli. *American*
Sala Thai. *Thai*
Sindbad's. *American*
Steve's Soul Food. *Soul food*
Stewart's. *American*
Traffic Jam. *American*
Tres Vite. *Italian*
Union Street. *American*
Van Dyke Place. *Mixed bag*
Vince's. *Italian*
The Whitney. *Mixed bag*
Xochimilco. *Mexican*

Detroit Beach

Detroit Beach Restaurant. *Pizza & pasta*

Dexter

Cousins Heritage Inn. *Mixed bag*

Dixboro

Lord Fox. *American*

Eastpointe

Cloverleaf Pizza. *Pizza & pasta*

Farmington, Farmington Hills

D. Dennison's Seafood Tavern. *American*
Ginopolis on the Grill. *Greek/American*
Macaroni Grill. *Italian*
Marco's. *Italian*
Nipponkai. *Japanese*
Steamers Seafood Grill. *Seafood*
Tandoor Asia. *Indian*
Thai Peppers. *Thai*

Mackinnon's

If ever a restaurant fit its setting, it's Tom Mackinnon's lace-curtained cafe on Northville's Victorian-themed Main Street. His place is inviting, from the entrance way leading past the small bar, to the brick-walled dining room done up in stained glass lamps and panels with a game bird theme.

126 E. Main Street, Northville.
(810) 348-1991.

Hours: Lunch, 11 a.m.-4 p.m. Mon.-Sat.; dinner, 5-10 p.m. Mon.-Thu., 5-11 p.m. Fri.-Sat. Closed Sun. and major holidays except Easter and Mother's Day.

Nonsmoking: 50 percent.

Full bar.   Major credit cards.

Expensive.

The woodsy paintings and lithographs are just right, considering how the chef/proprietor loves to serve game dishes. Choices include grilled mallard breast with figs, leeks and wild rice; duck with raspberry sauce; venison stew, and wild turkey tenderloin with spiced berry sauce.

There are always four soups and an array of oysters on the menu. Appetizers include a hot appetizer platter, which, oh joy, is not the usual assortment of fried munchies. This one has escargots, crab pasta, stuffed mushrooms and other nicely chosen morsels.

While prices have crept upward — many main courses are in the $23.95-$29.95 range — each selection is fully garnished with vegetables and potatoes. A house salad is included, too.

Desserts are lovely and the list is lengthy. Such choices as banana Wellington with caramel walnut sauce, mocha crepe with ice cream, lemon mist torte and sorbet of the day are merely a few.

Macomb Inn

45199 Cass Avenue, Utica.
(810) 726-0770.

Hours: Lunch, 11:30 a.m.-2:30 p.m. Tue.-Thu.; dinner, 5-10 p.m. Tue.-Thu., 5-11 p.m. Fri.-Sat. Closed Sun., Mon., Thanksgiving, Christmas Day and New Year's Day.

Nonsmoking: 80 percent.

Full bar.   AE, MC and Visa.

Moderate.

Consistency is one of the attributes of the fare served in this quaint house, which has a historic designation. It's been the site of one restaurant or another for more than 40 years.

Seventy can be seated in Macomb Inn's three small dining rooms, done up with white linens and fresh flowers. Lately, chefs Anthony Currie and Bob Bird have been in the kitchen turning out fresh fare on a changing menu. Featured dishes might include grilled hickory-smoked pork chops, tournedos with Roquefort, Michigan mixed grill of pork tenderloin, braised quail and duck breast, as well as fresh fish.

The theme is regional Michigan to some degree, but it departs from that. After all, key lime pie is not exactly a native Michigan dish.

When the restaurant opens for dinner on weeknights, early diners may snag a notable bargain. Dinner, including salad, dessert and coffee, is just $9.95 until 6:30.

Note that access may be difficult for wheelchair users because of the front steps leading to the entrance.

Maisano's

26139 Novi Road, north of Grand River, Novi. (810) 348-1647.

Hours: lunch, 11 a.m.-3 p.m. weekdays; dinner, 5-9 p.m. Tue.-Thu., 5-10 p.m. Fri.-Sat., 5-9 p.m. Sun. Closed major holidays.

Nonsmoking: 75 percent.

Full bar.   Major credit cards.

Reasonable.

Maisano's is a charming mom-and-pop establishment where guests feel like they are being entertained in someone's home. In this case, the home of Jackie and Frank Maisano, who never really intended to get into the restaurant business but love it. And it shows.

The two dining rooms flanking a mini-bar are done up in charcoal gray and pink patterned wallpaper, with brass and glass wall sconces (happily with dimmer switches) and a collection of framed black-and-white photographs of Maisano and Manzo family wedding parties dating back to 1924. (Jackie was a Manzo before her 1964 marriage to Frank — that wedding photo is displayed over the bar.)

The photographs are just the right note, adding warmth and nostalgia. Like the pictures, the recipes are also from the family archives. All the basic dishes, like lasagna and Italian sausage, marinara and meat sauces, are well-prepared and consistent because whoever happens to be in the kitchen follows the family guidelines.

The menu is relatively brief, offering eight or nine pasta dishes from spaghetti and meatballs to gnocchi, some veal and chicken dishes, with steak and perch rounding it out. There are daily specials, too, to keep the regulars happy.

At lunch, the menu takes on a deli flavor (the restaurant evolved from a three-table Italian deli and pop shop), with an Italian sub, and ham and turkey sandwiches among the choices, and soups, such as beef barley and clam chowder. Six choices of pasta are served with a fresh salad.

But evenings are really the time to get the full feeling of the friendly Maisanos and their staff. That's when the kitchen turns out the dishes that say "Italian restaurant" to most people.

Majestic Cafe

Part of the midtown restaurant mini-boom is this spruced-up room that once was known as the Gnome. The menu retains some of the Gnome's Middle Eastern slant — tabbouleh, falafel, stuffed grape leaves — but the scope has been broadened to include American dishes and some with a bit of Spanish flair.

The new approach at the Majestic is especially welcome. In place of the buttoned-up hideaway of the Gnome, the setting is open and fresh with huge expanses of glass left uncovered, rosy brick walls and shiny oak floors under a vaulted ceiling. Matisse-like murals seem appropriate to the artsy neighborhood.

☆ ☆ 1/2

4130 Woodward, Detroit.
(313) 833-0120.

Hours: 11 a.m.-11 p.m. Mon.-Thu. (late-night menu until 12:30 a.m.), 11 a.m.-12:30 a.m. Fri.-Sat. (late night menu until 2 a.m.); Sun. brunch, 11 a.m.-3 p.m. and dinner, 3-11 p.m. Closed Christmas Day and New Year's Day.

Nonsmoking: 50 percent.

Full bar.   AE, MC and Visa.

Reasonable.

Joe S. Zainea is the chef, turning out kafta burgers (ground lamb), four-bean hommus, vegetarian stuffed squash, artichoke- and mushroom-topped pizzas, chicken taquitos with black bean salsa, and mini meat and cheese pies.

Each weekday from 11 to 3, the 10-minute lunch menu is in force. Yes, the I'm-in-a-hurry types are promised their lunch within 10 minutes. Is this progress? I'm not sure.

Mandarin House

☆ ☆ ☆

2020 Wyandotte Street W., Windsor, Ontario. (519) 254-2828.

Hours: 11 a.m.-midnight daily.

Nonsmoking: 40 percent.

Beer and wine.   MC and Visa.

Reasonable.

Wei Ming Shen is the energetic man behind this simple but attractive spot that is part of a block full of intriguing Asian restaurants and shops. Shen's menu of Cantonese and Sichuan dishes is extensive, but he still offers a list of daily specials. His live lobster dish has become so popular, he offers it every day. Beef hot pot is another crowd pleaser.

It's hard to choose, however, because there are numerous interesting dishes. Among them are braised duck with seafood, meat or mixed vegetables; hot and spicy prawns; chicken with orange flavor, and double cooked pork.

M & M Cafe

☆ ☆ 1/2

13355 Michigan Avenue, Dearborn. (313) 581-5775.

Hours: 9:30 a.m.-7 p.m. weekdays. Closed Sat., Sun. and major holidays.

Nonsmoking: 20 percent.

Soft drinks only.   No credit cards.

Reasonable.

A laid-back, unpretentious aura permeates the two narrow storefronts behind an all-but-invisible facade in the shopping district on east Dearborn's Michigan Avenue. No, this place will never be a destination for the trendy crowd.

It's been a word-of-mouth kind of spot ever since Elaine and Maurice Lteif (pronounced Le-teef) opened it 11 years ago. The Lteifs met when both were part of the waitstaff at the Sheik restaurant in downtown Detroit.

Elaine wears jeans and T-shirts as she works alongside Maurice in the open kitchen behind the counter. This diner isn't cute. It doesn't try to recreate an era. It exists to provide fresh, nutritious fare to the schoolteachers, truck drivers, office workers and shoe sellers in the neighborhood.

The couple makes it look very simple feeding the equivalent of a very big family each weekday, from late breakfast through lunch and early dinner. Without seeming to try, the Lteifs give the place personality.

They make the homely tasks look easy, using just a grill, a broiler and a couple of burners on a gas stove, shaking a big, much-used frying pan over the flames.

Plucking fresh vegetables from a bin in the cooler, they put together salads that are beautiful simply because they gleam with freshness.

No wonder so many people prefer to sit at the counter where they can watch the raw ingredients transformed into steaming plates. They arrive, very democratically, on a first-come, first-served basis. I'm not sure exactly how the Lteifs keep it all straight, but they manage. They seem to know instinctively who has ordered what, calling out for the waitress to come and get each plate as it is finished, or serving it themselves.

And if Helen's tuna plate, wreathed with crisp, raw carrots, radishes and cucumbers, arrives before husband Ed's steak, that's fine. The regulars know that you get your food when it is ready.

Customers who don't choose to perch on one of the counter stools take a table in the room that parallels it.

Each day has its special, from Monday's stuffed peppers and Wednesday's spaghetti to Friday's grilled whitefish served with stir-fried vegetables and rice.

This is the very opposite of the slick, contrived restaurant experience. It is a rainy Tuesday kind of place, offering the simple comfort of the kind of American fare (with a Middle Eastern tinge) that families thrived on before the current era of frozen entrees, immersible pouches and conflicting work schedules.

Marco's

A traditional Italian-American menu is served by Marco Conte and members of his family. The setting, however, departs from the usual red, white and green and has an almost glitzy, commercial restaurant look.

Still, the spirit is a family one and people are welcomed warmly for the dishes we all grew up on: lasagna, red-sauced spaghetti, grilled veal chop and veal piccante.

 ☆ ☆ 1/2

32758 Grand River, Farmington. (810) 477-7777.

Hours: Lunch, 11:30 a.m.-3 p.m. weekdays; dinner, 3-10 p.m. weeknights, 4:30-10 p.m. Sat. Closed Sun. and major holidays except Easter.

Nonsmoking: 75 percent.

Full bar.   Major credit cards.

Moderate.

For 38 years, Enzo and Ann Conte served similar dishes at Rina's on Schaefer in Detroit. Marco wasn't even born when his parents founded the restaurant. And now that's his name over the door.

The beat goes on.

Margarita's Cafetal

 1/2

2479 Woodward Avenue, Berkley.
(810) 547-5050.

Hours: 11:30 a.m.-10 p.m. Mon.-Tue.,
11:30 a.m.-11 p.m. Wed.-Thu., 11:30 a.m.-
11:30 p.m. Fri.-Sat., 11:30 a.m.-9 p.m. Sun.
Closed Easter, Thanksgiving and Christmas
Day.

Nonsmoking: 100 percent.

Soft drinks only.   Major credit cards.

Reasonable.

The restaurant in the white-painted cement block building is the brainchild of Luis Gomez, who came to Detroit from his native Guadalajara when he was 15.

In a down-to-earth ambience, he and his staff serve well-prepared if familiar dishes like tacos, enchiladas and burritos, combination plates featuring the same, sides of beans and rice — the latter served hot, a news item right there — and vegetarian dishes.

Gomez wasn't familiar with the Berkley area when he bought the building, but he has discovered that the locals love meatless dishes. The first time I stopped by, I ordered one without even realizing that it didn't contain meat. The entomatadas were so good I didn't miss the beef one little bit. The dish consists of corn tortillas topped with ranchero sauce, diced onions, shredded cheese and lettuce, with beans and rice.

Other dishes I've enjoyed in a number of visits: tortilla soup, a nice relief from the crunchies, since this blend of chicken broth, vegetables and spices includes soft bits of corn tortillas; machacado (shredded beef with scrambled eggs, diced onion, green pepper and tomato); potato-stuffed flautas and Mexican fries (rounds of thinly sliced potato sprinkled with spices and baked).

Guacamole — one of the true tests of a Mexican kitchen — measures up, too. It is available extra-chunky for those who prefer it that way. The obligatory chips and salsa come unbidden to the bare-topped tables. There's a choice of salsas: mild, hot, three-alarm green, or pico de gallo (diced onion, green pepper, tomatoes, lime juice and cilantro).

The setting is modest, with the biggest part of the L-shaped quarters attractively done up with tables and chairs. But most people prefer to cram into one of five booths in what Gomez calls "the railroad car room," a narrow section just off the kitchen.

Brightly colored Chi-Chi's-like menus are just about the only false note at his Cafetal — a word that translates to "coffee house." Appropriately, lots of coffee drinks are available, along with just about anything non-alcoholic you can think of. That's until such time as Gomez can obtain a liquor license.

Maria's Front Room

Winning new fans since moving to Ferndale is the little Italian restaurant that once was a hangout in Detroit's Rosedale Park neighborhood. The atmosphere harks back to those days, with red-and-white checkered tablecloths, little shaded lamps on some tables, and a warm, friendly, casual feeling. Maria's manages to project a cozy, even romantic atmosphere. Of course, not when that family with five kids comes in and sits down at the next table.

The pizza is excellent here, and fans come miles for the freshly made, hot garlic bread. Pastas, veal and chicken dishes are solid, too.

All this place needs, and is working hard to get, is a blessing from the Michigan Liquor Control Commission. Wine is very much a part of the Italian food experience, and this gutsy fare calls out for it.

☆ ☆ 1/2

**215 W. Nine Mile Road, Ferndale.
(810) 542-7379.**

Hours: Lunch, 11:30 a.m.-2:30 p.m. weekdays; dinner, 4-9 p.m. Sun.-Thu., 4-10 p.m. Fri.-Sat. Closed major holidays.

Nonsmoking: 60 percent.

Soft drinks only.   MC and Visa.

Reasonable to moderate.

Mario's

Founded in 1948 by Mario Lelli, the restaurant that retains his name survived his retirement in 1980.

It's now run by Vince Passalacqua, son of Frank Passalacqua, who spends his time running another venerable Detroit institution, Carl's Chop House. Mario's vintage look with paintings framed in ornate fashion, wall sconces with little cloth lamp shades and mellow wood paneling is old Detroit all the way.

The rooms look pretty much the same as always, and so does the menu, offering such tried and true dishes as shrimp cocktail, prosciutto with melon, oysters Rockefeller, filet mignon, chicken cacciatore, scampi and sauteed chicken livers.

That's just a hint of the offerings on the big menus. A full dinner comes with an

☆ ☆ 1/2

**4222 Second Ave., Detroit.
(313) 832-1616.**

Hours: 11 a.m.-11 p.m. Mon.-Thu., 11 a.m.-midnight Fri., 4 p.m.-midnight Sat., 2-11 p.m. Sun. Closed Christmas Day and July 4.

Nonsmoking: 70 percent.

Full bar.   Major credit cards.

Moderate to expensive.

antipasto tray, classic oil-and-vinegar dressed salad, minestrone and pasta. Entrees also may be ordered on an a la carte basis.

Mario's has always been a pre- and post-theater spot. It has a big-city feeling about it that is quite appealing.

Note that there's usually live dance music on Friday and Saturday nights.

Mati's Deli

☆ ☆ 1/2

1842 Monroe, Dearborn.
(810) 277-3253.

Hours: 10 a.m.-6 p.m. weekdays, 10 a.m.-3 p.m. Sat. Closed Sun. and major holidays.

Nonsmoking: 100 percent.

Soft drinks only.   No credit cards.

Reasonable.

A 1926 gas station near Dearborn's historic district houses an offbeat deli that nostalgia buffs will love. The oddly shaped, black-trimmed white tile building set back from the street has room for just 30 under a muraled copy of Edward Hopper's "Nighthawks."

Lots of glass brick and a '30s color scheme of apple green, lavender and turquoise add to the nostalgic feeling, as do the padded stools from the old Woolworth's dining counter in downtown Detroit.

Proprietor Lou Weinstein kept the menu from a previous regime but added two important amenities: hand-cut, double-baked rye bread and meat sold by the pound. Along with the typical deli sandwiches, there are some lighter in fat and salt, including chicken breast on French bread or pita, and a mix of vegetables and cheddar on pita.

Weinstein bakes the cream cheese brownies himself, and in the summer, sets up umbrella tables seating 20 on a small deck.

Matt Brady's Tavern

Carrying on the family tradition in a very real way is Diamond Jim Brady's youngest son, Matthew. His saloon has virtually the same menu that was served on West Seven Mile near Greenfield for so many years by his late dad.

It's a simple but crowd-pleasing array: shrimp cocktail, Delmonico steak, Brady's chili, four versions of the burger, the "garbage" salad and a few sandwiches including the BLT. A couple of things depart from the past. The original Brady's never had fries. Matthew serves fries, and he's also added desserts.

The friendly spirit, however, very much harks back to the old days in Detroit. Everyone is made to feel very welcome. There's nothing the least bit pretentious here, either in menu or setting.

 1/2

31231 Southfield Road, Beverly Hills.   (810) 642-6422.

Hours: 11 a.m.-midnight Mon.-Thu., 11 a.m.-1 a.m. Fri.-Sat., noon-11 p.m. Sun. Closed major holidays.

Nonsmoking: 50 percent.

Full bar.   Major credit cards.

Reasonable.

Mesquite Creek Steakhouse

We've all seen this menu before, and for that matter, the slick southwestern style setting, too. But thanks to a sharp kitchen crew and proprietors who know about such extras as freshly squeezed orange and grapefruit juice, Greek salads made at tableside, certified Angus beef and drinks mixed with Evian water, it's quickly apparent that this restaurant is not what it might have seemed at first glance.

Chowder is made with mesquite-roasted corn, nicely served in a glazed pottery bowl and topped with chopped green onions. Guacamole salad — a nice twist on the usual guacamole and chips — comes with pico de gallo, a mix of chopped tomatoes, onions, fresh cilantro, Serrano chilies and fresh lime juice, as well as grated cheese and lettuce.

7228 Ortonville Road, Clarkston. (810) 620-9300.

Hours: Dinner only, 4-10 p.m. Mon.-Thu., 4-11 p.m. Fri.-Sat., 4-9 p.m. Sun. Closed Thanksgiving, Christmas Day, New Year's Day and July 4.

Nonsmoking: 75 percent.

Full bar.   AE, MC and Visa.

Moderate.

Entree choices include mesquite-smoked baby back ribs with the house jalapeno barbecue sauce, and large shrimp stuffed with Monterey Jack cheese and jalapeno peppers, wrapped in bacon and cooked over mesquite, as are many of the menu items.

Then there's the Cowboy Steak, a 20-ounce, bone-in hunk of rib-eye steak that is the most expensive dish on the menu at $19.95. Like other entrees, it comes with all the trimmings, starting with the biggest baked potato short of Morton's of Chicago or plump skin-on fries or grilled vegetables, and a choice of salads. An interesting Greek salad is just an extra $1.95.

Service by the enthusiastic staff is competent and friendly, and each expresses his or her own style with a personally chosen tie to set off red, green, beige or cream shirts and beige pants.

The people behind Mesquite Creek include Oakland County real estate man Brian Hussey Sr. and his son, Brian. The Husseys are putting together another Mesquite Creek Steakhouse at the Crowne Plaza Pontchartrain in downtown Detroit. It is expected to debut in spring of '95.

Michigan Star Clipper

☆ ☆ ☆

840 N. Pontiac Trail, Walled Lake.
(810) 960-9440.

Hours: Departing 7 p.m. Tue.-Thu. and Sat.; 7:30 p.m. Fri.; 5 p.m. Sun. Closed Mon. and Christmas Eve, Christmas Day and New Year's Day.

Nonsmoking: 75 percent.

Full bar.   Major credit cards.

Expensive.

This rolling restaurant has no bad tables. Everyone gets a well-scrubbed window through which to watch the scene as the sleek cars, built in '56 for the Pennsylvania Railroad, rumble slowly away from the station on the 8.9-mile line known as Coe Rail.

The relaxing, three-hour train ride offers the atmosphere of the long-gone dining car. Appointments are acceptable if not ultra-elegant and the food is well beyond what might be expected. At the speed of just eight miles per hour, the glassware doesn't even rattle as the waitstaff serves pre-dinner drinks.

No menus are presented. That's because guests choose one of three main courses when reservations are made. One option is always prime rib and the other two change. They might be marinated pork tenderloin, chicken stuffed with smoked oysters or grilled halibut with tomato and basil relish.

Accompaniments include hors d'oeuvre, soup, salad, vegetables and dessert.

Tickets are $68.50 on cars with entertainment, perhaps a murder mystery or a cabaret performance, and $53.50 on those without. A gratuity is not included, nor are alcoholic beverages.

This is an experience geared toward adults, not a family excursion.

Midtown Cafe

Blow-ups of celebrity portraits by photographer Linda Solomon are everywhere. Cher, Andy Warhol, Heather Locklear, David Letterman, Johnny Carson and even Linda herself — gaze down from the walls onto the marble-topped tables.

Seated is a casually dressed crowd nibbling grilled vegetables, thin-crusted pizzas, Caesar salads and baked Brie.

☆ ☆ 1/2

139 S. Woodward, Birmingham. (810) 642-1133.

Hours: 11:30 a.m.-11 p.m. Sun.-Mon., 11:30 a.m.-1 a.m. Tue.-Sat. Closed Thanksgiving and Christmas Day.

Nonsmoking: 50 percent.

Full bar.   AE, MC and Visa.

Moderate.

There's a much more laid-back feeling than was once the case at this balconied spot in the heart of downtown Birmingham. Once a see-and-be-seen kind of place, that element has seemingly faded into oblivion. And that's to the good. It's a more comfortable atmosphere now, and the staff is friendly, unpretentious and, thankfully, displays no attitude.

The menu includes daily specials like crab cakes with roasted pepper sauce, pasta of the day, grilled swordfish with spicy tomato sauce and smoked pork chops with three-bean salsa. There are a couple of steaks along with the chicken and veal dishes, and fancy tortes offered for dessert.

The photographs are numerous enough to be a little overpowering. I wasn't sure on my last visit just how much I liked having Mickey Rooney stare down on my plate. Of course, it could have been worse. It could have been Cher.

The Mini Restaurant

Thanh and Barbara Lam spent three weeks in Vietnam early in '95, and came back with a new resolve to make their restaurant as authentic as possible. Their delicious, sometimes spicy, always light and refreshing Vietnamese fare is offered on an all-day menu.

Many dishes are served in clear sauces or as soups. Broths are made from simmered chicken or beef bones.

475 University W., Windsor, Ontario. (519) 254-2221.

Hours: 11:30 a.m.-10 p.m. weekdays, 5-10 p.m. Sat. Closed Sun. and major holidays.

Nonsmoking: 35 percent.

Beer and wine.   Major credit cards.

Reasonable.

Congee, rice cooked to the consistency of cereal, is an alternative to steamed rice. Barbecued meats tinted red by spices are served atop platters of rice.

The long list of dishes ranges from spring rolls and deep-fried tofu to curries, fried rice combinations and such noodle dishes as duck on fried noodles, shrimp in black bean sauce on fried noodles, and rice stick noodles with beef, onions and bean sprouts.

No longer "mini," the original tiny storefront was enlarged a few years ago and now has more polished, bi-level quarters.

Mr. Paul's Chophouse

29850 Groesbeck, north of 12 Mile Road, Roseville. (810) 777-7770.

Hours: Lunch, 11:30 a.m.-4 p.m. weekdays; dinner, 5-11:30 p.m. Mon.-Sat. Closed Sun. and major holidays.

Nonsmoking: 50 percent.

Full bar.   Major credit cards.

Moderate.

Don't try to convince the patrons or staff here that red meat is in a decline. This long-standing steak house still serves impressive amounts of it and always has. From filet mignon and T-bone to prime rib and Chateaubriand for two ($38.50), from lamb chops to calves' liver, meat stars on the menu.

That's not to say that seafood isn't available. Steamed salmon, scallops and mussels are often on the specials list, along with whitefish, lobster tails and Dover sole on the printed list.

Service is stressed by the founding Paul Gogo family. People are taken care of very, very well and they show their appreciation by returning to this somewhat out-of-the-way spot year after year.

You don't expect to find a restaurant like this on a stretch of road that seems more conducive to industry. But here it is, and here it's been for decades.

The Money Tree

The history of this downtown restaurant reflects the city's ups and downs. The original flourished in the '70s, stayed afloat through most of the '80s, but sank in 1990. After a brief revival in '93, it died a premature death — and just in time for Christmas.

A more solid revival began around Christmas of '94. Now the place is alive and kicking, thanks to proprietor Jackie Grant, and as business warrants, she will offer more extensive hours.

☆ ☆ ☆

333 W. Fort, Detroit.
(313) 961-2445.

Hours: Lunch, 11:30 a.m.-3 p.m., cocktails until 8 p.m. Mon.-Thu.; lunch, cocktails and dinner, 11:30 a.m.-9 p.m. Fri.; dinner, 5-9 p.m. Sat. Closed Sun. and major holidays.

Nonsmoking: 100 percent in the dining room; smoking allowed in the bar.

Full bar.   AE, MC and Visa.

Moderate.

The menu offers a mixed bag of contemporary American dishes and some traditional Money Tree favorites, including baked French onion soup with its crust of Gruyere, Caesar salads and variations on the Caesar, and chicken strudel.

Other dishes from chef Paul Jackman's kitchen include Maryland crab cakes with tropical fruit relish, herb linguine with chicken and vegetables, and cheese-stuffed ravioli. There's usually an interesting fish or seafood selection, sandwiches and lighter dishes. Jackman's soups are wonderful, ranging from corn clam chowder and puree of root vegetables to wild mushroom.

The Friday dinner menu changes weekly, offering a choice of appetizers and a half dozen or so main courses with a seasonal approach.

The room has copper-topped tables, banquettes against the wall, photo murals of European scenes and a street view through window walls. In warm weather, there's a sidewalk cafe.

The Money Tree is a haven of civility. No crashing dishes and shouting counter people here. Its not-yet-30-year-old chef sends out artistic plates with tricolor sauces and bright fruit and vegetable relishes.

The intent is to be more than just a place to grab a quick sandwich, yet nothing that's going to intimidate anybody. And that's a very nice combination.

Mon Jin Lau

☆ ☆ ☆

1515 Maple Road at Stephenson Highway, Troy. (810) 689-2332.

Hours: 11 a.m.-midnight Mon.-Thu., 11 a.m.-1 a.m. Fri., 4 p.m.-1 a.m. Sat., 3 p.m.-midnight Sun. Closed Thanksgiving and Christmas Day.

Nonsmoking: 50 percent.

Full bar.　　　　　Major credit cards.

Moderate.

The prettiest room in the place is the nonsmoking area. It's just another reason to applaud Marshall and Marco Chin, who have brought their restaurant to fruition over the past couple of years.

The high-ceilinged room with its live trees, tall windows and French doors makes an appealing contrast to the darker, more intimate areas of the big restaurant. The room eventually will expand to include a garden just outside.

That's next on the schedule for the brothers, whose pan-Asian fare continues to pack them in at tables covered with glossy white paper. Service is by an all-Asian staff and that lends a properly authentic air to the proceedings.

Among recommended dishes on a menu that always includes a list of daily specials, are Singapore noodles, a dish described as "Chinese angel hair pasta" tossed with chicken and shrimp, green and red peppers, scallions and a hint of curry; Mongolian beef; pan-fried dumplings; Sichuan spicy shrimp; cashew seafood, and shrimp with lobster sauce.

An interesting wine list accompanies the well-prepared fare. That's one unusual feature for an Asian restaurant. Another is the pastry tray brought out at dessert time. No orange sherbet here.

This is a restaurant that caters to an upscale crowd.

Mongolian Barbeque

Exotic? Mongolian Barbeque may sound that way, but it's about as exotic as an Army-Navy surplus store.

The style of the restaurant fits right in with the kind of casual atmosphere and down-to-earth fare that is typical of towns like Royal Oak and Ann Arbor.

It's a simple premise. For $7.95 at lunch, $10.95 at dinner, patrons can have the fun of putting together an all-you-can-eat meal from combinations they choose themselves.

First, they visit the conventional salad bar, with a steaming pot of soup on one side. That revs up the appetite for the main course: a trip (or two or three) to the buffet table, where a selection of raw beef, lamb, turkey, pork, chicken, cod, calamari, shrimp and tofu is arrayed. Vegetables include green pepper, mushrooms, leeks, sprouts, onion, tomatoes, broccoli and pineapple.

Pots of sauces, oils and seasonings are the next stop. Garlic oil, sesame oil, barbecue and black bean sauces and smaller pots of dried herbs, ground ginger, black pepper and other spices may be chosen in multiples to add the final touch to the meat and vegetables.

Once a bowl is filled and seasoned, the diner takes it to one of the baseball-capped cooks wielding two-foot wooden sticks, like giant chopsticks, at a flat metal grill in the middle of the room. The cooks quickly stir-fry the food, put it into yet another clean bowl and hand it back.

At the table, each diner has a bowl of rice, carefully folded flour tortillas and chopsticks. Finish that off and he or she may return to start the whole routine over again. Note that three dozen international beers are available along with wine by the glass.

Proprietors are Amy and Bill Downs, both Michigan State University graduates, who spent time with the London, England Mongolian Barbeques (there are five) before returning home.

There's no denying the Downses have a hit on their hands.

Make that two hits.

☆ ☆ 1/2

310 S. Main Street, Royal Oak.
(810) 398-7755.

200 S. Main Street, Ann Arbor.
(313) 913-0999.

Hours: 11 a.m.-11 p.m. Mon.-Thu. (10 p.m. in Ann Arbor), 11 a.m.-midnight Fri.-Sat. (11:30 p.m. in Ann Arbor), noon-10 p.m. Sun. Closed major holidays.

Nonsmoking: 75 percent (Royal Oak), 90 percent (Ann Arbor).

Full bar.   AE, MC and Visa.

Reasonable.

Monte Bianco

☆ ☆ ☆

02911 Boyne City Road, Boyne City.
(616) 582-3341.

Hours: Dinner only, 5-10 p.m. Wed.-Sun. from mid-May to mid-June; 5-10 p.m. Tue.-Sun. from mid-June to Labor Day; 5-10 p.m. Wed.-Sun. from Labor Day to Oct. 20; 5-10 p.m. Fri.-Sun. from Oct. 20 to mid-May. Closed Thanksgiving, Christmas Eve and Christmas Day.

Nonsmoking: 50 percent.

Full bar.   MC, Visa and Discover.

Moderate.

Monte Bianco occupies the faintly Alpine structure that once housed the Nordic Bar in the resort town of Boyne City. Its appeal is its upscale Italian menu, something hard to find in the pine-scented north.

Husband-and-wife team Mary and John Kelly certainly have been encouraged by the reception their Italian fare has received since they returned a couple of years ago to Michigan from northern California.

After the chefs who had come with them departed, the Kellys found Glenn Gerring, like themselves a Michigander who had returned to his home state. He handles the menu of Italian dishes, San Francisco-style, with pastas that include linguine with prawns, scallops, mussels and roasted garlic in a spicy tomato sauce.

Other choices include grilled lamb chops with eggplant and balsamic vinegar chutney, and fresh fish, generally walleye or whitefish. A typical appetizer is pizza bread slathered with roasted garlic, cheese and rosemary.

Other interesting appetizers include an assertive carpaccio (the thinly sliced beef sparked with pepper, olive oil and a sharp mustard sauce) and grilled prawns with mint vinaigrette.

The most popular dish of all is the house-made ravioli with shrimp in a sauce of basil, cream and vodka. Not to be missed is what the house calls North Beach seafood soup, a tomato-based seafood soup of scallops, shrimp and mussels.

There's a perfectly adequate little wine list to go with the fare, and service is willing, in the friendly spirit of the north country.

The setting is not what counts at Monte Bianco. Done up in a monotone gray, with tables to the right and left of the bar, the dining room is pretty nondescript.

Monterrey

Monterrey, on Royal Oak's restaurant row, is more than just a holding tank for Tom's Oyster Bar on busy nights, though it occasionally functions that way. It has fans of its own for the Veracruz burrito, arroz con pollo, chicken and cheese quesadillas, spicy bean dip, and enchiladas, among other popular Mexican dishes on the affordable, a la carte menu.

It's an informal, comfortable place with seating on a couple of levels under a tin ceiling, high-intensity lights and offbeat works by sculptor Nick Van Kridjt. The undesigned look is exactly what Ron Rea says he went for in creating the setting. The brick walls look as if they might have been attacked by a subway graffiti artist, and that's all part of the loose feeling.

In spring and summer, the sidewalk cafe is almost always packed.

☆ ☆ 1/2

**312 S. Main, Royal Oak.
(810) 545-1940.**

Hours: 11 a.m.-midnight Mon.-Thu., 11 a.m.-1 a.m. Fri.-Sat., noon-11 p.m. Sun. Closed Easter, Thanksgiving and Christmas Day.

Nonsmoking: 70 percent.

Full bar.   AE, MC and Visa.

Reasonable.

Morels

One of my personal favorites, this regional Michigan spot offers fresh, appealing fare on a menu that is imaginative yet accessible.

Its only drawback is the office building setting in which it finds itself and its large size, which includes banquet rooms that are often in use. Despite the central atrium where fresh herbs and flowers grow during the warm months, Morels can't shake that commercial feeling.

The food, however, manages to make the setting irrelevant, at least to most people.

Typical of the offerings are such dishes as lamb and wild mushroom strudel, rock shrimp with spicy black beans, cedar-roasted salmon and Indiana duck with

☆ ☆ ☆

**30100 Telegraph Road,
Bingham Farms. (810) 642-1094.**

Hours: Lunch, 11 a.m.-4 p.m. weekdays; dinner, 5-11 p.m. Mon.-Thu., 5 p.m.-midnight Fri.-Sat. Closed Sun. and major holidays.

Nonsmoking: 90 percent.

Full bar.   Major credit cards.

Moderate.

fruit relish and polenta. Items, of course, change on a seasonal basis. A number of dishes are offered in small and large portion sizes.

The contents of the bread basket are more than supporting players. Bread and rolls are from the Sourdough Bread Bakery where Andrew McGrath works his magic for this restaurant and others in the Matthew Prentice stable.

Chef David Krystal is just the latest in a line of chefs who have managed to keep things remarkably consistent.

Moro's Dining

6535 Allen Road, just west of Southfield Road, Allen Park.
(313) 382-7152.

Hours: 11 a.m.-10 p.m. weekdays, 4-10 p.m. Sat., 2-8 p.m. Sun. Closed Thanksgiving, Christmas Day and New Year's Day.

Nonsmoking: 20 percent.

Full bar.   AE, MC and Visa.

Moderate.

Tom Moro has been successful in luring diners to his off-the-beaten-track restaurant for a number of years now. The little spot once was a major bargain — in fact, a few years back some patrons wanted to pay more than Moro asked for his well-prepared dishes.

Those bargain days are over. Now the prices at this interesting spot seating 80 are more in line with other Italian restaurants. Table-side cooking of scampi, veal and beef dishes, a popular element here, has escalated in price to $25 per person. The meal includes, of course, salad, soup, vegetable and potato.

Other dishes are less expensive. Veal Marsala and veal cutlet maison are $13.50. Certainly comparable in price to other places except, perhaps, to those who remember when entrees were less than $8. Pasta dishes are in the $8-$13 range.

Moro, who is of Hungarian descent, trained under former Mario's proprietor Mario Lelli. He shares the Detroit restaurateur's dedication to quality.

Morton's of Chicago

The glossy Morton's of Chicago tosses excess in our faces like a carefully aimed cream pie.

Even before the waiter arrives with the presentation cart to display slabs of raw meat, live lobster with a tendency to lurch at startled guests and an entire chicken spread-eagled on a plate under its plastic-wrap blanket — a look around the room establishes the premise.

☆ ☆ ☆

1 Towne Square, between Civic Center Drive and Lahser, Southfield. (810) 354-6006.

Hours: Dinner only, 5:30-11 p.m. Mon.-Sat., 5-10 p.m. Sun. Closed major holidays.

Nonsmoking: 40 percent.

Full bar.   Major credit cards.

Expensive.

Big.

And bigger.

Wine bottles, none smaller than a jeroboam. Idaho potatoes, each the size of a basketball shoe, piled in a basket. Beefsteak tomatoes so lush they look ready to pop their skins. Onions like softballs.

Even the roses in the flower arrangements are huge.

Slide into one of the handsome wood chairs at a white-covered table and glance at the table appointments. You realize that choosing your dining companions carefully is especially important at this steak house, where every place setting includes a wide-bladed, wood-handled knife.

Flames flicker on each table in a glass oil-burner held by a pewter animal. Closer inspection reveals that it is … a pig. (Knives and pigs are available for purchase.)

The presentation cart offers for viewing double filet mignon (for one, $27.95) and single-cut prime rib ($26.95). Porterhouse, weighing in at 24 ounces, makes New York sirloin seem comparatively dainty at a mere 20. Porterhouse for two ($59.90) is bigger than some newborns.

Sure, you may order chicken. A whole chicken. Or a 3½-pound lobster at $15.50 a pound (the current market price), unless you'd prefer a bigger one. They are available up to 5½ pounds.

Vegetarians, be forewarned: one glance at the presentation cart will have you running for the exit.

Note that the menu is completely a la carte. That $29.95 Porterhouse is just that. The potato is another $4.25. But trust me: you can split it. Ditto for the fat stalks of steamed asparagus at $6.95 or the bunch of broccoli at $4.25. Both come with Hollandaise sauce.

Care for dessert? A hot souffle — chocolate, Grand Marnier or lemon — will be suggested ($9.95 for two).

Service is very good and the staff seems eager to please.

That's Sinatra in the background. Always, and it really fits in this room.

I have to admit that I was at first somewhat turned off by this scene, but I've adapted. What Morton's does, it does very well. In an age when most restaurants are providing half portions and scaled-down menus, it takes the opposite direction.

There's something admirable about that. They know, at Morton's, what they want to do, and they do it. Their way. Sinatra would certainly approve.

Moveable Feast

☆ ☆ ☆

326 W. Liberty, Ann Arbor.
(313) 663-3278.

Hours: Lunch, 11:30 a.m.-2 p.m. Tue.-Fri.; dinner, 6-9 p.m. Mon.-Sat. Closed Sun. and major holidays.

Nonsmoking: 100 percent.

Full bar.   Major credit cards.

Moderate to expensive.

Dining in this airy, well-restored 1870s house is a civilized experience, not pretentious nor overdone but very comfortable.

The seasonally motivated menu in the hands of chef Andrew Kile offers a la carte choices or complete, fixed-price meals at $24.50, $29.50 or $36.75.

Typifying Kile's approach are such dishes as medallions of pork tenderloin with pine nut butter, grilled Florida swordfish with pesto sauce and grilled breast of chicken with port wine sauce. These are accompanied by fresh vegetables and interesting potato, rice and lentil side dishes.

The sourdough baguettes and desserts from warm chocolate tart to creme caramel are notable. The wine list is in keeping with the culinary ambitions of this superior spot.

Joe Muer's

☆ ☆ ☆ ☆

2000 Gratiot at Vernor, Detroit.
(313) 567-1088.

Hours: 11:15 a.m.-10 p.m. Mon.-Thu., 11:15 a.m.-10:30 p.m. Fri., 4:45-11 p.m. Sat. Closed Sun. and major holidays.

Nonsmoking: 50 percent.

Full bar.   Major credit cards.

Expensive.

Long before everybody's neighborhood bar and grill served catch of the day, there was Joe Muer's. A Detroit standard since Oct. 28, 1929, the bastion of fresh fish and seafood is family run and amazingly consistent.

Untouched by fads, the restaurant founded by cigar-maker Joe Muer as a seven-table oyster bar still adheres to principles established in a time when going out to dinner was a rare treat.

Single-page menus, on crisp white paper topped with the red-and-black lobster claw logo, change daily, offering some 30 varieties of fish and seafood — and it's all catch of the day.

Notable items include Florida stone crabs, Dover sole, baked deviled crabmeat and tiny bay scallops. All are served pristinely. No fancy garnishes, no carved vegetable trimmings. Just plain and simple — and excellent.

The setting is a series of brick-walled, oak woodwork-trimmed rooms hung with paintings. Diners sit in captain's chairs at white-covered tables or banquettes.

Musashi

Celebrating the 10th anniversary of his restaurant in '95, proprietor Koji Watanabe certainly has beaten the odds in this volatile business. His restaurant is extremely authentic and attracts many Japanese businesspeople.

In the early going, the clientele was, in fact, about 80 percent Japanese. Now more non-Japanese are coming to the spot on the second level of the Town Center, where the options include, of course, a sushi bar.

Watanabe prides himself on his

☆ ☆ 1/2

3000 Town Center, Evergreen north of 10 Mile, Southfield. (810) 358-1911.

Hours: Lunch, 11:30 a.m.-2 p.m. weekdays; dinner, 5:30-10:30 p.m. Mon.-Thu., 5:30-11 p.m. Fri.-Sat., 5-10 p.m. Sun. Closed major holidays.

Nonsmoking: 35 percent.

Full bar.   Major credit cards.

Moderate to expensive.

Wagyu beef (often called Kobe beef), the velvety-textured, well-marbled meat from a special breed of black cattle. It's raised in Kobe as well as other regions of Japan on a regimen of grain, beer and special massages.

The beef is available raw, as a sashimi appetizer ($15), grilled on a hibachi at the table ($20) and as an eight-ounce steak at $70.

Other options include nabemono (one pot) dinners, sukiyaki (thinly sliced sirloin, tofu, bamboo shoots and vegetables sauteed quickly at the table) and shabu shabu, a similar assortment boiled in broth.

The premises are scheduled for an update in honor of the anniversary.

New Hellas Cafe

☆ ☆

583 Monroe Street, Detroit.
(313) 961-5544.

Hours: 11 a.m.-midnight Tue.-Thu. and Sun., 11 a.m.-2 a.m. Fri.-Sat. Closed Mon., Thanksgiving and Christmas Day.

Nonsmoking: 50 percent.

Beer, wine and some mixed drinks.

Major credit cards.

Reasonable.

Solid Greek fare — the menu for which could be inscribed on the Greektown pavement, so ubiquitous is it in the neighborhood — is served here in this corner spot that has an especially friendly feeling.

Maybe it's the uncovered windows allowing a view of the street. That certainly helps, as does the strategic location kitty-corner from Old St. Mary's Church.

This place has lots of lamb, lots of feta, lots of flaming kasseri cheese, and a crowd most of the time at the tables and booths.

New Parthenon

☆ ☆

547 Monroe Street, Detroit.
(313) 963-8888.

Hours: 11 a.m.-3 a.m. Sun.-Thu., 11 a.m.-4 a.m. Fri.-Sat. Closed Christmas Day.

Nonsmoking: 25 percent.

Full bar. Major credit cards.

Reasonable to moderate.

Funny how this spot, so eye-catchingly glitzy when it debuted in '89, seems to have settled in. It's now just another doorway along a block where, if you are not into Greek cuisine, you are nearly out of luck.

Only a couple of other options are available along Monroe, but at least it's getting a little more diversified.

Few can argue, though, with the popularity of big beet- and olive-dappled Greek salads, of flaming kasseri cheese and hearty lamb dishes. These are all available here, along with some Greek statuary and murals to set the scene.

Seating is on several levels, just one of which is nonsmoking.

New Seoul Garden

The big blue-and-white building is visible from Northwestern Highway, yet has a can't-get-there-from-here look. Actually, it's easily accessible from Telegraph Road with two quick right turns just south of 12 Mile Road. Another way is to exit at Lahser from I-696 west, turn right on Lahser, then left on 11 Mile Road to the Northwestern Highway service drive.

☆ ☆ ☆

27566 Northwestern Highway service drive, Southfield. (810) 827-1600.

Hours: 11:30 a.m.-10:30 p.m. Mon.-Sat., noon-10 p.m. Sun.

Nonsmoking: 50 percent.

Full bar.   Major credit cards.

Moderate.

Both Korean and Japanese dishes are served, a cross-section of about 58 selections ranging from sushi to kalbi and bulgoki. The latter are Korean barbecue dishes featuring, respectively, boneless short ribs and slices of beef, served with rice and seasoned vegetables. The meat is cooked on the hooded tables with built-in gas burners. There are 26 such tables available.

Those who like spicy dishes should try kimchee chige, a spicy broth with pork and vegetables, served in a stoneware pot. Bi bim bap, a mix of beef and vegetables topped with a fried egg, is another favorite. Korean dishes are served with an array of small side dishes, including the pickled cabbage relish without which a Korean meal can't be served. That's kimchee. Other tidbits might include steamed watercress, bean sprouts and julienned radishes.

Chef Yueng Chan Kim has been with proprietors Byung and Giyung Chung since the beginning several years ago.

Nicky's

☆ ☆ 1/2

755 W. Big Beaver, just west of I-75,
Troy. (810) 362-1262.

Hours: Lunch, 11 a.m.-4 p.m. weekdays;
dinner, 4-11 p.m. Mon., 4 p.m.-midnight
Tue.-Thu., 4 p.m.-1 a.m. Fri., 6 p.m.-1 a.m.
Sat. Closed Sun. and major holidays.

Nonsmoking: 50 percent at lunch, 25 percent at dinner.

Full bar.   Major credit cards.

Moderate to expensive.

More recently, a simplified menu has gone back to the basics at this dimly lit spot. Nicky's has something of a supper club feeling because of its live music, now every night, and its dance floor.

The straight-forward American roadhouse-style dishes include baked salmon, veal Oscar, grilled lamb chops and prime rib. Among the appetizers are shrimp cocktail, baked and fried oysters and blackened beef tenderloin tips with bearnaise sauce. The bearnaise comes out again with the filet mignon and there it is again with the a la carte asparagus.

Dinner includes soup or the house or Caesar salad. Plates come nicely garnished with redskins, rice pilaf or vegetable du jour.

The menu at lunch is lighter but offers some of the same dishes.

Niko's Cafe

☆ ☆ ☆

1943 King Road, two blocks west
of Fort Street, Trenton.
(313) 676-0987.

Hours: 11 a.m.-9 p.m. weekdays, noon-9
p.m. Sat. Closed Sun. and major holidays.

Nonsmoking: 80 percent.

Soft drinks only.   MC and Visa

Reasonable.

Maybe the most encouraging part of the success of Niko's Cafe, which doubled its original size when it expanded into a second storefront in '94, is that it proves people really do respond to quality.

The fresh, creative fare at this blink-and-you'll-miss-it spot far outshines its obscure location and limited amenities.

Who would have expected to find, in this little place with its bare-top tables and lots of people stopping by for carry-outs, a memorable wild mushroom and angel hair pasta dish, just barely veiled in a light Madeira and cream sauce?

Or a Caesar salad so fresh and crisp its ribs of romaine and house-made croutons seem to leap off the plate? Or soups like carrot-leek bisque and tomato puree with fresh mint?

The staff in neat white chefs jackets seems to take a genuine interest in each guest and his or her choices at lunch or dinner.

All of this might surprise first-timers, but it's taken for granted by the regulars at Niko's — some 200 people who return again and again and whose faces are known to chef-proprietor Nicholas Palivos.

He is the spirit behind this pink-and-turquoise gem. As he puts it: "We're a small house with a big house attitude."

After 13 years of experience in a number of local restaurants and country clubs, Palivos opened Niko's in May 1990, and the menu has expanded steadily since then along with the space.

The quality of his pastas, chicken dishes, fresh sandwiches and salads — everything from linguine with broccoli, spicy perch sandwich to roasted garlic spinach salad — pay tribute to his mentor, Ernie DiMichele, now of Ernesto's in Plymouth, to whom Palivos credits much of his food philosophy.

Nipponkai

When the first Nipponkai opened in Clawson in 1984, it was the only truly authentic Japanese restaurant in the area. Done up in the soft colors and spare details typical of the Japanese decorative style, it had a dressy air about it.

After 10-plus years, it has settled in. Now Nipponkai is more of a neighborhood restaurant — and I mean that in the most complimentary way. It's comfortable, informal, less dependent on decor, and has become a favorite of both Japanese and non-Japanese alike.

As always when dining in an ethnic restaurant, I love seeing how many people who are not members of the particular ethnic group appreciate the fare. And there are usually lots of non-Japanese digging into sushi, miso, tuna teriyaki and even eel.

Yes, eel, served sliced atop seasoned rice in a bowl.

The seats at the small sushi bar are also filled on most occasions.

The newer, more elaborate sibling of the same name in Farmington Hills serves pretty much the same menu: a full range of Japanese dishes from the well-known tempura, chicken and beef teriyaki and sukiyaki, to less familiar dishes.

Both restaurants are run by Masayo Kimura, widow of founder George Kimura.

32443 Northwestern Highway, Farmington Hills. (810) 737-7220.

511 W. 14 Mile Road, Clawson. (810) 288-3210.

Hours: Lunch, 11:30 a.m.-2 p.m. weekdays; dinner, 5:30-10:30 p.m. Mon.-Thu., 5:30-11 p.m. Fri.-Sat. Closed Sun. and major holidays.

Nonsmoking: 25 percent.

Full bar.   Major credit cards.

Moderate to expensive.

Nisbet Inn

☆ ☆ 1/2

131 Elliott Street W., Windsor,
Ontario. (519) 256-0465.

Hours: 11 a.m.-11 p.m. Tue.-Sat., 2-10
p.m. Sun. Closed Mon. and Christmas Day,
Dec. 26 and New Year's Day.

Nonsmoking: 40 percent.

Full bar.   AE, MC and Visa.

Reasonable.

A dilapidated circa-1915 house that languished untended for years until it was bought by a pair of British-born sisters has been turned into a charming bed-and-breakfast. And all it took was eight years of hard work.

That's the effort Kim and Lynne Nisbet put into creating their inn, which has been open just a year, a block from busy Ouellette Avenue in downtown Windsor.

The finished product offers four antique-furnished bedrooms and a 10-foot bathtub on claw feet, plus a cozy dining room and bar that is just beginning to attract a clientele for simple but well-prepared food with a pub slant.

Lunch and dinner patrons are more than welcome in the first-floor rooms and garden of the brick house Kim Nisbet calls a late Victorian. The house does not have, however, the ornate froufrou that might be expected of the typical Victorian. Nor have the sisters gussied it up with the kind of cutesy decor often encountered in B&B establishments.

This one has a solid British feeling, including the five-seat bar constructed out of French doors, the subdued color scheme that shows off lots of mellow oak trim, the stone fireplace and the curving window seats. Subtle, deep-toned draperies are at the windows, and table settings are simple, giving a nice pub atmosphere to the place.

The menu spotlights such solid fare as fish and chips and chicken pot pie with a high hat of golden-brown puff pastry. One specialty is ploughman's lunch — cheddar cheese, pickled onion, green salad and bread. Daily specials might include baby pizza with grilled chicken and mushrooms. The house potatoes — boiled new potatoes pan-fried with garlic, butter and a handful of diced red peppers — are served with most entrees.

On the last Sunday of each month, Nisbet Inn offers a traditional roast beef and Yorkshire pudding dinner, complete to the sherry trifle or bread pudding for dessert. It's $12.95 (Canadian) and is served from 5 to 8 p.m. Reservations are needed for the Yorkshire pudding dinner.

Note that the house is not easily accessible to wheelchair users.

Norm's Eton Street Station

Train stations make great settings for restaurants. This former Grand Trunk Western railroad station on Birmingham's Eton Street, built in 1931 and given a $2.3 million renovation several years ago, is certainly no exception. It's on the National Register of Historic Places, to boot.

☆ ☆ 1/2

245 S. Eton, Birmingham.
(810) 647-7774.

Hours: 11 a.m.-10 p.m. Mon.-Tue., 11 a.m.-11 p.m. Wed.-Thu., 11 a.m.-midnight Fri., noon-11 p.m. Sat. and 10:30 a.m.-9 p.m. Sun. Closed major holidays.

Nonsmoking: 80 percent.

Full bar.   Major credit cards.

Moderate.

When the restaurant first opened, however, the food was no better than mediocre. Over the years, it's improved noticeably. First, it was chef Jeff Baldwin who sharpened the fare. Lately, it's been Mike Boyce working on an upgraded menu.

Among his additions are such dishes as whiskey pepper tenderloin tips with pasta and wild mushrooms, charred salmon salad with wild mushrooms atop spring lettuces, and such vegetarian items as grilled portobello mushrooms on potato bread. You might guess that he served a stint at Morels in Bingham Farms from that lineup, and he did.

Boyce likes to do game dishes and says he has had surprising success offering things like hasenpfeffer and wild boar as occasional specials.

In warm weather, the outdoor patio is an added element.

Ocean Grille

 1/2

280 N. Woodward, Birmingham.
(810) 646-7001.

Hours: Lunch, 11:30 a.m.-2:30 p.m. week-days; dinner, 5-10 p.m. Mon.-Thu., 5-11 p.m. Fri.-Sat. Closed Sun. and major holidays.

Nonsmoking: 90 percent.

Full bar.   Major credit cards.

Moderate.

Chef Tim Cikra's arrival in '94 at this heart of Birmingham spot has given it a new lease on life. Cikra, formerly chef at Morels in Bingham Farms, brings his respect for fresh ingredients and his regional approach to the menu.

As the name suggests, fish and seafood star on an extensive menu. In addition to that, there are eight to 10 daily specials, some of which are also from the waters. Despite the seafood slant, Cikra still likes to dish up Indiana duckling. His light, non-greasy treatment of the bird is exceptional.

Proprietor Craig Dilworth knows a little something about fish, too. He spent years with the C.A. Muer organization before opening his own restaurant, one flight down in an office building concourse.

Oceania Inn

Paul and Amy Leung's Ryan Road restaurant is a very authentic Cantonese spot, with a few Sichuan dishes, too. All of it is aimed at those who, whether by birth or inclination, have extensive knowledge of the fare.

The menu is lengthy and offers dishes not seen on the menus of more Americanized Chinese restaurants. These items include chicken and duck feet, sea cucumber and conch. That's certainly one reason why the clientele includes workers from other restaurants, who come here when their shifts are over. The long hours are another draw.

⭐ ⭐ 1/2

24845 Ryan Road, Warren.
(810) 756-4664.

Hours: 11 a.m.-2 a.m. weekdays, 10:30 a.m.-2 a.m. Sat.-Sun. Dim sum daily, 11 a.m.-3 p.m. weekdays, 10:30 a.m.-3 p.m. Sat.-Sun.

Nonsmoking: 50 percent.

Soft drinks only.   AE, MC and Visa.

Reasonable.

Old Mexico

☆ ☆ ☆

5566 Drake Road at Walnut Lake
Road, West Bloomfield.
(810) 661-8088.

Hours: 5-10 p.m. Mon.-Thu., noon-11 p.m.
Fri., 5-11 p.m. Sat. Closed Sun. and major
holidays.

Nonsmoking: 70 percent.

Full bar.   AE, MC and Visa.

Reasonable.

Proprietors Ramon
and Vicki Castaneda
and their son Tim have
a secret. They know
they'll have happy
customers if they
give them a little touch
of Acapulco with their burritos and
quesadillas.

So their premise is to create a fiesta
atmosphere to go along with the Mexican
dishes on the menu. Yes, it's a typical
Mexican restaurant menu, but done very
nicely here. As Tim Castaneda points out,
why kill yourself coming up with specials
when people are perfectly happy with their tortilla dishes slathered with sour
cream and melted cheese?

Jose Riojas plays latin jazz Thursday through Saturday nights, and that adds to
the fiesta feeling in a special way.

The Castanedas have a satellite spot in Livonia, on Five Mile Road between
Inkster and Middlebelt, but it does not have the same festive feeling as their place
in West Bloomfield.

O'Leary's Tea Room

☆ ☆ ☆

1311 Brooklyn, Detroit.
(313) 964-0936.

Hours: 9 a.m.-4 p.m. weekdays, 10:30
a.m.-3 p.m. Sun. Closed Sat. and major holidays.

Nonsmoking: 80 percent.

Full bar.   Major credit cards.

Reasonable.

The grass-roots
charm of this Corktown
spot comes from its
setting in antique-filled
small rooms in two
adjoining houses, the simple,
unpolished but kind service
and the authentic Irish dishes emerging
from chef Gene Ameriguian's kitchen.
His name may not sound Irish, but after a
bite of his soda bread, scones, Killarney
green pea soup, shepherd's pie, lamb
shanks and bread pudding, you'll think
he is.

Those who enjoy high tea may have it from 2 to 4 p.m. each weekday, but it
must be arranged in advance.

The trellised garden in back is shaded with old grapevines and is a popular spot
for lunch when the weather permits.

Not quite adjoining O'Leary's, but almost, is Eph McNally's Sandwich Shoppe, on the corner of Brooklyn and Porter. The place serves soups, salads and deli sandwiches from 10 a.m. to 4 p.m. weekdays. It's also run by O'Leary's proprietor Jane McNally, who created this little Irish corner a few years ago.

Om Cafe

The fare here is totally meatless and offers only occasional dairy products and no refined sugar. Om Cafe does, however, offer fish, which is part of a macrobiotic diet.

The lunch menu offers lighter dishes, like miso, lentil and bean soups, vegetarian chili and sandwiches, including the tempeh burger. Among the more substantial items in the evening is a macrobiotic plate consisting of brown rice and adzuki beans (small dried beans), assorted vegetables and sea vegetables. It's $7.95.

☆ ☆ 1/2

23136 N. Woodward, Ferndale. (810) 548-1941.

Hours: Lunch, 11 a.m.-2:30 p.m. and dinner, 4-9 p.m. Mon.-Sat. Brunch, 10 a.m.-1 p.m. on 1st, 2nd and last Sun. of month. Closed other Sun. and major holidays.

Nonsmoking: 100 percent.

Soft drinks only.   No credit cards.

Reasonable.

A number of freshly squeezed vegetable and fruit juice concoctions have been added to the tea and coffee drinks on the menu.

It should be noted that despite its dedicated vegetarianism, this is not a grim place. Non-vegetarians will also feel comfortable stopping by for a moment of relief from the high-fat bandwagon — at least for one meal.

ONE23

Not a tremendous number of people have put this Grosse Pointe Farms spot on their regular dining list. And that's too bad. Because it is an excellent restaurant.

The main problem is that its location on the strip of shops known as "the hill" is not exactly the beaten track for the majority in the metro area. And the highly contemporary setting, with its skylights, huge glass sculptures against brick walls and bi-level construction, can seem cold. It's difficult to feel you are in a "theater" setting — which so many people demand of restaurants.

You have to perch in the clubby little bar at the rear in order to have that feeling. In the dining room, sight lines are good only from a couple of the big banquettes.

Rather than be concerned about who might be seated on the other side of the Pewabic tile and walnut banquette, diners would do well to concentrate on the contemporary American dishes emerging from Chef Michael Trombley's kitchen.

It's been more than two years since Trombley arrived on Kercheval to be sous-chef to Zachary Smith. It wasn't long before he inherited the top job, and slowly began giving the menu his own stamp. That means a regional approach.

Still, Trombley's smart enough to know he must please two kinds of diners. The old guard wants traditional dishes like seared tournedos of beef with mushroom sauce and garlic whipped potatoes, and it's a dish he is happy to provide. There's also a more adventuresome group that goes for his seared ahi tuna with fresh mango and coconut coulis or rock shrimp and angel hair pasta with hearts of palm.

The menu is well balanced with choices, and there's always a burger available on a multi-grain roll — that's a nice touch. Proprietors Lynn and Stanley Day always insist that people dress the way they wish and order that same way, too. If someone wants an appetizer pizza (and this one is more than a couple of mouthfuls) with a salad, so be it. Casual dress is fine here, though the dining room has a deceptively dressy look.

The menu is rewritten monthly and very much reflects the season. Little touches are telling: the ancho chile dressing that varies the traditional Caesar salad, the vinaigrette the chef calls "citronette" because it contains lemon and lime juice instead of vinegar (he drizzles it over roasted loin of swordfish), the fried sage in the leek and potato soup. These are indications of Trombley's attention to detail.

Still more goodies: the "diver" scallops brought up from the deep by divers instead of nets, thereby retaining their perfect shape; the maple syrup and dark beer sauce on slices of pork loin, and the excellent warm bread accompanied by a butter square that has a bit of fresh green dill pressed into its surface.

Desserts range from an earthy, caramel-sauced bread pudding dotted with dried cherries and pecans to the kind of elaborate creations of chocolate truffle cream that make people groan with pleasure. Service is completely professional.

Opus One

For the first time in its eight-year history, this luxurious restaurant had a change in the hierarchy of the kitchen early in '95. Tim Giznsky inherited the wire whisk from Peter Loren, who moved on to the kitchen of a new Farmington Hills restaurant.

Fans of the marble and etched-glass lavished place in downtown Detroit didn't have to worry, however. Giznsky had

☆ ☆ ☆ ☆

565 E. Larned, Detroit.
(313) 961-7766.

Hours: Lunch, 11:30 a.m.-3 p.m. weekdays; dinner, 5:30-10:30 p.m. Mon.-Thu., 5-11 p.m. Fri.-Sat. Closed Sun. and major holidays.

Nonsmoking: 70 percent.

Full bar.   Major credit cards.

Expensive.

worked closely with Loren at Opus since the beginning, so the beat goes on without a hitch.

The style at Opus One fits its decor. The food is meticulous in both composition and presentation. Sauces are rich — but the kitchen is quite willing to put them on the side, or omit them entirely should the guest prefer.

Like any talented chef, Giznsky has his own signature dishes. In the early going, they include sauteed breast of Michigan pheasant with roasted vegetables atop white beans in basil cream; char-grilled medallions of veal with truffle Madeira sauce, and potato-crusted lamb with roasted garlic and rosemary sauce. He says he will changed the menu monthly to reflect what is seasonal.

House-smoked salmon, and breads and pastries made right on the premises — of course! — are all part of the upscale approach here under proprietors Jim Kokas and Ed Mandziara. One or both of them usually can be found at the door.

They like to call the Opus style "American cuisine with a French flair." Need I say that service by the well-dressed staff is in keeping? Everyone is pretty much made to feel like a VIP in the rooms at 565 E. Larned.

Kokas and Mandziara are in the process of putting together their second restaurant, in partnership with Mike and Marian Ilitch. Jake's on the Lake, a casual seafood restaurant, is at the intersection of Orchard Lake Road and Pontiac Trail. It's the former Buster's Bay. Chef Gary Gryzwacz will be in charge of the kitchen when the restaurant opens in spring of '95.

Orchid Cafe

☆ ☆ ☆

3303 Rochester Road, north of Big
Beaver, Troy. (810) 524-1944.

Hours: Lunch, 11 a.m.-3 p.m. Mon.-Sat.;
dinner, 3-9 p.m. Mon.-Sat. Closed Sun. and
major holidays.

Nonsmoking: 100 percent.

Soft drinks only.   Major credit cards.

Reasonable.

Named for the flowers grown as a hobby by Thi Nguyen, husband of proprietor Maria Nguyen, this serene spot has blossomed like Thi's orchids since it opened in '91.

Despite the storefront location, it's a serene spot with an artistic feeling. Niceties include linens in the evening and attractive place settings.

Many now-familiar Thai dishes are on the menu, including gai pad ped (sauteed chicken with hot curry, eggplant, peppers, onions and coconut milk), tod mun (spicy minced fried chicken patties with cucumber salad) and pad Thai, the noodle dish that seems to be a particular favorite locally.

House specialties include royal crispy rolls, which are crunchy rolls of rice paper wrapped around ground chicken and shrimp, bean threads, onions and water chestnuts; angel wings, deboned chicken wings stuffed with onion, lemongrass and onions, and ginger-sauteed shrimp.

☆ ☆ ☆

20273 Mack, Grosse Pointe Woods.
(313) 884-4144.

19355 W. 10 Mile Road, Southfield.
(810) 357-3399.

1360 S. Woodward, Birmingham.
(810) 642-5775.

Hours: 7 a.m.-9 p.m. daily (Grosse Pointe
Woods); 7 a.m.-4 p.m. daily (Southfield);
6:30 a.m.-9 p.m. daily (Birmingham).
Closed Christmas Day.

Nonsmoking: 70 percent (80 percent in
Birmingham only).

Soft drinks only.   No credit cards.

Reasonable.

Original Pancake House

Breakfast is what these cheerful restaurants do best. Not to be confused with chain pancake houses, these make everything from scratch and offer a truth-in-menu approach. Real cream, real butter, real maple syrup and real oranges in the orange juice are just part of the everyday plan. If something isn't fresh, they'll tell you.

As the name states, pancakes of every possible description are on the menu, from huge puffy baked creations filled with apples or garden vegetables to silver dollar-sized pancakes.

Service is friendly and efficient. The Original Pancake House is a rarity in that people are willing to line up for Saturday and Sunday breakfast with relative equanimity.

Overtures, an Eatery

If you judged this place solely by its sign, its size and its cottage exterior, you might dismiss it as a quaint little tea room.

Not so. Overtures, an Eatery has an interesting menu of dishes with an international approach, everything from the familiar Greek and Caesar salads to Indonesian sate of chicken with coriander peanut sauce, Brie en croute flavored with Dijon mustard and Jamaican jerk shrimp. Stars on the seafood list are shrimp and salmon.

1107 Lesperance Road, Tecumseh, Ontario. (519) 979-0010.

Hours: Lunch, 11 a.m.-5 p.m. Tue., 11 a.m.-3 p.m. Wed.-Sat.; dinner, 5-11 p.m. Wed.-Sat. Closed Sun., Mon. and major holidays.

Nonsmoking: 70 percent.

Full bar.   MC and Visa.

Moderate.

The range of dishes is the style of Glenn van Blommestein, who was born in the Netherlands, spent much of his early childhood in Indonesia and moved to Canada in '67. He enjoys surprising people with his multifaceted approach to cooking.

His wine list is in keeping. Choices come from places like Australia and Chile as well as France, Italy, Germany and the United States.

Paint Creek Restaurant

☆ ☆ 1/2

4480 Orion Road, between Adams
and Rochester roads, Goodison.
(810) 651-8361.

Hours: Dinner, 5-10 p.m. Tue.-Sat.; breakfast, 9 a.m.-2 p.m. Sun. Closed major holidays except Easter.

Nonsmoking: 75 percent.

Full bar.   Major credit cards.

Moderate.

Being asked to wait for a table is not such a bad thing during the summer months. Here, one way to while away the time is to cross the little bridge over Paint Creek and meander along the woodsy trail shaded by elms and willow trees. The trail extends for 11½ miles, but chances are the wait won't be quite that long.

The restaurant in a cider mill in Goodison — the oldest settlement in Oakland County, Est. 1827 — offers a country village setting that belies its proximity to the split-levels and shopping plazas of Rochester.

Its creek-side deck is shaded by a very old elm, "one of the last of the big trees," says Jerry Mancour. He runs the restaurant and cider mill along with his wife, Lucy, and daughters Jane, Carol and Tracy. Though the deck has been the setting for several weddings, Jerry Mancour says with a sigh that it's usually either too hot, too cool or too mosquito-y to make it work regularly for dining outside.

The good news is that the adjoining dining room's big windows offer virtually the same view: the creek on one side, the big waterwheel churning lazily on the other. Its motion actually provides enough power to light some of the lights in the dining room.

You might expect to find more atmosphere than solid sustenance in a spot like this. Happily, that's not so. It's a restaurant where virtually everything is house-made, from stocks and hollandaise sauce to five salad dressings, notably creamy apple with smoked cheddar cheese. Bread is baked on premises, and in the fall when the first McIntosh, Paula Red and Jonathan apples come in, the cider mill adds its element to the bucolic scene.

One of the best times to visit is at Sunday breakfast (a fixed price $10.50). Choices include fresh fruit and pastries, eggs Benedict, chicken strudel, malted Belgian waffles with strawberries and seafood crepes.

Dinner is from a creative menu that spotlights the apple in such dishes as apple- and pecan-stuffed chicken breast with cider brandy sauce. But not everything includes apples. There are pastas and a recommended dish of grilled loin of pork with wild mushrooms, rosemary, Dijon and white wine reduction.

Although there has been a mill on the property since 1835, the original structure burned down in 1875. This is the third building in the progression, but it retains a comfortable, vintage feeling.

Palio

Italian food is so popular, the owners of Gratzi, a thriving Italian restaurant on Ann Arbor's South Main Street, felt confident in opening another right across the street. Palio is virtually in the shadow of its bigger sibling. But it doesn't seem to matter.

Once the Quality Bakery, and for a while the Quality Bar, the space now houses a lively trattoria that has the combined atmosphere of an espresso bar and an Italian grocery store. It is lower key than Gratzi, and its menu is shorter, lighter and more country-style rustic.

☆ ☆ ☆

**347 S. Main, Ann Arbor.
(313) 930-6100.**

Hours: Dinner only, 5-10 p.m. Mon.-Thu., 5 p.m.-midnight Fri.-Sat., 4-9 p.m. Sun. Closed Thanksgiving, Christmas Day and New Year's Day.

Nonsmoking: 85 percent.

Full bar. AE, MC and Visa.

Reasonable to moderate.

Patrons encounter the open kitchen as soon as they come through the door. Cooks juggle saute pans in full view.

The retro-feeling dining rooms have a color scheme that features an apple green right out of a '40s dinette. There are some faintly art deco hanging lamps and shelves holding bottles of oil, tins of cookies, bags of pasta and cans of tomatoes.

The friendly, casual atmosphere is enhanced by the immediate arrival at each table of a basket of crusty country bread, to be dipped into rosemary-spiked olive oil. Bread is a recurring theme here. The antipasti include grilled garlic bread with tomatoes, anchovies, capers, oregano and basil, as well as toasted bread with grilled Asiago cheese flecked with fresh thyme. Cubes of bread are in the salad, along with arugula, tomatoes, onions and fresh basil, and a round of bread is immersed in the wonderful Tuscan vegetable soup.

I've always thought a just-about-perfect meal is comprised of good bread, a green salad, thick peasant soup and a glass of red wine. If you're so inclined, this meal can be put together very successfully here.

The menu goes much beyond that, of course. Its list of sturdy pastas, for example, includes penne with red and yellow peppers, green olives, tomatoes, capers and bacon, and ravioli filled with veal and spinach in pecorino cheese sauce.

Specialties include roasted lamb with fresh rosemary and garlic, served with herb-roasted potatoes and sauteed spinach; mixed grill of chicken breast, pork tenderloin, Italian sausage and jumbo shrimp, and grilled salmon with lemon garlic sauce.

It almost goes without saying that various espressos and cappuccinos are available, along with a nice list of Italian wines. Wine tasting dinners take place February through April and September through December on the second Tuesday of the month.

Paparazzi Ristorante

☆ ☆ 1/2

6263 Orchard Lake Road, West Bloomfield. (810) 855-3993.

Hours: 11:30 a.m.-9:30 p.m. Mon.-Thu., 11:30 a.m.-11 p.m. Fri.-Sat., 4:30-10 p.m. Sun. Closed Thanksgiving and Christmas Day.

Nonsmoking: 80 percent.

Full bar. AE, MC and Visa.

Reasonable.

An unpretentious Italian restaurant along West Bloomfield's restaurant row, this small spot is run by Steve and Olga Stojanovski, who took over from its original owners in '94.

The open kitchen is the domain of Anthony Middlebrook. Despite that first name, he can't claim Italian heritage but certainly cooks that way.

You might discern a hint of the Maria's Front Room style here. Maria's proprietors, Joan and Carl Orlando, now in Ferndale, helped put this place together originally. The freshly made garlic bread is in that tradition.

Main dishes include seafood marinara; salmon with sun-dried tomatoes, olives, fresh basil and garlic; eggplant Sorrentino, a favorite dish in local Italian restaurants, made with ricotta and angel hair pasta; ravioli stuffed with meat or cheese; spinach tortellini in pesto sauce, and thin-crusted pizzas.

The setting, as the name suggests, is awash in celebrity photos and old cameras.

Passage to India

☆ ☆ 1/2

3354 W. 12 Mile Road, Berkley. (810) 541-2119.

Hours: Lunch, 11:30 a.m.-2:30 p.m. weekdays; dinner, 4:30-10 p.m. Sun.-Thu., 4:30-10:30 p.m. Fri., 1-10:30 p.m. Sat. Closed July 4, Thanksgiving, Christmas Day and New Year's Day.

Nonsmoking: 20 percent.

Full bar. Major credit cards.

Reasonable to moderate.

Northern Indian dishes and a few Bengali selections are served by Mohamed Ahmed and Kazy Uddin, who grew up together in Bangladesh and have worked in this country in New York and Nashville. Uddin's kitchen turns out tandoori dishes, as well as shrimp, lamb, chicken and vegetable curries; biryanis (rice specialties), and hot fresh breads.

The room is lit softly by candlelight and fancy chandeliers. Cream-colored walls are accented with Indian art work set into mosque-shaped cutouts. This setting creates an exotic feeling, in keeping with the fare.

Much of the food is intense with flavor. It's often impossible to pick out individual spices. The mulligatawny soup, a puree of lentils with a touch of tomato, is an example. No single spice overpowers another. It's the masala (blend of spices) that offers the appeal.

The formally dressed all-Indian, all-male staff is unfailingly courteous. The reserved, almost silent way each serves, bringing food on rolling carts padded with white linen, is refreshing in an age of T-shirts and tennies.

A dish that can be especially recommended is the shrimp poori — but ask about the size of the shrimp on a given day. It's a puffy round of fresh hot bread, one of several made here, accompanied by a fragrant dish of pan-fried shrimp with green beans and fresh cilantro. When the shrimp are spooned atop the bread, the bread deflates and becomes a wrapper for the pungent shrimp.

Another good side dish at dinner, or as a main dish at lunch, is shag ponir. The mix of fresh spinach, cubes of homemade cheese and spices is served with rice pilaf.

Be assured that if you ask for the medium spice level, you will get a very noticeable level of heat. That's as far as I have delved on the spice chain. I suspect that Uddin's "hot" is exactly that.

Those not totally comfortable with the Indian experience are advised to relax and order the dinner for two. It comes complete with an array of typical dishes, including deep-fried onion fritters, the multi-layered white bread paratha, as well as a chicken and a lamb dish, eggplant with ginger and spices, and rice pudding for dessert. The charge is $23.95 with meat, $21.95 without meat.

The Peacock

 In '94, a number of improvements were made at Terry and Aji Ahluwalia's Indian spot in its unlikely location on a Dearborn side street. The bar was shrunk in order to make room for more table seating. And the dining room was divided into separate areas for smokers and nonsmokers — even more important than the addition of new chairs and carpeting. Sundays were added to the schedule.

The formerly a la carte menu has been adjusted, too. Along with steamed rice, dinner now comes with dal, a pureed lentil soup, and naan, hot flat bread made in the charcoal-fired clay oven called a tandoor.

The menu offers a number of curries, and such vegetarian dishes as green

☆ ☆ ☆

4045 Maple, Dearborn.
(313) 582-2344.

Hours: Lunch, 11 a.m.-2:30 p.m. weekdays; dinner, 5-10 p.m. Mon.-Thu., 5-11 p.m. Fri.-Sat., 4-9 p.m. Sun. Closed major holidays.

Nonsmoking: 75 percent.

Full bar.   Major credit cards.

Reasonable.

beans masala and baked eggplant with tomato and onions. Other choices include tandoori chicken or mixed grill.

Curries are made from blends of spices, not the dreaded curry powder, and the heat level of the fare ranges from mild to very hot. It's the diner's preference.

Pegasus Taverna

**558 Monroe, Detroit.
(313) 964-6800.**

Hours: 11 a.m.-2 a.m. Mon.-Sat., 11 a.m.-midnight Sun. Closed Thanksgiving and Christmas Day.

Nonsmoking: 50 percent.

Full bar. Major credit cards.

Moderate.

Some of the biggest, glossiest four-color menus in town are presented to diners at this busy Greektown spot, with its brick walls, woodwork and array of mismatched hanging lamps. The open kitchen is in the very front of the place.

Some American dishes have been added to the Greek selections, so you may have a BLT or hamburger at lunch as well as a gyros or moussaka (the layered eggplant and ground meat dish). There's Maurice salad and the classic Greek.

Lamb dishes include lamb simmered in tomato sauce and spices, lamb simmered with vegetables, roasted lamb with potatoes. And on and on.

The lively spot on the ground floor of Trappers Alley appeals to those who like big, bustling restaurants.

Peking House

**215 S. Washington, Royal Oak.
(810) 545-2700.**

Hours: 11 a.m.-10 p.m. Mon.-Thu., 11 a.m.-midnight Fri., noon-midnight Sat., noon-10 p.m. Sun. Closed Thanksgiving.

Nonsmoking: 50 percent.

Full bar. Major credit cards.

Moderate.

The north suburban crowd discovered this well-run Chinese restaurant after it was renovated a couple of years ago into a handsomely sophisticated restaurant.

No dangling red lanterns here. Pastel linens, soft, indirect lighting, and fresh flowers are the setting for Mongolian chicken, Singapore rice noodles, sweet and sour pork, crispy twice-cooked duck and shrimp with garlic sauce. The Cantonese and Sichuan selections are nicely pared down to a reasonable number. This is not one of the bedsheet Chinese menus.

The courteous staff is impeccably dressed in white shirts and tuxedo trousers, and trundles the dishes to the table on carts. In addition to the Asian specialties, there are American entrees and desserts, but why come here for those, I always wonder.

A number of dishes are spicy, or at least the menu indicates that. I've found, however, that you have to be very specific in ordering to get much of a spice level here.

The two dining rooms are divided into smoking and nonsmoking areas that are quite separate, and typical of the genre, children are treated well here.

Pepino's

Joe Bernardi still comes in every day to do the ordering and make the soups and sauces at the restaurant he and his wife, Helma, put together after he retired as chef at Ford Motor World Headquarters in Dearborn.

Bernardi was famous for his hamburger made of ground New York strip — a burger Henry Ford II often had on his plate.

☆ ☆ 1/2

118 Walled Lake Drive, Walled Lake. (810) 624-1033.

Hours: Dinner only, 5-9:30 p.m. Mon.-Thu., 5-10:30 p.m. Fri.-Sat. Closed Sun. and major holidays.

Nonsmoking: 65 percent.

Full bar.   MC and Visa.

Moderate.

At Pepino's, Bernardi is even more famous for a couple of dishes: rainbow trout in brown butter sauce and char-broiled lamb chops marinated in rosemary and garlic.

Puerto Rican black bean soup is another specialty at this warm and friendly place. It's on the menu every day.

The Bernardis celebrated their 52nd wedding anniversary in early '95, every bit as devoted to their restaurant as to each other.

Peppina's Ristorante

1128 Dix, Lincoln Park.
(313) 928-5523.

Hours: 11 a.m.-10 p.m. Tue.-Thu., 11 a.m.-11 p.m. Fri., 4-11 p.m. Sat., noon-10 p.m. Sun. Closed Mon., major holidays and one week over July 4.

Nonsmoking: 50 percent.

Full bar.   Major credit cards.

Reasonable to moderate.

Italian soul food. That's the best description of the fare at this Downriver standby. One bite into the tender depths of a parsley-flecked meatball or some oil-and-garlic-dappled spaghetti noodles or a spoonful of robust minestrone telegraphs this message.

This is Italian food from the hallowed list that includes Marsalas, Toscas, Piccatas and Parmigianas, and of course, pizzas.

The minestrone here is blended from 18 different vegetables. The rolls, topped with a sprinkling of poppy seeds and grated Parmesan, are freshly made. So are the pastas, salad dressings and concoctions on the homey-looking dessert tray. Fresh is a key word.

This venerable establishment is still run by the woman who started it all with a drive-in and eight-table spot in 1953. Mary Fontana Deardorff, whose daughter Paula Deardorff joined her in the enterprise a number of years ago, knows how to dish up the gutsy, old-fashioned fare.

As might be surmised, some of the kitchen help have chalked up pretty impressive statistics with the place. That consistency is part of the reason for Peppina's longevity. Mother and daughter insist that everything be measured, so that the sauces and soups are always the same regardless of who is cooking in the kitchen at the moment.

In addition to the solid fare, Peppina's has another drawing card — two fireplaces, one of rough-cut amethyst, the other of rose quartz. Mary Deardorff's Fontana family was in the mining business for some time in Thunder Bay, Ontario, and the sparkling minerals displayed in the restaurant reflect the clan's continuing interest.

The cozy dining room boasting the rose quartz fireplace is set off from the main dining room, and offers a quieter setting. There are table linens rather than bare tabletops, and a complimentary relish tray. It is a smoking section, by the way (not that everyone must smoke). Those who want to get away from the family-style hubbub in the main room may ask for a table here, with a surcharge of $1 per person. It's worth it.

Phoenicia

Sameer Eid's restaurant is one of the better-known Middle Eastern spots in town. He's been serving the cuisine of Lebanon in the area for nearly 25 years, so he naturally knows his way around the kitchen.

His specialties include kibbee nyee (lean, ground raw lamb seasoned with onions, herbs and cracked wheat), baked kibbee, artichokes stuffed with meat and pine nuts and baked in yogurt sauce, and a mixed plate of stuffed grape leaves, stuffed cabbage and baked kibbee.

Perhaps because of the upscale clientele, there's also char-broiled sweetbreads in butter, garlic and shallot sauce; rack of lamb; swordfish kebabs and sauteed frog's legs, scallops and shrimp, as well as a fresh catch of the day.

While Phoenicia has a higher price structure than at other Middle Eastern restaurants, it offers more amenities and Eid's devotion to top quality ingredients.

Entertainment is an added element Thursday through Saturday evenings, when a small combo provides soft, romantic music.

☆ ☆ ☆

588 S. Woodward, Birmingham. (810) 644-3122.

Hours: 11 a.m.-10 p.m. Mon.-Thu., 11 a.m.-11 p.m. Fri.-Sat. Closed Sun. and major holidays.

Nonsmoking: 80 percent.

Full bar.   Major credit cards.

Moderate.

Pike Street Restaurant

After working with chef Brian Polcyn for more than six years, Derin Moore was able to take over the kitchen at this downtown Pontiac spot in fairly seamless fashion. When Polcyn moved on to Acadia full time in '93, Moore was the logical successor.

Their philosophies are similar: both believe that the freshest of ingredients and as many local products as possible should be the underpinning of their fare.

They love to serve game dishes, and each believes in a "learning" kitchen, where culinary students apprentice and pick up skills.

It's a from-scratch kitchen that makes stocks and *pates* and does its own smoking of salmon and sausage. The menu is American, but shows influences from

☆ ☆ ☆ ☆

18 W. Pike Street, Pontiac. (810) 334-7878.

Hours: Lunch, 11 a.m.-3 p.m. weekdays; dinner, 5-10 p.m. Mon.-Thu., 5-11 p.m. Fri.-Sat. Closed Sun. and major holidays.

Nonsmoking: 50 percent.

Full bar. Major credit cards.

Expensive.

around the world.

For example, the pan-seared sea scallops get an Asian twist with vegetable won ton and barbecue glaze; crispy duckling is served with quinoa, a grain from Asia, and roast rack of lamb is accompanied by roasted potato and eggplant chili.

Still more interesting dishes: char-broiled pork medallions with spiced applejack sauce and quince compote, sauteed pickerel in pecan crust, roast leg of venison with wild mushroom, and lentil ragout.

Moore's work with the U.S. Culinary Olympics team is giving him broader knowledge of regional American cooking, too.

One change Moore admits to is that his portions are somewhat smaller than Polcyn's. The price structure has been lowered slightly, though it is still expensive by most people's standards.

The restaurant occupies a sturdy 1893 building that has the look of being indestructible.

Pita Cafe

☆ ☆ ☆

25282 Greenfield Road, south of I-696, Oak Park. (810) 968-2225.

Hours: 11 a.m.-10 p.m. Sun.-Wed., 11 a.m.-11 p.m. Thu.-Sat. Closed Thanksgiving and Christmas Day.

Nonsmoking: 75 percent.

Soft drinks only.   MC, Visa and Discover.

Reasonable.

Ali Chahine brought his brother Talal's winning menu from Dearborn's La Shish to this side of town, and the freshly squeezed juices and well-prepared Middle Eastern fare is just as popular in this small cafe.

The menu offers all the Lebanese favorites from shish kebab to hommus and tabbouleh. Among favorite dishes of the Oak Park clientele are shish tawook (marinated and grilled chicken breast) and sauteed lamb with mushrooms, tomatoes and carrots.

There's wonderful lemonade — the real thing — among 15 different fresh juices and juice combinations.

The setting is modest but the quality of the cuisine is superior.

Plunketts Bistro-Bar

Who would have believed that the tiny Chez Vins would, in just a few years, segue into this big restaurant occupying three storefronts on Chatham Street? Happily, it retains the warm Chez Vins spirit under wife and husband team Karen Behune Plunkett and Michael Plunkett.

The European style open front with its series of doors allows an indoor/outdoor feeling when the weather permits.

☆ ☆ 1/2

28 Chatham Street E., Windsor, Ontario. (519) 252-3111.

Hours: 11 a.m.-midnight Mon.-Wed., 11 a.m.-1 a.m. Thu.-Sat., 3-10 p.m. Sun. Closed major holidays.

Nonsmoking: 50 percent.

Full bar.   AE, MC and Visa.

Reasonable.

In any weather, the menu continues its international approach. Dishes range from bruschetta topped with tomato, garlic and basil, and spicy black bean cassoulet, to vegetable lasagna and chicken fajitas.

There are lots of what the Plunketts call "small dishes" for those who like to graze, as well as solid main dishes. These include the most popular choice of all: grilled chicken with sun-dried tomatoes and sauteed vegetables atop linguine. Another favorite here is the lamb, chicken and sausage mixed grill with spicy house-fried potatoes.

Beer fanciers may have a tasting of four draught beers for $5 (Canadian), and there are also a number of wines by the glass.

The area that once was Chez Vins has been preserved for diners who like a more intimate atmosphere.

Polish Village

☆ ☆ 1/2

2990 Yemans, Hamtramck.
(313) 874-5726.

Hours: 11 a.m.-2:30 p.m. Mon., 11 a.m.-8 p.m. Tue.-Sat., 1-7 p.m. Sun.

Nonsmoking: 50 percent.

Full bar.   No credit cards.

Reasonable.

One of the best values around can be found in this Hamtramck cellar, where a solid, full-course meal will set you back all of $5.25. That's the price tag on the Polish plate: stuffed cabbage, dumplings, sausage, sauerkraut and potatoes, plus salad or one of the solid soups like dill pickle, chicken noodle or cabbage and potato soup.

There are several dishes even less expensive than that. Service is snappy to a fault and food arrives quickly to the tables. Never mind that the napkins are paper and the plates and accessories of the serviceable variety.

This is a pleasant room, with old glass panels over the bar where Okocim Pils, a hearty Polish lager, is available along with more familiar brews. The house wines may not be on the Wine Spectator's list, but a glass costs just $2.

Proprietors Ted and Frances Wietrzykowski took over the restaurant more than 10 years ago.

Portofino

☆ ☆ 1/2

3455 Biddle, Wyandotte.
(313) 281-6700.

Hours: 11 a.m.-10 p.m. Mon.-Thu., 11 a.m.-11 p.m. Fri.-Sat.; Sun. brunch, 11 a.m.-2 p.m. and dinner, 2-9 p.m. (open one hour later each day in the summer). Closed Christmas Day and New Year's Day.

Nonsmoking: 50 percent.

Full bar.   Major credit cards.

Moderate.

Chef Kevin Binette, whose roots are in New England, has brought a level of consistency to this big restaurant on the water. He has a nice touch with fresh catch items from mahi-mahi to swordfish, as well as with chicken and pastas. Prime rib is another of his specialties.

Clam chowder is available every day, and there are a couple of additional choices of soups. Sandwiches, salads and lighter dishes are there for those who don't want a major meal. Bread is made on premises.

The dining room seats 200 — and there is room for 200 more on the patio during the summer season.

Prickly Pear

While other restaurateurs have found southwestern cuisine a tough sell, Gary Pearce and Mary Miller's 50-seat restaurant has won plenty of fans with a black bean/salsa/chorizo approach.

Perhaps it's the small size of this place that allows the sometimes misunderstood fare to be accepted. The casual spot is done up in the cheery sunset colors of the southwest, with chili pepper ristras and vibrantly painted art works setting the scene.

In the summer, the courtyard garden doubles the size of the restaurant with its extra seating.

Pearce is particularly adept at soups, among them roast garlic and onion with pepper croutons, butternut squash, and corn chowder. Pastry-wrapped dishes include empanadas filled with chicken, as well as fajitas and enchiladas.

Specialties that go farther afield are blue corn crabcakes with green chili chutney, red pepper fettuccine with grilled chicken breast tossed in cilantro pesto, and Navaho fry bread with chorizo chili.

The house-made ice cream is a delight.

328 S. Main, Ann Arbor.
(313) 930-0047.

Hours: Lunch, 11:30 a.m.-2:30 p.m. Tue.-Sat.; dinner, 5-10 p.m. Tue.-Thu., 5-11 p.m. Fri.-Sat. Closed Sun. and major holidays.

Nonsmoking: 90 percent.

Full bar.   Major credit cards.

Moderate.

Pronto! 608

☆ ☆ ☆

**608-610 S. Washington, Royal Oak.
(810) 544-7900.**

Hours: 10 a.m.-10 p.m. Mon.-Thu., 10 a.m.-midnight Fri., 9 a.m.-midnight Sat., 9 a.m.-10 p.m. Sun. Closed Thanksgiving and Christmas Day.

Nonsmoking: 100 percent.

Full bar.   Major credit cards.

Reasonable.

Whenever I'm asked about my favorite Royal Oak restaurants, this one is always on the list. It's a genuinely friendly, down-to-earth place, with three dedicated proprietors who divide up the duties and make the place work. The fresh fare is rarely disappointing.

Salads are popular here, including Mediterranean chicken, Nicoise, turkey cashew, French potato and cucumber salmon. Among the hot entrees, the chicken pot pie is a classic, and so is Pamela's Southwest Burger. It's named, like a lot of the sandwiches, for a regular patron. And regular patrons there are in droves.

That's a tribute to Bill Thomas, Jim Domanski and Tom Murray, the people behind Pronto, and their enthusiastic staff.

There are two parallel rooms, with the little bar in the back seating just a few people. When the liquor license was granted, the partners tried a two-pronged approach, with a more elaborate menu served in the room with the bar. Somehow, it didn't fit. So, unabashed, they just made the whole place one restaurant.

They know what works.

In warm weather, the sidewalk cafe seating is extremely popular.

Rachelle's on the River

This colorful spot, run by the bright and personable husband and wife team of Rachelle Bonelli and Jim Bloch, can be approached by land or by water. Located on the Pine River, it's the reworking of a dilapidated old bar.

Dilapidated no longer, there's a cheerful bright yellow-and-blue decor and the recent addition of movie posters featuring eating and drinking. "Breakfast at Tiffany's?" Of course.

☆ ☆ ☆

**119 Clinton Street, St. Clair.
(810) 329-7159.**

Hours: 11:30 a.m.-9 p.m. Wed., 11:30 a.m.-10 p.m. Fri.-Sat., noon-9 p.m. Sun. Closed Mon. and Tue. (except June, July and August) and Thanksgiving and Christmas. Summer hours: 11:30 a.m.-10 p.m. Mon.-Thu., 11:30 a.m.-11 p.m. Fri.-Sat., noon-9 p.m. Sun.

Nonsmoking: 75 percent.

Full bar.   AE, MC and Visa.

Reasonable to moderate.

Rachelle's also features a triangle theme, carried out from the shape of breads and burger buns to a three-cornered cake known as the Earthquake and a drink called the Bermuda Triangle.

Clearly, Rachelle and Jim know how to show people a good time, and have since they opened the place in '87.

Lately, they say, New York strip steak seems to be making people happy, though that and such dishes as smoked breast of chicken in a creamy sauce atop pasta, might not seem to fit the current low-fat craze in this country. Pastas are perennially popular here. So are fish of all sorts and the baby back ribs.

Raja Rani

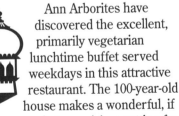

Ann Arborites have discovered the excellent, primarily vegetarian lunchtime buffet served weekdays in this attractive restaurant. The 100-year-old house makes a wonderful, if somewhat surprising, setting for the subtle Indian fare served by Loveleen Bajwa.

Her Indian fare is notable and the fragrance of spices wafting through the rooms quite seductive. The lunch buffet

☆ ☆ ☆

**400 S. Division, Ann Arbor.
(313) 995-1545.**

Hours: Lunch, 11:30 a.m.-2 p.m. weekdays; dinner, 5:30-10 p.m. Mon.-Sat. Closed Sun.

Nonsmoking: 85 percent.

Full bar.   MC, Visa and Diner's Club.

Reasonable.

is notable. For $6.95, it offers eight main dishes, six of which are vegetarian, along with salad and hot Indian bread.

The a la carte menu is also very affordable, with dishes ranging from $7 to $13. Bajwa is happy to discuss the menu with guests. She believes Indian cuisine is best enjoyed by sharing several dishes rather than concentrating on just one choice.

Rattlesnake Club

300 Stroh River Place, Detroit.
(313) 567-4400.

Hours: Lunch, 11:30 a.m.-2:30 p.m. weekdays; dinner, 5:30-10 p.m. Mon.-Thu., 5:30-11 p.m. Fri.-Sat. Closed Sun. and major holidays except Easter and Mother's Day.

Nonsmoking: 75 percent.

Full bar. 　　　　　Major credit cards.

Expensive.

Jimmy Schmidt is Detroit's best-known chef in cities around the country. Part of his fame comes from his involvement with Share Our Strength, the Washington, D.C.-based hunger relief organization, and from his work with the James Beard Foundation in New York, and the Chefs Collaborative 2000, a nationwide educational effort promoting minimally processed foods. Schmidt is very much an activist for causes he believes in.

His restaurant on the river offers top-of-the-line fare consistent with his reputation. The airy space offers a contemporary feeling from the art and photography displayed on the white walls to the sophisticated table settings and massive flower arrangements that break up the room. The place is fresh, crisp and upbeat.

Menus carry each day's date, and that is the foundation of Schmidt's philosophy. He believes in serving what is fresh and seasonal, and says simply, "Food should taste terrific and be good for you."

Probably few of the denizens of the Rattlesnake Club worry about nutrition when they are dining here, so it's a good thing the chef does it for them.

Typical of his approach are such dishes as arugula, apple and baby red lettuce with goat cheese in cider vinaigrette; cracker crust pizzas topped with fennel and artichokes; grilled wild mushrooms with garlic, parsley and balsamic vinegar; gravlax of salmon with apple and fennel salad (he does love fennel) and swordfish grilled with grapefruit, fried ginger and chives.

Desserts are outstanding. The hot fudge sundae achieves its pinnacle in the Rattlesnake Club treatment and there are many other chocolate and fruit treats typical of Schmidt's style. These include, of course, his signature white chocolate raviolis with hazelnut anglaise.

Wines are chosen by sommelier Madeline Triffon, a refreshingly unpretentious and devoted staffer. She is in charge of wines for all of the Schmidt restaurants, which currently number five, including the Rattlesnake Grill in Denver.

The restaurant's name was chosen simply to denote energy. There's plenty of it in this notable riverside spot.

Red Hawk Bar & Grill

The menu at this self-described "neighborhood bar & grill" has become even more wide-ranging than it was when the restaurant opened three years ago. The basic sandwiches and burgers approach has been augmented with a number of salads, including the Caesar in its various mutations. Other popular dishes include Beijing duck quesadillas, avocado with crabmeat hash and grilled chicken breast served as an alternative to the house burger.

☆ ☆ 1/2

316 S. State, Ann Arbor.
(313) 994-4004.

Hours: 11:30 a.m.-11 p.m. Mon.-Wed., 11:30 a.m.-11:30 p.m. Thu.-Sat., 11:30 a.m.-10 p.m. Sun. Closed major holidays except Labor Day.

Nonsmoking: 100 percent.

Full bar.　　　　　MC, Visa and Discover.

Reasonable.

Specials are added to the menu on a weekly basis, and usually include a fish or pasta, as well as a pizza and salad of the week.

If you are looking for a solid burger joint, this could be it. The seven-ounce burgers are notable and served with such accompaniments as guacamole, grilled peppers, Vermont ham and smoked mozzarella.

The rectangular, high-ceilinged storefront has settled in comfortably. The cherry wood booths and trimmings against restored brick walls might have been there for decades.

The long beer list includes everything from Anchor Steam to Red Stripe. Generous glasses of wine are poured from a by-the-glass list that manages to include France, Italy, Michigan, California and Washington.

The reasonable price range is yet another plus. Nothing on the menu goes higher than $12.95. Add to this the clientele itself, which ranges from the newest U-M freshmen to those grizzled old-timers who seem to have arrived one September day in the '60s and never left.

Rikshaw Inn

☆ ☆ 1/2

**6407 Orchard Lake Road,
West Bloomfield. (810) 851-6400.**

Hours: 11:30 a.m.-10:30 p.m. Tue.-Thu.,
11:30 a.m.-11 p.m. Fri.-Sat., 4-10 p.m. Sun.
Closed Mon. and July 4 and Thanksgiving.

Nonsmoking: 70 percent.

Full bar.   Major credit cards.

Moderate.

Proprietor David Lum loves to mix Caesar salads at table side and often does. *This* is a Chinese restaurant?

Yes, indeed.

In fact, the average diner is probably going to like it better than less accessible restaurants. Rikshaw Inn is definitely a cut above the average strip mall Chinese eatery, but it doesn't pretend to be offbeat.

Caesar salad is just the first clue, along with the French onion soup that doesn't just share but heads the list of soups. Standard Chinese restaurant dishes, typified by egg foo yong, sweet-and-sour pork and chicken chow mein, are unabashedly offered.

These dishes are on the menu because many people like them. Even though Lum employs a Chinese kitchen staff capable of doing some very good orange beef, sizzling rice soup and mussels with black bean and oyster sauce, this restaurant is really more American than Chinese.

Places are set with silverware. It's the rare customer who requests the paper-wrapped chopsticks. Salt and pepper shakers are on the tables along with soy sauce. Coffee seems to be poured just as often as tea, and the big bar at the back of the room is dominant in the slick, black-and-white room.

Chef/proprietor Lum has been in America for a number of years now. He was born in Canton, China, but grew up in Canada. He learned to cook his favorites, the continental dishes, at a Toronto hotel. Among them: Dover sole with lemon butter and almonds, filet mignon, and rack of lamb. These dishes are available along with the steak kow and moo goo gai pan at the Rikshaw.

Risata

Risata offers a contemporary, Italian-flavored menu in a multi-level setting that includes a roof-top bar seating 100. Though Risata may sound something like risotto, the Italian rice dish, its name — which means laughter in Italian — was chosen because of the restaurant's location under the same roof as Detroit's Second City comedy troupe.

☆ ☆ ☆

Woodward at Montcalm, Detroit. (313) 965-9500.

Hours: Dinner only, 5-8:30 p.m. Wed.-Thu. and Sun., 5-11:30 p.m. Fri.-Sat. Closed Mon. and Tue. and major holidays.

Nonsmoking: 66 percent.

Full bar. Major credit cards.

Moderate.

Architect Victor Saroki, who likes to let the bare bones of buildings show through, designed the restaurant setting. It has exposed steel girders and duct work, concrete ceilings, slate and stained-wood floors and dramatic indirect lighting that picks out the vibrant colors of the painted surfaces.

The structural effects are very much a part of Risata's appeal. Soaring 17-foot ceilings and windows lead the eye to an open staircase rising to several levels above.

The first level, entered through revolving doors from Montcalm Street, is dominated by a circular, honey-colored stone bar. Red-stained wooden stools are pulled up to the bar, with soft purple glove-leather seats at vantage points along the uncovered windows.

The menu has been kept brief and to the point. As executive chef Mike McFarlen observes, when you are serving 350 people (that's capacity), it's a good idea to be concise.

McFarlen and his brother John are in charge of the cuisine, which features such dishes as oysters on the half shell with garlic/horseradish sauce and corn and tomatillo relish; grilled focaccia, topped with herbs, olive oil and rock shrimp; spinach salad, and four-cheese tortelloni.

Other choices include grilled medallion of turkey, blackened swordfish, whitefish with herb-nut crust and mashed potatoes, and steak au poivre.

Ristorante di Maria

☆ ☆ ☆

2080 Walnut Lake Road,
West Bloomfield. (810) 851-2500.

Hours: Dinner only, 4:30-10 p.m. Mon.-
Thu., 4:30-11:30 p.m. Fri.-Sat., 3-9 p.m.
Sun. Closed major holidays.

Nonsmoking: 80 percent.

Beer and wine.　　　　　　AE, MC and Visa.

Moderate.

Avid restaurant diners simply love this little place, and have packed its 50 seats since it opened in the early '80s. The small dimensions are probably one reason why the place is so popular. There's something about having to fight for a table that seems to make it all the more desirable.

But the kitchen is certainly reliable, turning out the kind of gutsy Italian fare practically everybody loves. In addition to such pastas as linguine with tuna and meat, and spinach- and cheese-stuffed canneloni, there are more and more fish and seafood choices. Some of them: snapper with black and green olives, lobster tail in spicy red sauce and scampi in garlic and butter.

The all-Italian wine list is a nice touch.

Ristorante di Modesta

☆ ☆ ☆

29410 Northwestern Highway,
Southfield. (810) 358-0344.

Hours: Lunch, 11:30 a.m.-3 p.m. weekdays;
dinner, 5:30-10 p.m. Mon.-Thu., 5:30-11
p.m. Fri.-Sat., 5:30-9 p.m. Sun. Closed
major holidays.

Nonsmoking: 80 percent.

Full bar.　　　　　　Major credit cards.

Expensive.

What is it about Italian food that attracts chefs from other heritages? There are several great Italian chefs around town who happen to have been born in other countries, and Hamad Kouka of this restaurant is one of them. The native of Egypt is as talented with the fare of sunny Italy as anyone born on its shores.

Yes, he did spend several years in Florence before coming to the United States, first to New York, then to Michigan. He has been the mainstay of the kitchen here since '88.

Certain of his dishes are classics. The eggplant appetizer, for instance, stuffed with ricotta and spinach and lightly dressed with fresh tomato sauce. Others are the grilled shrimp with mustard sauce, and marinated tuna with olive oil and lemon.

Kouka offers eight treatments of veal, from simple sliced veal with porcini mushrooms to grilled veal chop topped with tomatoes, garlic and arugula. His arugula salad is as popular as Caesar with the regulars. Pastas may be ordered in two sizes, and they include angelhair with vegetables and fettuccine with fresh salmon.

Like many other restaurants in the area, there is a healthy approach with such dishes as broiled whitefish, whole wheat pasta with basil, and marinated chicken breast enlivened by a lemon, basil and fresh tomato sauce.

The airy setting is scheduled for an update in '95, says proprietor Manuel Chavez.

Ritz-Carlton Grill Room

Relatively small and clubby, the Grill Room became the hotel's only public dining space when the hotel closed the larger dining room a couple of years ago and added it to its banquet space.

This was a smart move because the other space was, frankly, pretentious and not nearly so comfortable as the Grill Room. Cozier and warmer, it has an old-hotel feeling to it.

In addition to daily specials the Ritz likes to call "signature items," the menu

300 Town Center Drive, Dearborn. (313) 441-2000.

Hours: Breakfast, 6:30 a.m.-11 a.m. daily; lunch, 11:30 a.m.-2:30 p.m. Mon.-Sat.; dinner, 6-10 p.m. Mon.-Thu. and Sun., 5:30 p.m.-midnight Fri.-Sat.; Sun. brunch, 10:30 a.m.-2:30 p.m.

Nonsmoking: 75 percent.

Full bar. 　　　　　　　Major credit cards.

Expensive.

includes such traditional dishes as prime ribs of beef, Dover sole and rack of lamb, all served very nicely with appropriate garnishes.

There is a luncheon buffet each day ($16.75) and the Sunday brunch has the highest price tag in town at $30.

Service and luxury are hallmarks of the Ritz, and sometimes the staff overwhelms with its attention to the guests' needs. But who's complaining? Given the lack of same in so many areas of life, it's a welcome perk.

River Crab

☆ ☆ ☆

1337 N. River Road, St. Clair.
(810) 329-2261.

Hours: 11:30 a.m.-10 p.m. Mon.-Thu., 11:30-11 p.m. Fri.-Sat.; Sun. brunch, 10 a.m.-2 p.m. and dinner, 3:30-9 p.m. (In summer, hours extended one hour later.) Closed Christmas Eve, Christmas Day and New Year's Day.

Nonsmoking: 70 percent.

Full bar.   Major credit cards.

Moderate.

What an ideal setting for fresh fish and seafood. This spot perched on the St. Clair River is known for such dishes as live Maine lobster and yellow-fin tuna.

As at other C.A. Muer restaurants, the menu also extends to pastas, ribs and steaks. Still, it's difficult not to be tempted by one of the eight to 12 fresh fish offered each day in this well-run spot.

The multi-level setting was recently freshened with new carpeting, white tablecloths and burgundy napkins, but this is a casual rather than formal restaurant.

A summertime feature is live music on the deck on Wednesday evenings. The deck is also a great spot for having drinks and appetizers.

Rochester Chop House and Oyster Bar

☆ ☆ ☆

306 N. Main Street, Rochester.
(810) 651-2266.

Hours: 11 a.m.-10 p.m. Mon.-Thu., 11 a.m.-11 p.m. Fri.-Sat., 1-9 p.m. Sun. Closed major holidays except Easter.

Nonsmoking: 75 percent.

Full bar.   Major credit cards.

Moderate.

As the name indicates, there are two options here: sitting in the casually comfortable oyster bar known as the Kabin Kruser or in the slightly more elaborate dining room in the rear.

The oyster bar is the cozier of the spots, and my favorite. Bins of ice hold oysters, clams and mussels along with bottles of beer and wine. Diners have a view into the kitchen. No need to ask about the menu here — it's seafood all the way. The back room offers steaks, chops and chicken dishes.

The restaurant is a sibling of its across-the-street neighbor, Kruse and Muer on Main. Proprietor Bill Kruse is a former C.A. Muer staffer who was a close friend of the much-missed Chuck Muer.

Rocky's of Northville

Wildlife art works set the tone at this casual, woodsy spot that was once Northville Charley's. Niceties create the special feeling. They include everything from big mauve and green linen napkins to wood carvings to the fieldstone fireplace. Dining is in a series of lodge-like dining rooms that fan out from the bar, which is the only room that allows smoking.

Fish and seafood are served here, yes, but there are other options: lamb shanks, baby back ribs and pastas that include linguine with clam sauce. Wild game dishes — venison, moose, duck — are spotlighted from time to time.

The menu runs the gamut from a simple burger at $5.25 to surf and turf at $24.95. Potato-crusted whitefish ($12.95) is the No. 1 seller.

The Rocky of the title is Chuck Rachwitz, formerly corporate chef for the Chuck Muer organization. Rachwitz is especially proud of his children's menu, which includes choices among pastas, shrimp and chicken for the under-12 set.

A second Rocky's is opening in Brighton in spring of '95 at the Oak Pointe Country Club.

☆ ☆ ☆

41122 W. Seven Mile Road, Northville. (810) 349-4434.

Hours: 11:30 a.m.-10 p.m. Mon.-Thu., 11:30 a.m.-11 p.m. Fri.-Sat., 1-9 p.m. Sun. Closed Christmas Day and New Year's Day.

Nonsmoking: 75 percent.

Full bar.   Major credit cards.

Moderate.

Roma Cafe

This Eastern Market area spot does not concern itself with the latest trendy dishes. Roma Cafe relies on the veals and pastas that have been popular here for more than 50 years.

In fact, a restaurant has been in its building for more than 100 years. Proprietor Hector Sossi's family took over in 1936, so there is real continuity to the red-and-white, two-story building.

Roma's two rather sedate-looking dining rooms flank a small, antique-like bar. Aside from that ornately carved bar, there is nothing particularly eye-catching about the setting. But that

☆ ☆ ☆

3401 Riopelle, Detroit. (313) 831-5940.

Hours: 11 a.m.-10:30 p.m. weekdays, 11 a.m.-midnight Sat. Closed Sun. and major holidays.

Nonsmoking: 50 percent.

Full bar.   Major credit cards.

Moderate.

unpretentiousness is part of its appeal.

A real Detroit tradition is to get a group together to sit at one of Roma's solid tables and have the black-suited, old-school waiters bring platters of familiar Italian fare.

Perennially popular dishes include lasagna and spaghetti alla Roma, both using the house meat sauce, and the classic veal Marsala and chicken Parmesan.

The Monday night buffet, from 5 to 9, offers an array of items, such as chicken cacciatore, Italian sausage, pastas, eggplant, fresh fruit and cannolis. The buffet is a value at $14.75.

Rowe Inn

☆ ☆ ☆ ☆

**County Road 48, Ellsworth.
(616) 588-7351.**

Hours: Dinner only, 6-10 p.m. daily (until 9 p.m. Nov.-April). Closed Thanksgiving and Christmas Day.

Nonsmoking: 80 percent.

Full bar.   AE, MC and Visa.

Moderate to expensive.

The cozy, 50-seat inn on a hilltop was the first to serve gourmet fare in the north country.

Rowe Inn, under founder and still-proprietor Wes Westhoven, is acknowledged as the catalyst that inspired others to raise the level of cuisine offered in the Lake Michigan countryside.

Chef Kathy Ruis is a veteran of eight years at the rustic inn. While her menu changes constantly, her solid Midwestern style is epitomized by such dishes as beef tenderloin with morels, rainbow trout roulades with morels, grilled duck breast with sweet and sour cherry sauce, and grilled pork tenderloin with a seasonal fruit sauce.

Morels are a continuing theme, with pecan-stuffed morels served during May or whenever the mushrooms are available.

The price of entrees, $19.50 to $29.50, includes soup, salad and a refreshing fruit ice. Among the a la carte desserts, the all-time favorite is the white chocolate brownie. Dried cherry ice cream is another winner.

The wine cellar is exceptional with about 1,200 wines in stock. Westhoven loves to talk wine with guests.

The Rowe, as the artistic neon sign calls it, has a number of special dinners during the year. Call Westhoven and he'll tell you all about them.

R.P. McMurphy's

What's the secret of success at this interesting spot? Chef Todd Sutherby puts it succinctly: "We give people what they want."

That means straightforward fare, from a menu of popular dishes with quite a fish and seafood slant. The clam chowder is locally famous. So is the bayou shrimp wrapped in bacon and jazzed up with Cajun spices. The chicken piccante has its fans, too, and steak is always available.

☆ ☆ 1/2

2922 Biddle Avenue, Wyandotte. (313) 285-4885.

Hours: 11 a.m.-11 p.m. Mon.-Thu., 11 a.m.-1 a.m. Fri.-Sat. Closed Sun. and major holidays.

Nonsmoking: 25 percent.

Full bar. Major credit cards.

Reasonable.

R.P. McMurphy's is consistent. Its chef has been around for 13 years now, so people know what to expect. The menu remains the same all day and virtually everything may be ordered in two portion sizes.

This vintage spot in a three-story red brick building is interesting both architecturally and decoratively. The setting is pure turn-of-the-century saloon (it has been a bar since the '30s), from its patterned tile floor to the deep-hued larger Pewabic tiles on its walls. The long, brass-trimmed bar shares a room with dusky murals, an interpretation of Pieter Bruegel's "The Wedding Dance" executed above the tile work.

In the dining room at the back of the building, the words "Established in 1979" are inscribed as part of that room's mural. They seem at least 100 years old, but '79 is simply the year that current owners Chris Doulos and John Rusu took over.

They chose to name their spot for the Jack Nicholson character in "One Flew Over the Cuckoo's Nest," a favorite movie of theirs.

Russell Street Deli

☆ ☆ ☆

2465 Russell Street, Detroit.
(313) 567-2900.

Hours: 11 a.m.-2:30 p.m. weekdays, 9 a.m.-2:30 p.m. Sat. Closed Sun. and major holidays.

Nonsmoking: 100 percent.

No bar. No credit cards.

Reasonable.

Here's the place to eat on Saturday mornings at the Eastern Market. The deli has a fresh foods approach that transcends the ordinary. Pancakes do not come from a mix, French toast is made with thick raisin bread, hash brown potatoes are free of grease.

The long narrow room is completely unpretentious, and you might get your orange juice served in a paper cup. But the food is well-prepared by chef/proprietor Bob Cerrito, a self-described foodie who trained, among other places, in the kitchen of the Rattlesnake Club. He says he learned a tremendous amount during the five-month stint.

His from-scratch cooking with a seasonal, regional approach includes simple pasta dishes, meat loaf and an array of deli sandwiches at lunch during the week. Those Saturday breakfasts are from a menu that features wonderful pancakes with Michigan maple syrup he buys from the farmer who taps it, French toast, egg-topped corned beef hash and an array of omelets.

Russian Bear

Once in a while, someone still mentions the old Russian Bear, a restaurant that dates back to the late '30s. It was a few steps down from the sidewalk in downtown Detroit, a downtown that was full of nightlife. To hear people talk, it must have been a wonderfully atmospheric place — or was it just that at the time, anything foreign seemed exotic and compelling?

The Russian Bear's blinis and stroganoff were never replaced by another restaurant with a Russian theme until '94, when a new Russian Bear popped up in a suburban strip mall. Midnight in Moscow is pretty hard to achieve in that setting. But Alex and Svetlana Stuck, Russian emigres from Odessa, are trying hard to accomplish it.

☆ ☆ 1/2

6303 Orchard Lake Road, West Bloomfield. (810) 855-9229.

Hours: Lunch, 11:30 a.m.-3:30 p.m. weekdays; dinner, 5-10 p.m. Mon.-Thu., 5-11 p.m. Fri.-Sat.; Sun. brunch, 11:30 a.m.-2:30 p.m. and dinner, 5-9 p.m. Closed July 4, Labor Day, Christmas Day and New Year's Day.

Nonsmoking: 50 percent.

Full bar.   Major credit cards.

Moderate.

They've disguised the quarters with bright pieces of peasant-y art from their homeland. Decorative effects range from an intricately carved bear-motif bench at the entrance to an array of paintings, samovars and colorful fringed shawls. These just barely manage to disguise the arched brick and wood space that once housed R.I.K.'s.

The menu includes some Russian dishes and a few that are unabashedly American — like the Russian Bear burger and the tuna salad sandwich at lunch.

Those who want to delve a bit into the ethnic style may order blinis (buckwheat pancakes) with red or black caviar, cabbage rolls, Ukrainian style borsch, chicken Kiev and shashliks (the Russian shish kebab) of lamb, sturgeon, pork or vegetables.

Beef stroganoff is on the menu, of course. It's served in a bowl accompanied by a plate of crisp shoestring potatoes, mushrooms and onions. The stroganoff can be ladled over the vegetables or eaten separately.

House salads come with most main courses, and they are appealing heaps of greens, carrots, beets and mushrooms. The choice of dressings includes roasted pepper buttermilk, sour cream chive and a pale pink Russian.

The Stucks deserve kudos for adding a missing ethnic entity to the local dining scene, including live music on Friday and Saturday evenings.

St. Clair Inn

☆ ☆ ☆

500 N. Riverside Drive, St. Clair.
(810) 329-2222.

Hours: Breakfast, 7 a.m.-10:30 a.m. Mon.-Sat., 8 a.m.-noon Sun.; lunch, 11:30 a.m.-4 p.m. Mon.-Sat.; dinner, 5-9 p.m. Mon.-Thu., 5-11 p.m. Fri.-Sat., 1-9 p.m. Sun. Closed Christmas Day.

Nonsmoking: 75 percent.

Full bar.   Major credit cards.

Moderate.

No one would suggest that the venerable St. Clair Inn toss aside its steadfastly traditional appearance and menu for a fling with that notoriously fickle companion, trendiness. It simply wouldn't fit the character of the rambling English Tudor inn, whose history of hospitality dates to 1926.

But a parting of the clouds around that hallowed menu has occurred since the arrival of chef Jay Martin.

The changes are subtle but noticeable on the menus in the five dining rooms that meander along the inn's river side. First, of course, you must duck under the hanging plants suspended from the ceiling in sturdy brown-twine cradles.

Then you note that the crock of orange cheese spread and basket of bread sticks and cellophaned crackers still arrive at the tables along with ice water.

So some things never change.

But others have: now diners looking for fare beyond shrimp cocktail may choose smoked bluefish *pate* and smoked salmon, or a rich cream of wild mushroom soup with a dash of sherry (one of four soups available each day).

Alternatives to the routine tossed salad include ruffled greens enlivened with dried cherries and chopped pecans in a dressing that has joined the hallowed French-ranch-Thousand Island trio: raspberry vinaigrette. Salads, it should be noted, are a la carte.

The inn still dishes up the baked or french-fried or hash brown potato choice with entrees, but an added starter is a wild rice blend.

Many customers still seek out the slabs of prime rib. Some nights it seems every other table is opting for beef. Other selections might include sauteed duck breast and roasted duck leg with port wine and raspberry sauce; pickerel roasted with pesto crust, served with tomato relish, and grilled chicken breast with fettuccine and fresh vegetables.

Like the hanging plants, the dessert list is dated: mostly ice cream concoctions including parfaits or old-fashioned apple or cherry pie.

But in both cases, that's what the customers want. This is a very traditional place, where people come back precisely because they want to recapture an earlier era.

Sala Thai

For far too long, Detroiters have had to travel to find foreign fare of almost any kind. So the arrival of Sala Thai was more than welcome.

The restaurant occupies two attractively renovated storefronts. They're done up in purple and white and brightened with travel posters of Thailand and portraits of the Thai royal family.

Tables are covered in patterned fabric from Thailand, neatly hand-stitched along the borders. Cooks in purple T-shirts work in view behind the counter in one dining room. The adjoining room is a little more secluded from the activity, which can get pretty frenzied as flames leap around the woks.

And who is wearing those T-shirts? For one, Ahrapin (Bell) Pradithavanij, who will be remembered from Siam Spicy in Royal Oak. She sold Siam Spicy to a friend to move to Panama City, Fla., then found the location not terribly receptive to her country's cuisine.

Now she's back helping former husband Arkom (Eddy) Pradithavanij, who is one of four partners running the restaurant. He, in his Thai garb, might be remembered from Ferndale's Bangkok Cafe as well as Siam Spicy. The other partners are non-Thais David and Larry Wood and Frank Kirby.

The same menu is offered at both lunch and dinner, with just a small price hike in the evening. Lovers of Thai food will find the fare familiar. Appetizers include delicate spring rolls with sweet-and-sour sauce, peanut-sauced chicken *satay,* and soups ranging from a couple of hot-and-sour versions to a mixed vegetable with tofu.

Stir-fries dominate the list of entrees. In two visits, a couple of them stand out in a satisfying array of choices: pad prik khing, a mix of hot curry, string beans and a choice among several meat or seafood options, and pra ram long song, which is broccoli, cabbage and peanut sauce with a chosen meat or seafood, in this case, shrimp. Plenty of steamed rice accompanies.

While there are similarities to both Chinese and Indian fare, Thai cuisine has its own identity. Sour, salty, hot and sweet flavors can be combined in a single dish, but not every dish is spiced at scorch level, of course.

"Sala" means refuge or sanctuary. It also means good things for downtown Detroit.

☆ ☆ 1/2

1541-1543 E. Lafayette, Detroit.
(313) 567-8424.

Hours: 11 a.m.-9 p.m. Mon.-Thu., 11 a.m.-10 p.m. Fri., 4-10 p.m. Sat. Closed Sun. and major holidays.

Nonsmoking: 75 percent.

Soft drinks only. AE, MC, and Visa.

Reasonable.

2621 Squirrel Road, Auburn Hills.
(810) 373-0940.

505 N. Woodward, Birmingham.
(810) 644-8977.

6565 N. Telegraph Road, Dearborn
Heights. (313) 278-4060.

22611 Gratiot Avenue, Eastpointe.
(810) 775-4477.

G-322 Miller Road, Flint.
(810) 732-1070.

1650 E. 12 Mile Road,
Madison Heights. (810) 542-3281.

24299 Novi Road, Novi.
(810) 348-3930.

29110 Franklin Road, Southfield.
(810) 357-8877.

13499 Dix-Toledo Road, Southgate.
(313) 246-5900.

43734 Schoenherr Road,
Sterling Heights. (810) 247-2782.

2650 Orchard Lake Road,
Sylvan Lake. (810) 662-5776.

2750 Haggerty Road,
West Bloomfield. (810) 960-0570.

Hours: 11 a.m.-10 p.m. Mon.-Thu., 11
a.m.-11 p.m. Fri.-Sat., 1-9 p.m. Sun. Closed
Thanksgiving and Christmas Day.

Nonsmoking: 50 percent.

Full bar.   Major credit cards.

Reasonable.

Salvatore Scallopini

People love
these friendly
spots created by
the Bongiovanni
family. From the
first one in Madison
Heights, it wasn't long before Salvatore
Scallopini's red, white and green colors
were popping up all over town. The
founding family still runs the restaurants
in Eastpointe, Madison Heights,
Southfield, Sterling Heights and West
Bloomfield. The others are franchised.

The menus are interchangeable.
Pastas are the specialty, and one of the
better deals around in the $4.95 lunch or
$6.95 dinner. The meal includes freshly
made spaghetti, rotini, fettuccine, shells
or mostaccioli with choice of six sauces, a
fresh green salad and bread.

There are many other options,
including grilled chicken breast with
sauteed green beans and polenta,
steamed mussels, fried calamari, scampi
in garlic butter and ravioli, but I find
myself ordering pasta every time.

The settings are all alike — colorful
and attractive in a mama's kitchen style
— with just a couple of exceptions. The
Eastpointe location, boasting Ron Rea's
designer touch, is especially appealing
with its marble-topped bar and Italian
posters.

Sandpiper

The view from the dining room of this tri-level, lakeside restaurant is lovely, and so is the food. Surprising might be another word for chef Daniel Graves' fare. He came from Chicago to take over the kitchen about a year ago, and continues the high standards set by his predecessor, Ed Westerlund.

Proprietor Pat Eldean is very devoted to her contemporary spot. The menu has a bit of a southwestern/New Orleans twist, and the combinations of flavors are lively and unusual. For instance, roast duck comes with a persimmon grits cake and cherry-Chianti sauce, wild turkey sausage enlivens the gumbo, catfish is crusted with cornmeal and ancho chiles, and sirloin is rubbed with coriander and served in Chianti-peppercorn sauce.

That upbeat menu, coupled with the setting, ought to make more people sit up and take notice. This is one of western Michigan's prime spots. If only that lake were a little bigger.

2223 S. Shore Drive, Macatawa. (616) 335-5866.

Hours: Lunch, 11:30 a.m.-2 p.m. weekdays (noon-3 p.m. Sat. from Memorial Day to Labor Day); dinner, 5-8:30 p.m. Mon.-Thu., 5-9:30 p.m. Fri.-Sat.; Sun. brunch, 10 a.m.-2 p.m. and dinner, 5-9 p.m. from Memorial Day to Labor Day only, with closing time one hour earlier on other days. Closed Christmas Day, New Year's Day and Sun. between Labor Day and Memorial Day except for Mother's Day.

Nonsmoking: 100 percent.

Full bar.   Major credit cards.

Moderate.

Sanremo Mediterranean

The unassuming, neighborhood- and family-spirited spot is perched on an obscure corner in Windsor's Little Italy section.

It's as basic as the fish market around the corner — the very market that provides its bill of fare. Frank Aiuto runs the market, his son Ross and Ross' wife, Enza, the restaurant. A second market in Leamington is in the hands of Dina Aiuto, Frank's wife.

The premise is so simple it's brilliant:

900 Erie Street E., Windsor, Ontario. (519) 252-1292.

Hours: Lunch, noon-2 p.m. Mon.-Sat.; dinner, 5-9 p.m. Tue.-Thu., 5-10 p.m. Fri.-Sat., 1-8 p.m. Sun. Closed Easter, Christmas Day and New Year's Day.

Nonsmoking: 50 percent.

Full bar.   Major credit cards.

Reasonable.

The restaurant serves fresh fish and seafood directly from the market, taking advantage of three weekly deliveries of a wide range of fish from around the globe.

Fish are prepared in just three ways — chargrilled, fried or sauteed — and served with the house pasta, Sicilian tomato and garlic.

Soups follow the theme. There is a tomato-based fish soup, a creamy fish bisque and a wonderful clam chowder — though probably not for those who equate clam chowder with the thick, white, library pasty clam-chowder-on-Friday variety.

This chowder is a flavorful soup with whole clam shells as well as pieces of clam in the parsley-flecked broth. No thickening, no potatoes.

Ross Aiuto says the family is trying to present fish pretty much the way it is served in the small towns of Sicily, coastal towns such as San Vito Capo, his father's home, and Poggioreale, where his mother was born.

Simplicity is a key. Aside from the hot sauce for peel-and-eat shrimp, there are virtually no sauces. Just big juicy wedges of fresh lemon to be spritzed on the fish. Salads are equally simple, just lettuce and tomato with a choice of dressings.

The blackboard menu at Sanremo includes names of fish most people have never heard of, such as conger eel, turbot, skate wing, kingfish, red mullet. That's in addition, of course, to the especially popular swordfish and red snapper as well as lobster, smelt, monkfish and shark.

Two evenings each week are devoted to buffet-style spreads. On Fridays, shrimp and mussels star, and on Sundays, there is a potpourri of fish and seafood along with such accompaniments as squid salad, chunks of salted tuna with wrinkled Mediterranean olives, and peel-and-eat shrimp with heads on.

The bar at Sanremo is a friendly neighborhood hangout, with darts and pool table, an array of gelati and a hissing espresso machine.

Schuler's

115 S. Eagle, Marshall.
(616) 781-0600.

Hours: Lunch, 11 a.m.-4 p.m. Mon.-Sat.; dinner, 4-9 p.m. Mon.-Thu., 4-10 p.m. Fri.-Sat.; Sun. brunch, 10 a.m.-2 p.m. and dinner, 1-9 p.m. Sun. (dinner hours extended one hour during the summer). Closed Christmas Day.

Nonsmoking: 75 percent.

Full bar.   Major credit cards.

Moderate.

The fourth generation of Schulers now runs the venerable restaurant, and they have slowly, very slowly, allowed the menu to develop a more contemporary style. It's still solid American fare, but in '94, along came Chris Hessler, who trained with Milos Cihelka at the Golden Mushroom.

Hessler has made a major difference in the cuisine. Where there might have been filet mignon with sauteed mushrooms, there's now medallions of veal with wild mushrooms, garlic and shallots. Rainbow trout comes with a crabmeat stuffing and champagne sauce, wood-grilled breast of free-range chicken with apple cider-maple glaze — and it's all part of the movement toward fresh ingredients, from fish to seasonal vegetables. Of course, you may still have the famous prime ribs of beef that come with seconds on the house.

Even that sundae-laden dessert list has seen progress. Hessler does flans, sorbets, creme caramel and warm cherry cobbler.

What hasn't changed is the polite, pleasant attitude of the help. The workers at Schuler's know how to make people feel welcome.

Schuler's began as a 20-seat restaurant in 1909. Now more than 300 may be seated in a series of rooms in the Calhoun County town. It's about 107 miles west of downtown Detroit.

Sebastian's Grill

Greg Ervin, a long-time cohort of chef Jimmy Schmidt, now runs this bistro-like restaurant in the heart of the Somerset Collection. He's both chef and general manager for proprietor Matthew Prentice, meaning that he has to keep an eye on the front of the house as well as the kitchen.

Ervin has pared down the menu somewhat from the beginning, now offering such solidly American dishes as turkey scallopini with grilled leeks and caramelized apples, plank-roasted whitefish with walnut crust and chive sauce, and roast Indian duckling. There are pastas, pizza and risotto as well.

Somerset Collection, Big Beaver at Coolidge Road, Troy. (810) 649-6625.

Hours: 11 a.m.-10 p.m. Mon.-Thu., 11 a.m.-11 p.m. Fri.-Sat., noon-5 p.m. Sun. Closed Easter, Thanksgiving and Christmas Day.

Nonsmoking: 85 percent.

Full bar.   Major credit cards.

Moderate.

Bread at this restaurant, as at all the Prentice spots, is not to be missed. It's from the Sourdough Bakery in Pontiac, where Andrew McGrath turns out memorable loaves.

The earthy approach of Sebastian's Grill has developed nicely over the years. Service is friendly and informal as befits a restaurant in a mall, even if this mall is called a "collection."

It's perfectly fine to order salads or sandwiches at both lunch and dinner, and shopping bags tucked under the table are OK, too.

Seoul Garden

☆ ☆ ☆

2101 15 Mile Road at Dequindre, Sterling Heights. (810) 264-4488.

Hours: 11:30 a.m.-10:30 p.m. weekdays, noon-10:30 p.m. Sat., 11:30 a.m.-10 p.m. Sun.

Nonsmoking: 60 percent.

Full bar.   Major credit cards.

Moderate.

Korean and Japanese dishes share the menu at this artistic restaurant, the creation of Jay and Ihn Kyung Park. Of the selections, a little more than half are Korean. They include kalbi (marinated short ribs), one of the barbecue dishes prepared at tableside; gyoza (fried beef dumplings) and a number of the popular hot-pot dishes, some of which are resonantly spicy.

Side dishes provide a contrast to that heavy emphasis on meat. Kimchee and white radishes, seaweed and bean sprouts are served in little dishes.

The room's amenities include one of the most attractive sushi bars in the area. Some of the lithographs and paintings in the room are Ihn Kyung Park's own work.

Shari at the Willard Hillton

☆ ☆ ☆

1506 W. Beaver Road, Auburn. (517) 662-6621.

Hours: Dinner only, 6-10 p.m. Mon.-Sat. Closed Sun. and major holidays.

Nonsmoking: 90 percent.

Full bar.   AE, MC and Visa.

Moderate.

Don't tell Shari Baird her restaurant is in the middle of nowhere. It just seems that way to those who don't expect to find a notable restaurant adjacent to farmers' fields, haylofts and silos.

The premises, the former Beaver Hotel and Saloon (1890), is pretty easily accessible to those in Midland and Bay City, as well as people heading north or south on the freeway. It's just a few miles from I-75.

Culinary Institute-educated Baird, along with her husband, John, who runs the front of the house, offer a weekly changing menu. It may include such dishes as hickory-grilled beef tenderloin with mustard horseradish sauce; chicken stuffed with wild rice, grapes and pesto; mixed grill of chicken, sausage and beef filet with three sauces, or grilled shrimp with strawberry butter.

There's always a pasta, pizza and soup of the evening, and lots of fresh salads. Vegetables, garlic and herbs are grown organically, especially for the restaurant.

Desserts range from house-made ice cream to several chocolate fantasies.

Interesting special events dot the calendar, from beer and wine dinners to Michigan wine and food festivals.

Shin Shin

Windsor and Detroit residents alike simply love this 70-seat spot with its wonderful food. Sichuan and Peking dishes are the specialty of Julia and Ming-Li Hsu, whose restaurant has chalked up 10 years in business.

☆ ☆ ☆

978 University W., Windsor, Ontario. (519) 252-1449.

Hours: 11:30 a.m.-10 p.m. Mon.-Thu., 11:30 a.m.-11 p.m. Fri.-Sat., 11:30 a.m.-9 p.m. Sun. Closed Christmas Day.

Nonsmoking: 70 percent.

Full bar.   AE, MC and Visa.

Reasonable.

Vegetarians are ecstatic when they see the array of vegetable and bean curd dishes, and there are always a few specials in addition to the printed list. However the Hsus accomplish it, they are adept at providing spice levels that are subtle and fully realized at the same time. There will be no harsh hits from over-seasoned food here.

It's hard to choose notable dishes on a menu that seems to be all specialties. If forced to choose, I'd have to recommend chicken with garlic flavors, sauteed green beans, Sichuan soup, shrimp with dried hot pepper sauce, eggplant with garlic sauce, and beef with orange flavors.

Truthfully, I'd be willing to accept almost anything this couple dished up. On the basis of food alone, this spot rates four stars. But realizing that the modest table appointments and lack of amenities might appear a drawback in some minds, I've given Shin Shin an overall three star rating.

Siam Kitchen

★ ★ ★

2509 Jackson Road, Ann Arbor.
(313) 665-2571.

Hours: Lunch, 11:30 a.m.-2 p.m. Tue.-Thu.; dinner, 5-9 p.m. Tue.-Thu., 5-10 p.m. Fri.-Sat. Closed Sun., Mon. and major holidays.

Nonsmoking: 75 percent.

Beer and wine.   Major credit cards.

Reasonable.

Thai restaurants were a rarity in Michigan when Phorn Thep Dhitirojana relocated here with his family. It was 1982, and even as they were remodeling the space in the Westgate shopping strip, people stopped by to inquire if they were going to serve "real Thai." They were. And they still do.

The food of Thailand is now familiar to many people, as Thai restaurants have proliferated in this country. For a good introduction to the fare, try the dinner combinations at Siam Kitchen. Including soup, appetizer and main dish, the meals range from $11.25 to $16.75.

The menu is complete without being overpowering. It offers such appetizers as spring rolls and chicken satay, soups including favorites tom yum goong (shrimp, mushrooms, lemongrass, chili and lime juice) and tom kha gai (chicken, chili, the ginger-like galanga, lime juice and coconut milk), rice and noodle dishes and a full range of stir-fries and curries of beef, pork and chicken.

Siam Spicy

★ ★ 1/2

2438 N. Woodward, Royal Oak.
(810) 545-4305.

Hours: Lunch, 11 a.m.-2 p.m. Tue.-Fri.; dinner, 5-10 p.m. Tue.-Thu., 5-11 p.m. Fri.-Sat., 5-9 p.m. Sun. Closed Mon. and major holidays.

Nonsmoking: 100 percent.

Soft drinks only.   AE, MC and Visa.

Reasonable.

The most popular dish at this well-run spot continues to be good old number 23 — the stir-fry with garlic, black pepper and a choice of beef, chicken, pork, shrimp or squid — just as it has been for years.

The red and green curries, such as gang pa, gang pa nang and gang mus sa mun also have their fans. *Gang*, which means curry, is a key word on Thai menus. Other words to remember: *pad* (saute), *pak* (vegetables), *pla* (fish) and *prik* (peppers).

The spice levels are resonant, and if you want fiery food, you need twist no arms at this little place. Sukanda Karczewski and her staff will be happy to deliver.

A second Siam Spicy opened in March of '95 at 32425 Northwestern Highway in Farmington Hills.

Sindbad's

A Detroit riverside standby since 1949, Sindbad's is still run by the family of the late Buster Blancke, who founded it with Hillaire (Van) Van Hollebeke. Marc, Brian and Denise Blancke, with backup from their mother, Noella, carry on in pretty seamless fashion. The menu is a basic American waterfront bill of fare, with lots of fresh fish, steaks and burgers and an option to have breakfast any time of day. Perch is still the favorite dish.

During the summer, there's live entertainment from Wednesday through Sunday in a second floor room. It offers banquet space during the winter.

☆ ☆ 1/2

**100 St. Clair, Detroit.
(313) 822-7817.**

Hours: 11 a.m.-11 p.m. Sun.-Thu., 11 a.m.-1 a.m. Fri.-Sat. (in summer, hours extended to 1 a.m. seven days a week). Closed Easter, Thanksgiving, Christmas Day and New Year's Day.

Nonsmoking: 50 percent.

Full bar.   Major credit cards.

Reasonable to moderate.

601 Bistro

Behind the bright blue neon script spelling out the name in the window is a 34-seat haven operated by Diane Gauthier and associate Keith Kozak. That's it; they cover both the front and back of the house.

Gauthier says cooking is something she always loved to do, even as a child. The charming 34-seat spot they run is not for those who want to dash in for a fast meal. It's a place to relax for a while. By the same token, it certainly isn't one of those spend-the-evening places where cobwebs form while people wait for their food.

601 Pelissier Street, Windsor, Ontario. (519) 252-0143.

Hours: 11 a.m.-4 p.m. Mon.-Tue., 11 a.m.-9 p.m. Wed., 11 a.m.-10 p.m. Thu.-Fri., 4:30-10 p.m. Sat. Closed Sun. and major holidays.

Nonsmoking: 50 percent.

Full bar.   Major credit cards.

Reasonable to moderate.

What's interesting about the menu is that some of it sounds pretty cut and dried: Cajun salmon, chicken teriyaki stir-fry, lasagna, tuna pasta salad. What comes from the kitchen, however, is not at all routine. The fare is fresh, obviously cooked *a la minute* and nicely garnished.

He shops for meat, fish and wine, takes the orders and serves every table, sometimes lending a hand in the kitchen, often making the butterscotch cake for dessert. She shops for fresh produce and does most of the cooking in the minuscule kitchen, including whipping up the Amaretto and slivered almond sauce that enhances Keith's butterscotch cake.

He'll suggest a variation for the soup she makes each day from chicken stock, using whatever fresh vegetables are on hand and handfuls of herbs. The two love to use tarragon, thyme, chives, basil, lots of garlic and a touch of curry.

Both also enjoy improvising recipes for sauces and trying out their ideas on each other. A favorite dish is pork tenderloin medallions. The tender meat, sauteed in cream sherry, demi-glace and a bit of cream, is topped with a few diced tomatoes and capers.

The lunch menu includes such dishes as Caesar and Greek salads; bruschetta topped with olives, capers, garlic and tomatoes, or simply with rosemary and garlic; pita sandwiches, and sauteed shrimp atop noodles.

Some of the same dishes appear at dinner, along with a marinated New York strip steak and jumbo shrimp in white wine and garlic. These are the two most expensive entrees at $16.95 and $17.95, respectively. Main dishes are accompanied by fresh vegetables and a choice of soup or salad. French three-onion soup is a specialty.

The neat, uncluttered place with its burgundy walls, mirrors, white lace valances and big flower painting by Gauthier is attracting a nice little following.

Spago Ristorante

☆ ☆ 1/2

690 Erie Street E., Windsor, Ontario.
(519) 252-1626.

Hours: Lunch, 11:30 a.m.-2 p.m. Tue.-Fri.; dinner, 5:30-9:30 p.m. Mon., 5:30-10:30 p.m. Tue.-Fri., 5-10:30 p.m. Sat., 4:30-9 p.m. Sun. Closed Christmas Day, Dec. 26 and New Year's Day.

Nonsmoking: 35 percent.

Full bar.   AE, MC and Visa.

Reasonable to moderate.

Perched at second floor level is the main dining room at this two-pronged Italian restaurant. On the street level is Spago European Cafe, a more casual place open each day from 4 p.m. to midnight or later. It serves pastas, pizzas, Italian sandwiches and specialty coffees.

Spago itself upstairs offers a haven of peach-covered tables for more elaborate dishes and a more soothing atmosphere. When weather permits, diners may sit at 10 tables on the outdoor terrace, which offers a view of busy Erie Street and its little bit of Italy in Windsor.

The Spago menu includes several veal dishes, char-broiled filet seasoned with olive oil and herbs, fresh mussels steamed in wine and usually a fish of the day. There are a number of pasta dishes, of course.

Spago means "string" or "thread" in Italian.

Sparky Herbert's

Every neighborhood should have a hangout like this one. It's unpretentious and informal, yet has food that goes well beyond the neighborhood designation. There are several seating choices: the bar, for those who like to rub elbows with their neighbors, the more secluded, candle-lit wine cellar to the left of the entrance, and the high-ceilinged back room with its array of art works and mottled walls that look like the bindings on old books.

☆ ☆ ☆

15117 Kercheval, Grosse Pointe Park. (313) 822-0266.

Hours: Lunch, 11:30 a.m.-5 p.m. Mon.-Sat.; dinner, 5 p.m.-midnight Mon.-Sat.; Sun. brunch, 11:30 a.m.-2:30 p.m. and dinner, 3-10 p.m. Closed major holidays except Easter.

Nonsmoking: 50 percent.

Full bar.   MC, Visa and Diner's Club.

Moderate.

The menu offers a full range of dishes. For those who want just a burger or a salad, there's a nice list of lighter fare. It's typified by the smoked salmon sandwich on black bread with cheese, capers and red onion or the sirloin salad over mixed greens with horseradish dressing. The more extensive menu includes such dishes as grilled lamb chops, Cajun-crusted yellow-fin tuna and even Dover sole.

A popular feature is the Twilight Supper ($9.95), no longer just featured for the early bird set, but offered throughout the evening. It's a choice of salad or soup and one of three entrees.

Darrell Finken is the proprietor of the place that always seems to draw a crowd, regardless of weather conditions. Chef Joe Arcand, in the kitchen for years, lends a needed sense of continuity.

Spice of Thai Express

☆ ☆ 1/2

515 S. Lafayette, Royal Oak.
(810) 543-7210.

Hours: 11 a.m.-10 p.m. Mon.-Thu., 11 a.m.-11 p.m. Fri.-Sat., 2-9 p.m. Sun. Closed major holidays.

Nonsmoking: 50 percent.

Soft drinks only.　　　Major credit cards.

Reasonable.

The atmosphere — nothing fancy. The service — competent, unembellished. But the spicy fare offered here can be absolutely addictive.

This little spot, like many others around town, dishes up fresh Thai fare and fluffy steamed rice from its open kitchen. The menu offers some 40 dishes, including many now-familiar favorites like pad Thai, tom yum, chicken satay and cashew chicken.

There are usually a couple of daily specials, and spicy catfish shows up often on the board. A favorite with many people is panang, a type of curry that features a choice of chicken, beef or pork in a sauce of chili paste, coconut milk and sweet basil.

The price structure is gentle and the spice level is left to the diners' discretion. They'll dish it up as hot — or as mild — as you want it.

Stage & Company

☆ ☆ ☆

6873 Orchard Lake Road,
West Bloomfield. (810) 855-6622.

Hours: 10 a.m.-10 p.m. Tue.-Thu., 10 a.m.-11 p.m. Fri., 10 a.m.-midnight Sat., 11 a.m.-10 p.m. Sun. Closed the eight days of Passover, Rosh Hashanah, Yom Kippur and Thanksgiving.

Nonsmoking: 60 percent.

Full bar.　　　AE, MC and Visa.

Moderate.

Steve Goldberg, son of Harriet and the late Jack Goldberg, is now proprietor of the famous deli established by his parents many years ago. In the family tradition, he offers a long list of deli sandwiches from the triple deckers named after Broadway shows to the combinations — named after Broadway shows — to plain singles on rye with no fancy titles.

There are omelets, smoked fish, chopped liver, classic chicken soup with noodles, rice, matzo ball or kreplach — and the Swanky Frankie, that vintage favorite.

This is a reliable spot with a loyal clientele, and it deserves all the applause it gets.

Station 885

An interesting twist is the return of chef John P. O'Connor, who began his culinary career right here in the mid-'80s when he was still in high school. "I learned to cook french fries at Station 885," he says. Then it was on to work for the Rattlesnake Club for several years. Now he's back with the title of executive chef, capable of much more than french fries.

O'Connor brings both regional and seasonal touches to the basic menu at the former train station, now owned by the Costanza family. Fresh fish and seafood turn up on the special board, and so do such dishes as duck sausage with penne and fresh basil, and pheasant with wild mushrooms.

What did he learn from Jimmy Schmidt at Rattlesnake? "Everything I know," says O'Connor.

Located in the Old Village section of Plymouth, the station takes full advantage of its nostalgic setting on the tracks. One dining area under the eaves is approached via a romantic spiral staircase, and toy trains make the circuit around tracks set high on the walls in two of the dining rooms.

☆ ☆ 1/2

855 Starkweather, Plymouth. (313) 459-0885.

Hours: 11 a.m.-11 p.m. Mon.-Thu., 11 a.m.-midnight Fri.-Sat., 10:30 a.m.-10 p.m. Sun. Closed Easter, Christmas Day and New Year's Day.

Nonsmoking: 65 percent.

Full bar. Major credit cards.

Reasonable to moderate.

Steamers Seafood Grill

Steamers' seafood menu seems to have captured the imagination of the hard-to-please crowd that makes or breaks restaurants on the Orchard Lake Road corridor.

The room is white, deep green and rust, with slick white paper covering tables set with commercial-size containers of sea salt and pepper. Silverware comes wrapped in thick, terry cloth dish towels. It's a setting just right for shellfish, lobster and seafood stews.

30685 W. 12 Mile Road, Farmington Hills. (810) 442-2531.

Hours: 11 a.m.-10 p.m. Mon.-Thu., 11 a.m.-11 p.m. Fri.-Sat., 4-9 p.m. Sun. Closed major holidays.

Nonsmoking: 50 percent.

Full bar. Major credit cards.

Moderate.

Chowders and gumbos, steamed mussels and clams, buckets of shrimp and reasonably priced lobsters star on chef Joe Lewis' menu. He manages to combine Boston and New Orleans in his approach, offering an authentic version of dirty rice, good crab cakes and lobster pan roasts (called "saffron cremes" here).

For good measure, Lewis tosses in the San Francisco treat, cioppino, the American answer to bouillabaisse. With daily changing ingredients, it is one of the most popular dishes here.

With most entrees, Steamers includes a bowl of coleslaw — the crispy variety bright with red cabbage — or a mixed green salad, both to be self-served out of big metal bowls.

Garlic-basil butter accompanies long, skinny loaves of bread served in a paper bag. You can take leftover bread home if there is any. Not likely. Issuing fresh and hot from the convection oven every 10 minutes, the bread is pretty irresistible stuff.

Among the recommended dishes: a tasting of three soups — Cuban black bean, seafood chowder and gumbo; shrimp steamed in Louisiana spices; the crab cakes, and the saffron lobster creme. The latter comes in versions with shrimp, chicken, scallops or more lobster, in a creamy lobster broth.

Stelline

 ☆ ☆ ☆

Somerset Collection, Big Beaver at Coolidge, Troy. (810) 649-0102.

Hours: Lunch, 11 a.m.-5 p.m. Mon.-Sat., noon-5 p.m. Sun.; dinner, 5-10 p.m. Mon.-Thu., 5-11 p.m. Fri.-Sat. Closed Thanksgiving and Christmas Day.

Nonsmoking: 90 percent.

Full bar.   Major credit cards.

Moderate.

Stelline is such a handsome restaurant it doesn't seem like the kind of place where people would feel comfortable in shorts and tennis shoes. But I've seen it there, along with more chic ensembles, on the diners at this sophisticated restaurant. Stelline is, after all, situated in a mall, an elegant mall, but a mall nonetheless.

Once seated, however, it's easy to forget the shopping frenzy all around. John Buffone's urbane design uses flying buttresses, sculptured columns and a warm yellow color scheme set off by touches of red oak and deep blue and green tapestry. It has such touches as a subtle star pattern that runs along the walls and a diamond pattern in black and silver in the woodwork. It is his best design to date. And Robert Schefman's stunning mural spanning two walls draws every eye.

That's the setting for the colorful dishes of grilled mushrooms, polenta, pastas, pizzas, risotto and salads of fennel, orange and ruffled greens. This is a menu that has become more and more a signature of chef Jimmy Schmidt. He simply loves Mediterranean fare, and it is served at three of his five restaurants.

The star-shaped pasta for which the restaurant is named naturally turns up as one of the items on the menus. The tiny, grain-like stars are served in a sauce that is much lighter than it sounds, blending rock shrimp, ginger cream and Parmesan. And that's pretty much the premise: dishes that are imaginative but relatively simple.

Dishes I've especially enjoyed include an appetizer of calamari fried crisp-tender along with crunchy little circles of lemon, a touch of fennel seed and flat-leaf parsley, and an airy summer antipasto that bears absolutely no resemblance to the salami-laden dish of yore.

This antipasto includes fennel stems (a Schmidt favorite), tiny sculptured whole carrots, equally petite scallions and an array of artichokes, tomato wedges, radishes and the tiniest of black olives. Other winners: the caprina pizza, its firm crust topped with black olives, sun-dried tomatoes and mozzarella and goat cheese; grilled chicken breast with squares of red pepper- flecked polenta, and sirloin grilled with peppercorns, garlic, lemon and rosemary.

Madeline Triffon's all-Italian wine list is especially appealing. Like the fare, it is light and bright.

Steve's Back Room

A Middle Eastern market in front, a cozy little restaurant in back. It's a simply wonderful combination because of the high standards of Theresa and Steve Kalil, who run the original in Harper Woods. Son Steve carries on the family tradition in the newer West Bloomfield location, which is still in its infancy. It's just a little glitzier than it needs to be, so it lacks the simple comfort of the east-side spot.

The Lebanese menu is meticulously handled. Everything on it is a specialty, from the fresh, herb-dappled salads to the lamb shish kebab, which is the best around. Dishes are attractively presented and the quality is exceptional.

☆ ☆ ☆ ☆

19872 Kelly Road, Harper Woods. (313) 527-5047.

7295 Orchard Lake Road, West Bloomfield. (810) 851-1133.

Hours: 11:30 a.m.-9 p.m. (Harper Woods); 11:30 a.m.-10 p.m. Mon.-Thu., 11:30 a.m.-11 p.m. Fri.-Sat. (West Bloomfield). Closed Sun. and major holidays at both locations.

Nonsmoking: 50 percent.

H.W.: Soft drinks only.   AE, MC and Visa.

W.B.: Full bar.   AE, MC and Visa.

Reasonable to moderate.

Some of the more unusual dishes, in addition to the excellent but oh-so-familiar ones, are squash stuffed with ground lamb and rice in tomato sauce, eggplant topped with lamb, onions and pine nuts, lamb curry and swordfish kebabs. Mujadarah, a stew of lentils, cracked wheat and onions, is especially popular with vegetarians. You may simply count on the fact that everything you order is going to be as good as it gets.

Steve's Soul Food

☆ ☆ 1/2

8443 Grand River, Detroit.
(313) 894-3464.

Hours: 11 a.m.-9 p.m. daily. Closed Memorial Day, Labor Day and Christmas Day.

Nonsmoking: 50 percent.

Soft drinks only.　　　　AE, MC and Visa.

Reasonable.

Steve Radden has been dishing up chicken and greens on Grand River for more than eight years now, in a setting he has gradually upgraded and enlarged. Classic soul food is the premise, from barbecued baby back ribs and smothered chicken to turkey wings in gravy, meat loaf and short ribs of beef. It's all served cafeteria style.

My favorite part of any soul food meal has always been the sides. It's no different here, with the top-notch sides including macaroni and cheese, collard greens, yams and string beans.

A nightclub called the Fountain Room was added recently, and offers cocktails and entertainment Wednesday through Sunday. Alcoholic beverages are not available in the cafeteria.

Stewart's

☆ ☆ ☆

4265 Woodward at Canfield, Detroit.　(313) 832-3200.

Hours: 11 a.m.-8 p.m. Sun.-Thu., 11 a.m.-midnight Fri., 4:30 p.m.-midnight Sat. Closed major holidays.

Nonsmoking: 75 percent.

Full bar.　　　　AE, MC and Visa.

Moderate.

Lots of little restaurants like this one should be dotting the city streets — places where chefs and owners aren't afraid to put their individual touches on the menu and in settings just as idiosyncratic as the fare.

Maybe that will be true some day. But for now, such places are the exception, rather than the rule. So it's of more than passing interest that Ron and Natalia Stewart, backed by a corporation made up of family members and friends, opened this place. Ron was the chef at the nearby Union Street for some time before going out on his own in '93 and adding another element to the neighborhood.

Stewart's has been a surprising hit, attracting a varied audience. Diners range from symphony-goers who swear by the place for pre-concert dinners, to Wayne State University professors, bartenders and waiters on breaks from nearby restaurants, musicians, artists and downtown office workers.

The restaurant is on the first floor of the building that once housed the jazz room called Alexander's. It was gutted and rebuilt, with much of the work done by the principals themselves. You have to be multi-talented in the restaurant business these days.

The absence of a professional decorator turns out to be a plus in this case. A decorator probably wouldn't have chosen the color scheme of pale banana yellow and a rather strange shade of blue, but it works.

And it's obvious that the collection of memorabilia, things like offbeat china pieces, cocktail shakers and vintage fishing lures, is the real thing. Stained glass panels add another element to the bar and the former cappuccino bar, now a carpeted dining area featuring neoclassic cocktails and live music on Friday and Saturday evenings.

The upbeat, contemporary feeling to the place is very much aided and abetted by the friendly staff. After trying out informal and formal menus in the early going, the Stewarts streamlined the offerings into a single menu. Now there are a number of daily specials in addition to such standbys as "black and bleu" whitefish, which is sauteed whitefish with a blue corn chip crust and a dab of bright chili mayonnaise on top; grilled farm-raised sturgeon; peanut- and curry-marinated yellow-fin tuna atop mixed greens, and pan-seared rainbow trout. All of them have been served here since day one.

The house soup now is seafood chowder, and there's also French onion, whose revival seems to have caught on again just like martinis. Sandwiches include the catfish Reuben — these people do love fish — as well as the club and grilled chicken marinated in rosemary and mustard.

Streetside Seafood

The former Richard & Reiss has been transformed into a cozy seafood spot. Wooden floors, random-patterned rough brick walls — designer Ron Rea had to convince the bricklayer to do them that way — and cracked white finishes give the place a been-here-forever look.

It has room for just 60 — including the seats at a copper and wood bar. As befits the small quarters, the menu is pared down, too.

☆ ☆ ☆

**273 Pierce, Birmingham.
(810) 645-9123.**

Hours: 11 a.m.-11 p.m. Mon.-Thu., 11 a.m.-midnight Fri.-Sat., 4:30-10 p.m. Sun. Closed major holidays.

Nonsmoking: 70 percent.

Full bar.   AE, MC and Visa.

Moderate.

Dishes include almond-crusted rainbow trout, tomato-fennel seafood stew, blackened catfish and sauteed lake perch, as well as chowders and bisques, shrimp cocktail and oysters.

Proprietors Bill and Judi Roberts, who also ride herd on the nearby 220 and also Beverly Hills Grill, decided to make something more of their once-popular but slightly faded breakfast/lunch spot. They felt Birmingham would welcome a casual little fish place. And they're right.

There's something about a restaurant with small dimensions that appeals to a lot of people. If this place had twice as many seats, it could undoubtedly fill them, but the cozy feeling would be lost.

Sweet Lorraine's Cafe

29101 Greenfield Road, Southfield.
(810) 559-5985.

303 Detroit Street, Ann Arbor.
(313) 665-0700.

Hours: 11 a.m.-10 p.m. Mon.-Thu. (an hour later in summer), 11 a.m.-midnight Fri.-Sat., noon-9 p.m. Sun. (11 a.m.-10 p.m. Sun. in Ann Arbor). Closed July 4, Thanksgiving, Dec. 24, Christmas Day and New Year's Day.

Nonsmoking: 90 percent in Ann Arbor, 75 percent in Southfield.

Full bar.   Major credit cards.

Moderate.

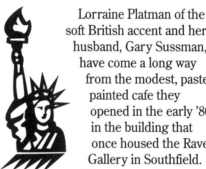

Lorraine Platman of the soft British accent and her husband, Gary Sussman, have come a long way from the modest, pastel-painted cafe they opened in the early '80s in the building that once housed the Raven Gallery in Southfield. Platman, cooking in the kitchen, and Sussman, the front of the house expert, make a good team.

That's especially important since they expanded to Ann Arbor. Both cafes, done up in eccentric colors — no wimpy pastels for the couple anymore — serve virtually the same menu now, with just a couple of exceptions.

Variety, freshness, taste and color are the premise. Appetizers include crab won tons with apricot-hot mustard sauce, rotini noodles tossed in a spicy sesame-peanut sauce, and a variation of Caesar salad topped with fried clams.

Some of the main dishes are Jamaican jerk steak — the jerk marinade and poppyseed salad dressing are now sold to go in attractive packaging — as well as roast chicken with mashed Yukon Gold potatoes with spinach and glazed carrots. And if you love the Yukon Golds as much as I do, you can also get them in a side dish of potato salad.

A vegetarian entree is de rigueur at both locations.

The Southfield cafe is getting a bar with lots of seating. Ann Arbor started out with one right in the middle of the room, which is on the lower level of a building near the Ann Arbor Farmers Market.

Both cafes are casual. There's a third little spot in Madison Heights, mostly for carry-out, in addition to these full-service restaurants.

Tandoor Asia

About 60 percent of those who come to Tandoor Asia are Indian — and that says something about the noticeably fresh food, which is prepared to order.

When the curries, biryanis and masalas do arrive at the table, one's patience is rewarded. The dishes come arrayed attractively on thalis (large round metal platters), making it easy to share, or in karahis (covered pans set over a flame). The presentation adds much to the authenticity of this Indian dining experience, as does the Punjabi and Hindi music in the background.

29210 Orchard Lake Road, Farmington Hills. (810) 932-0531.

Hours: 11 a.m.-10 p.m. Mon., Wed. and Thu.; 11 a.m.-11 p.m. Fri.-Sat.; noon-9 p.m. Sun. Closed Tue. and major holidays.

Nonsmoking: 70 percent.

Soft drinks only.

MC, Diner's Club and Visa.

Reasonable.

This authenticity is exactly what proprietor Jatinder Sandhu wants for his non-Indian clientele, not a watered-down version of his native cuisine.

I've been impressed with a number of dishes, including the lamb vindaloo, chunks of tender lamb with potatoes in a hot curry sauce; the dal makhni, herbed lentil stew, and onion kulcha, one of a number of irresistible hot breads. Several of the breads are made in the tandoor (clay oven). The bread is slapped directly on the oven walls and cooked at intense heat. In addition to the onion kulcha, diners may choose from among 11 other varieties of the round white bread naan. It can be ordered plain or stuffed with potatoes, the house-made cheese or minced lamb.

The weekday lunchtime buffet at Tandoor Asia is a notable value. For a mere $5.95, diners may choose whatever they wish from an assortment of meat and vegetarian dishes, fluffy rice pilaf dotted with bright green peas, pickled vegetables, and — brought to each table directly from the kitchen in order to keep them hot and fresh — tandoori chicken and fresh naan.

Three little bowls of chutney on the buffet — hot, medium and mild — can be used to season the main dishes. Prepared mild to medium in order to serve a wide variety of tastes, the hot chutney livens up the dishes for those who want more heat.

The array, which changes daily, even includes dessert. Sometimes, it's the soothing rasmajal, a pudding-like sweet made of cheese, rose water, milk and pistachios. The a la carte drinks include spiced Indian tea; lassi, a yogurt drink in three varieties — try the mango — and American soft drinks.

Despite the storefront setting and bare tabletops, everything is served with some style. Linen napkins help, and so do the Indian art works displayed on the walls. So why are all those people flocking into Burger King, which looms just to the south of this interesting spot? It's obvious Sandhu and his cousin and partner Parminder Sandhu have their work cut out for them.

Tapawingo

☆ ☆ ☆ ☆

9502 Lake Street, Ellsworth
(616) 588-7971.

Hours: Dinner, 6-9 p.m. daily, July 1-Labor Day; 6-9 p.m. Wed.-Sun., Labor Day through mid-Nov.; 6-9 p.m. Thu.-Sun. Dec. 26 through mid-March; 6-9 p.m. Wed.-Sun. mid-April through June 30. Closed mid-March to mid-April and mid-November through Christmas Day.

Nonsmoking: 100 percent.

Full bar.   MC and Visa.

Expensive.

Harlan (Pete) Peterson was firmly rooted in his Ford engineering career until a trip to France opened his eyes to another world.

The beauty of Paris, its open-air markets and its appreciation of wonderful food so captured him that he switched his career path and signed on as an apprentice in the kitchen at Rowe Inn. After working his way up to the head chef's post at the restaurant in the little town of Ellsworth, he went off on his own.

And so Tapawingo evolved, in the same little town. Peterson sat down at his drawing board in 1983 and put together the plan for his own restaurant as a giant design project. He bought a former summer home on tiny St. Clair Lake in Ellsworth. His research revealed that the place had been called Tapawingo, an Indian name denoting tranquility. He decided to keep it.

That meticulous approach still shows in the freshness and quality of the fare served at Tapawingo, dishes that are often inspired by Peterson's travels and enlivened with surprising little touches of Thailand or Mexico or Italy.

Peterson always uses as many local ingredients as possible, from morels and watercress growing wild in the area to the herbs and pheasants raised by nearby farmers. Still, he loves to add an unusual spice or other exotic touch. "I like to challenge taste buds," he says.

If any Tapawingo dish is typical, it might be rack of Colorado lamb with Gorgonzola polenta, or perhaps small whole chicken roasted with herbs and honey mustard atop braised Swiss chard. The ideas — and the menu — change constantly, of course.

Dinners at Tapawingo include an appetizer and salad. The desserts spotlighting fruit are wonderful, even more so than the chocolate creations, and vary from strawberry-rhubarb cobbler to chocolate-cherry truffle torte with fresh black cherry ice cream.

The wine list is in keeping with the food, and always features several wines by the glass. This serene restaurant has developed into one of the best in the Midwest. Some people make an annual pilgrimage or two to this little farming town, which also boasts House on the Hill. It's a wonderful bed and breakfast just up the slope from Tapawingo.

Taste of Thailand

Taste of Thailand is right up there in the higher echelons of local Thai restaurants. It's not just a little storefront serving up stir-fries, but an upscale spot that happens to have an ethnic menu, and one that doesn't just repeat what we've seen before.

The greeting you receive is in the British accent of London-born Michael Hall, who runs the front of the house. In the kitchen are his wife, Primprau, and her sister Wannee Shaw. They have the authentic accents of the southeast Asian country whose cuisine has swept America.

☆ ☆ ☆

2755 University Dr., Auburn Hills. (810) 373-4422.

Hours: Lunch, 11 a.m.-2 p.m. weekdays; dinner, 4:30-9 p.m. Mon.-Thu., 4:30-9:30 p.m. Fri.-Sat. Closed Sun. and major holidays.

Nonsmoking: 100 percent.

Full bar. AE, MC and Visa.

Moderate.

Appetizers here include a combination platter of spring rolls, satay, stuffed chicken wings, shrimp rolls and beef on skewers. Main courses range from rice with crayfish, served either mild or spicy, the Thai specialty Boxing Stadium chicken, which is marinated, grilled chicken, and tamarind sauce-topped whole fish.

There are curries, like panang (beef simmered in coconut milk) and noodle dishes, as well as Songkhla chicken, a half chicken marinated in coconut milk, peanuts, brown sugar and spices, then grilled. Songkhla is the name of the sisters' hometown.

The simple room is neat and well kept, in keeping with the quality of the refined fare. Features of the decor include handsome art work, big white linen napkins in fancy folds atop the tables, and little bursts of color in the multi-colored parasols along one wall.

In what has become almost expected at Thai restaurants, the plates have an artistic look. There are trimmings of lettuce ruffles and finely sculpted vegetables, like the perfect rose made from a tomato or the cucumber that mimics a bird on the wing.

In both setting and fare, Taste of Thailand simply exudes a good feeling.

Terry's Terrace

☆ ☆ 1/2

36470 Jefferson at Crocker,
Harrison Twp. (810) 463-2671.

Hours: 9 a.m.-10 p.m. Mon.-Thu., 9 a.m.-midnight Fri., 7 a.m.-midnight Sat., 7 a.m.-10 p.m. Sun. Open an hour later in the summer. Closed Thanksgiving and Christmas Day.

Nonsmoking: 75 percent.

Full bar.   AE, MC, Visa, Discover.

Reasonable.

It's elementary, really: Take a completely unpretentious, down-to-earth setting, load it up with pop-style antiques (which get dusted every day), hire cheery staffers who don't get rattled easily, then add a long menu of basic American dishes at a price structure that reminds one of a much earlier time.

That's appears to be the game plan at Terry Owens' place. Food quality is admirable for the price range, and diners know a good deal when they see one.

In addition to the big printed menus, there's a sheet in the middle of each table noting the specials of the day.

About 20 varieties of fresh fish are listed, including yellow-fin tuna, whitefish, monkfish, grouper and Boston scrod. Other possible selections are veal with artichoke hearts and seafood fettuccine.

An average dinner, with all the trimmings, is priced at $8.95. The accompaniments include a basket of house-baked rolls, a crisp salad or soup of the day (perhaps split pea or steak-and-potato), and a choice of french fries, redskins or mashed, baked or hash browned potatoes.

Thai Bistro

☆ ☆ ☆ ☆

45620 Ford Road at Canton Center Road, Canton. (313) 416-2122.

Hours: Lunch, 11:30 a.m.-2:30 p.m. weekdays; dinner, 4:30-9 p.m. Sun.-Thu., 4:30-10 p.m. Fri.-Sat. Closed major holidays.

Nonsmoking: 70 percent.

Beer and wine.   Major credit cards.

Reasonable to moderate.

Despite its location in an obscure shopping strip so far west on Ford Road that the next stop is a grove of trees, this is a four-star restaurant.

For people who crave the complex, spicy and altogether fascinating fare of Thailand, the drive will be well worth it.

Brothers Lek and Noi Phromthong and Lek's partner, Lada Sripinyo, landed at this remote location partly because of one of the most avid fans a chef could hope to have.

Louis Mika, an art director at a Troy firm, met the brothers when both were working at the Royal Thai Cafe on 14 Mile and Crooks roads. Noi was chef and Lek was manager. Mika got so hooked on Noi's meticulously prepared dishes, he had lunch at the Royal Thai every day for an entire year — surely some kind of culinary record.

So what was Mika to do when the Phromthongs told him they intended to move on to a restaurant of their own, with more space and a bigger kitchen? Well, if he couldn't have lunch from Noi's menu, he figured he might as well have dinner. He encouraged them to locate in a place that would be convenient to his home in Plymouth.

That's how the brothers turned up in a modest Canton Township shopping strip in late February of '94. The simple but attractive room is done up with eye-catching framed art works from Thailand, low-hanging contemporary lamps, and a rose-and-gray color scheme set off by black tables and chairs.

Noi's food is impeccable, from the array of delicate yet intensely flavored sauces on his red, green and yellow curries to the triangular-shaped pastries filled with curried chicken, peas and sweet potato to the stir-fries of mushrooms, baby corn and green onions. With very few exceptions, everything on the menu can be prepared for vegetarians, without meat or fish.

Soups live up to the level of the entrees, notably the tom yum. This spicy soup can be ordered not just with the usual chicken or shrimp in its lemongrass-and-lime-scented depths, but also with vegetables or other seafood choices.

Some of the food is from recipes by Noi's mother, Sutkhet Phromthong. An outstanding dish features plump stir-fried shrimp with chunks of tender Asian eggplant and sweet basil, with several layers of flavor discernible. As with most items on the menu, the shrimp dish may be ordered at a variety of heat levels. The range is from extra mild — no chili peppers — through mild with a hint of heat, medium, hot and extra hot — the latter two for "seasoned professionals only," advises the menu with a touch of humor. Or maybe not.

Since each Thai restaurant seems to have its own definition of levels of heat, it takes some trial and error before a diner can order with confidence. Here, medium is just about right for someone who likes heat but wants to avoid the paralyzing kind.

There hasn't been a hint of grease on any dish I've tried, including sometime-offenders like spring rolls, dumplings, curry puffs and other deep-fried items. One special favorite is an appetizer of rice cakes with a memorable sauce using coconut milk, cilantro, minced pork and shrimp. It's not listed on the menu but sometimes available.

Noi, a university-trained chef, is ready to prepare many additional dishes to the 40-some on the printed list. Some people just leave the ordering to him.

With all of the help lent by Louis Mika, he did give the brothers one piece of bad advice. He wanted them to name the place Beau Thai. They were smart enough to say no to that one.

Thai House

☆ ☆ 1/2

25223 Gratiot, north of 10 Mile
Road, Roseville. (810) 776-3660.

Hours: 11 a.m.-9:30 p.m. Mon.-Thu., 11
a.m.-10 p.m. Fri., 4-10 p.m. Sat. Closed
Sun. and major holidays.

Nonsmoking: 90 percent.

Full bar.   AE, MC, Visa.

Reasonable.

Quite typical of the Thai restaurants in the area, Pipop Leodhuvaphan's place isn't fancy, but does offer more than just four walls. Sculptures, textiles, coins and jewelry from Thailand are displayed throughout the L-shaped room, giving people a little taste of Thailand's culture along with its food.

Pipop has won a measure of fame with his Mr. and Ms. Hot Cooked Contest each October, when chile-popping patrons coolly consume some of the hottest food in the world without batting an eye.

Thai House doesn't just offer the usual mild, medium and hot choices. There are seven spice levels to choose among at the restaurant — very mild, mild, mild-up, medium, medium-up, hot — and at the peak of spiciness, extra hot.

Don't try that one unless you are very brave.

Thai Palace

☆ ☆ 1/2

22433 Michigan Avenue, Dearborn.
(313) 278-5252.

Hours: 11 a.m.-10 p.m. Mon.-Thu., 11
a.m.-11 p.m. Fri.-Sat., 3-10 p.m. Sun.
Closed major holidays.

Nonsmoking: 90 percent.

Soft drinks only.   Major credit cards.

Reasonable.

Thai dishes are served in a tiny, serene room fragrant with basil and lemongrass and chilies. Along with several noodle and rice dishes, the menu includes tiny, delicate spring rolls; a full range of soups and salads, and chicken, beef and seafood combinations in Thai curries and stir-fries.

Service is friendly and caring by members of the interrelated Yang families from Laos, cousins Tony and Pao Yang and their wives and children. Just 40 may be seated at the booths and tables.

The colorful, attractively served platters of food include fresh, house-made noodles, resonant broths and sauces, and pristinely fresh vegetables. The No. 1 dish on the menu is pad Thai, a mixture of rice noodles, shrimp, bean sprouts, salty radish, egg, peanuts and green onion.

The atmosphere changes subtly from noon to night. By day, it is casual, with paper napkins and soup served in little cups from the kitchen. At night, the lights soften. Out come linen napkins and soup is served in flame-spewing tureens for a little romance.

It's hard to resist coconut ice cream for dessert, especially for those who've traveled the spicy path, but the Yangs also offer something less familiar: banana cake Thai style. It is like a steamed pudding of sticky rice and banana wrapped in a banana leaf.

Thai Peppers

Despite its location in a modest strip mall, the interior of Thai Peppers offers a pleasant surprise: it is softly illuminated with indirect lighting and decorated with a collection of Thai artifacts and antique furniture.

The chef here is Alongkot Artharamas. His years of experience include stints at such Bangkok hotels as Dusit Thani, several Thai restaurants in Houston, and the Bangkok Club in Southfield, now closed. He left Bangkok Club to open Thai Peppers with his wife, Somruedee, known as Dee.

☆ ☆ ☆

29402 Orchard Lake Road, south of 13 Mile Road, Farmington Hills. (810) 932-9119.

Hours: Noon-10:30 p.m. Sat.; buffet lunch, 11:30 a.m.-2 p.m. weekdays; dinner, 5-10 p.m. Mon.-Thu., 5-10:30 p.m. Fri. Closed Sun. and major holidays.

Nonsmoking: 65 percent.

Soft drinks only.   Major credit cards.

Reasonable to moderate.

The lunch buffet he provides is a great way to sample the wares. The dishes are fresh and attractive with recognizable ingredients. The food doesn't just sit there either: it is frequently replenished.

Set up attractively on a table under a gleaming swag of gold lame on the wall high above, the buffet table offers a changing array of dishes. It always includes a soup, an appetizer and a fresh salad of cucumbers, lettuce and tomato with the chef's special herb house dressing. A noodle dish, a hot and spicy dish and a mild one, fried rice and steamed rice are other components. They even toss in dessert, all for $6.25.

Interesting dishes include the bite-sized pork- and chicken-filled dumplings known as kahnom jeep; beef with green curry; eggplant and green beans, and noodles with red peppers. Steamed jasmine rice, a fragrant long-grained white rice, comes with just about everything.

Eating buffet style is the closest approximation to dining the authentic Thai way. In Thailand, dishes are shared. However, it's not the only way. Those who prefer may order from the menu at lunchtime, and it offers a completely different selection from the buffet. For example, there are a couple of excellent soups: tom yum, a spicy broth with chicken or shrimp and mushrooms, and tom kha, redolent of coconut milk, herbs and mushrooms.

What the menu calls "set lunches" include soup, rice and main course, ranging from stir-fried chicken with vegetables and garlic to a highly spiced red or green curry dish.

The spice level at Thai Peppers is indicated by exclamation marks. One is spicy, two is hot, three is hot-with-a-burn and four, extra hot. At dinner, you can hit an even higher spice level.

The dinner menu is more extensive. In addition to the expected stir-fries and curry dishes, it encompasses such choices as sweet and sour fish, steamed fish with ginger and vegetables, and everybody's favorite, the noodle dish called pad Thai.

House specialties include crispy duck atop a bed of greens (seasoned at the three exclamation mark spice level), as well as a mildly spiced baked duckling filled with cilantro root, herbs, garlic, peppercorns and orange peel.

Thai Village

☆ ☆ 1/2

12414 Hall Road, just east of Van Dyke, Sterling Heights. (810) 726-9060.

Hours: Lunch, 11 a.m.-3 p.m. Mon.-Thu.; dinner, 5-9:30 p.m. Mon.-Thu., 11 a.m.-10:30 p.m. Fri., 5-10:30 p.m. Sat., 5-9:30 p.m. Sun. Closed major holidays.

Nonsmoking: 45 percent.

Full bar.   Major credit cards.

Reasonable.

The premises once housed a country-French restaurant that never managed to catch on. That hasn't been the case with its successor, the Thai spot that opened early in '90. It's made a go of it, as have so many Thai restaurants in the metro area. Menus offer appetizers of delicate spring rolls, tod mun (minced spiced chicken patties served with a cucumber and ground nut sauce) and beef satay (thinly sliced marinated beef on wooden skewers).

Soups are resonantly spicy, especially a wonderful shrimp and lemongrass blend. The list of main dishes runs the gamut from chicken plus four (stir-fried chicken with pineapple, ginger, onions and green peppers) to stir-fried rice noodles with broccoli and eggs, and crispy fish with slivers of ginger.

Presentation is emphasized. The platters of food are ornamented with intricately carved vegetables, including birds cut from carrots.

Not to be missed is the wonderfully icy coconut ice cream dolloped with peanuts. It's the perfect finale.

Proprietors Surawud Preyawan and Yongyuth Sonjeow ventured out on their own after spending time in the kitchen at Bangkok Cuisine.

Thanasi's Olympus

Thanasi's takes a home-style approach to Greek cooking.

Certainly, the familiar cry of "Opa!" echoes through the bi-level restaurant. As I discovered on my first visit, the flaming cheese style of cuisine, made famous locally by Detroit's Greektown — egg-lemon soup, Greek salads and roast lamb — is alive and well across the river.

☆ ☆ 1/2

1204 Tecumseh, Windsor, Ontario.
(519) 977-6650.

Hours: 11 a.m.-10 p.m. Mon.-Thu., 11 a.m.-midnight Fri.-Sat., noon-10 p.m. Sun. Closed Christmas Day and Dec. 26.

Nonsmoking: 50 percent.

Full bar.   Major credit cards.

Reasonable.

But a closer look at the menu reveals a number of items not on that oh-so-familiar list. The dishes prepared from the recipes of Maria Pontikis, mother of proprietor Nick and wife of Athanasios, are what give Thanasi's its special feeling.

Maria Pontikis hails from the island of Schinousa — "a dot, a rock in the Aegean" her son calls it. The family came to Canada when Nick, who was born in Athens, was just 9 years old.

A noticeable family warmth permeates the place. There is much more of a relaxed approach here than is found in the often frantic Monroe Street spots. At Thanasi's, there are no black-suited waiters with gruff exteriors. Diners may sit back and enjoy the food without a thought about how long they are holding a table, and they can ask the proprietor to order for them if they are unsure about what to choose.

Nick Pontikis loves to take away the menus and bring out some of his favorite dishes. That often includes bifteki, spiced ground beef patties; barbecued quail, butterflied to make it easy to pick up in the fingers, and some of the wonderful, spicy sausage made especially for Thanasi's. He might also suggest salted cod, pan-fried and served with skordalia (mashed potatoes and garlic) and house-made pickled beets.

Other items Pontikis is proud of are the lamb chops sprinkled with oregano and lemon, the pork and chicken kebabs (all served with both rice and roasted potatoes in the Greek style), his mother's spinach pie, stewed beef and stuffed grape leaves.

Dinners-for-two are appealing. There are four combinations, including a range of dishes right down to house-made desserts, tagged from $29.95 to $39.95, and that's in Canadian money.

With this cuisine, it's almost impossible not to order some appetizers to pass around the table. The appetizer platter includes a sampling of several dishes, including meatballs, hot sausage, artichoke hearts, olives and feta cheese, or the wonderfully garlicky dips: skordalia, tarama (whipped caviar), tzatziki (yogurt, garlic and cucumber) and melitzanosalata (eggplant, garlic and seasonings.) It's enough garlic to make you think you've stumbled into the festival in Gilroy, Calif.

This is not at all a formal restaurant, despite its statuary, columns and fountains. Napkins are paper, for instance. Service is by fresh-faced young women who exude a believable enthusiasm about the fare. Dress is casual.

One dining room is accessible. The rest rooms are not.

Thomas Edison Inn

 ☆ ☆ 1/2

500 Thomas Edison Parkway,
Port Huron. (810) 984-8000.

Hours: Breakfast, 7-10:30 a.m. weekdays, 7-11 a.m. Sat., 8-11 a.m. Sun.; lunch, 11:30 a.m.-4 p.m. Mon.-Sat.; dinner, 5-10 p.m. Mon.-Thu., 5-11 p.m. Fri.-Sat., 3-9 p.m. Sun.; brunch, 11:30 a.m.-3 p.m. Sun. Open an hour later for dinner in the summer. Closed Christmas.

Nonsmoking: 75 percent.

Full bar.   Major credit cards.

Moderate.

The vista of river traffic makes a nice counterpoint to the Victorian chairs, splashy flower prints, etched glass and globe lights in the dining room at this hotel and conference center in the shadow of the Blue Water Bridge.

The menu is American contemporary, with such dishes as seafood pasta, grilled swordfish, veal chop, breast of duckling and, of course, prime ribs of beef and steak, to tie in with the widely varying tastes of the clientele.

Four soups are offered at both lunch and dinner, and they range from fisherman's chowder to Michigan onion. At lunch, there's an array of salads, sandwiches and lighter entrees, with an emphasis on fish and chicken. Michael Bade is the executive chef.

Dining in a room this size — it seats 325 — hardly can be called intimate, but then inns of this size aren't exactly the place to go in search of a hideaway.

Tom's Oyster Bar

Tom Brandel has fine-tuned his concept steadily since opening the first of his oyster bars in '85: great fresh oysters on the half shell, many from aqua-farmers around the country, a blackboard chalked with maybe 23 varieties of fish that could all be called catch of the day, with everything served in a completely informal setting.

That means bare wooden floors, dark wood walls and tin ceilings with spinning fans and schoolhouse lamps. Bentwood chairs are pulled up to round tables covered in blue-and-white-checked vinyl cloths. Burgees deck the walls, along with New Yorker magazine covers.

These signature touches were transplanted to Royal Oak when the

☆ ☆ ☆ ☆

15402 Mack, Grosse Pointe Park.
(313) 884-6030.

Hours: 11 a.m.-11 p.m. Mon.-Thu., 11 a.m.-midnight Fri.-Sat., 5-10 p.m. Sun.

318 S. Main, Royal Oak.
(810) 541-1186.

Hours: 11 a.m.-midnight weekdays, 11 a.m.-1 a.m. Sat., noon-11 p.m. Sun. Closed Super Bowl Sun., Thanksgiving, Christmas Eve, Christmas Day, New Year's Day.

Nonsmoking: 50 percent in Grosse Pointe, 25 percent in Royal Oak.

Full bar.　　　　　　　Major credit cards.

Reasonable to moderate.

second of the oyster bars opened in '94, along with the typical Brandel trimmings of redskin potatoes, corn on the cob and coleslaw. The latter is always served, along with cocktail sauce, in fluted paper cups.

I've heard people complain about those paper cups. To me, they're as much a part of the oyster bar experience as the tray of hot sauces and the outsized goblets filled with oyster crackers on every table. And so are the packets of Wash 'N Dri's for sticky fingers and big, high-quality paper napkins. It's all fine with me, because it's completely in keeping with the comfortable, unpretentious setting.

Brandel was able to snag the services of Michael Houlihan, a chef with a wealth of experience, when the Royal Oak outpost opened in '94. Houlihan's skills allow the oyster bar to buy fish in volume for both Royal Oak and Grosse Pointe Park, and for the upcoming third place scheduled to open in Southfield in '95.

Chalked on the big entree board could be choices like lightly breaded sauteed whitefish, sauteed tilapia, blackened catfish, grilled swordfish and ginger or Cajun shrimp.

In Grosse Pointe Park, the menu is under the direction of another fine chef, Bill Osborne. He likes to do oyster pan roasts rich with chunks of fresh tomato, onions and spices, as well as seafood-pasta combinations that change every day. These might include shrimp pesto, shrimp and scallops with lobster sauce, and tomato-basil fettuccine.

Other interesting dishes that might be spotted on the board at either place include Jamaican jerk chicken, oyster corn fritters, and shrimp and chicken curry.

You may count on getting fresh oysters from the raw bar, peel-and-eat shrimp, smoked fish appetizers, and even a few beef selections. Six or seven varieties of the fresh oysters are standard. Available by the piece or the dozen, they are served with wedges of lemon and cocktail sauce topped with freshly ground horseradish.

There's a long list of beers, some nice wines by the glass, and a full house most of the time at these well-run places.

The Southfield location is at the corner of Northwestern Highway and Franklin roads, the site of the old Vineyards restaurant. I can't imagine that it will be any less appealing than the other two oyster bars.

Tom Brandel has this particular genre down pat.

Too Chez

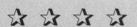

27155 Sheraton Drive, Novi.
(810) 348-5555

Hours: Lunch, 11:30 a.m.-2:30 p.m. Mon.-Sat.; dinner, 5:30-10 p.m. Mon.-Thu., 5:30-11 p.m. Fri.-Sat. Closed Sun. and major holidays.

Nonsmoking: 75 percent.

Full bar.   Major credit cards.

Moderate.

Started as Raphael's in 1983, this restaurant wowed its diners with food as art. The name changed to Chez Raphael in 1986, after leaving the tight quarters in the Sheraton Oaks Hotel for a more luxurious space in its own nearby building.

In 1990, the place was re-born as Too Chez, with a much more contemporary approach, and a price structure that is less than half of what it was in the more opulent days. A humorously eclectic setting and a simplified menu makes the restaurant accessible to far more people.

Chef Greg Upshur's personality and style fit the quirky, eccentric look of the place. Elements include columns painted in a Pucci-like pattern of shock colors, picture-less picture frames suspended over the fireplace, lamps constructed from champagne magnums and an entire chalkboard-and-memorabilia wall. Bright mosaic tile insets in the floors add more flippant character.

The food from the huge kitchen makes diners sit up and take notice, just as their eyes are caught by the room's eccentricities.

Lunch and dinner menus are presented in loose-leaf notebooks that also include the wine list. The small course/large course theme is followed. Among the small courses might be Cajun shrimp cocktail, escargot with roasted garlic, mushroom gratin, house-smoked salmon and baked chevre and polenta.

On the more substantial side are such choices as roast pork loin, rack of lamb and Black Angus beef with jalapeno jack cheese and roasted potatoes.

Available at both lunch and dinner are whole wheat-crusted pizzas and a more and more pastas, such as angel hair with fresh tomato sauce.

The word eclectic was coined for this place. The relaxed scheme lets long-time maitre d' Achille Bianchi wear slouchy suits and patterned tie-less shirts rather than an uptight tux.

Traffic Jam

Partners Ben Edwards and Richard Vincent complement each other perfectly in running a restaurant that has chalked up an amazing 30 years in business. Edwards is behind the scenes fixing the equipment and baking bread, beer or cheese, while Vincent is right up front, with his energy and patter, making people feel comfortable. The urban-artifact lavished place seats 240, but certainly doesn't have the feel of a restaurant that large.

511 W. Canfield at Second, Detroit. (313) 831-9470.

Hours: 11 a.m.-3 p.m. Mon., 11 a.m.-9 p.m. Tue.-Wed., 11 a.m.-10:30 p.m. Thu., 11 a.m.-midnight Fri., 5 p.m.-midnight Sat. Closed Sun. and major holidays.

Nonsmoking: 80 percent.

Full bar.   MC, Visa and Discover.

Moderate.

Computer-generated menus change bi-weekly here, with a continuing emphasis on the fresh, creative, spicy (up to a point) and international. There are always four or five salads, including spinach and Caesar, sandwiches like the basil and tomato broil, the Jamburger, Tex-Mex lentil burger and maybe an Italian hoagie.

Traffic Jam's freshly baked bread is legendary — and so far beyond wheat and rye that it sometimes takes three menu lines to describe.

Cheese is made in-house as well and, finally, the brew-pub law allows beer brewed on the property across the street to be served at the restaurant. There are three house beers on tap. A sampler of each is $4.25.

Main dishes might include a barbecued chicken breast with potato wedges and coleslaw, eggplant and pasta bake, or a curried broccoli and onion dish with an Indonesian flavor.

Desserts are emphasized, and if you don't order a chocolate and ice cream concoction, bread pudding or hot apple strudel — just a sampling of what might appear on the menu — you'll ruin Vincent's day. And don't think he won't notice.

Trattoria Bruschetta

27790 Novi Road, Novi.
(810) 305-5210.

Hours: Lunch, 11 a.m.-2 p.m. Mon.-Sat.; dinner, 5-11 p.m. Mon.-Thu., 5 p.m.-midnight Fri.-Sat., 5-9 p.m. Sun. Closed Christmas Day.

Nonsmoking: 80 percent.

Full bar.   Major credit cards.

Moderate.

Hotel restaurants are rarely as cheerful and upbeat as this one, with its well-spaced tables, red-and-white checkered tablecloths peeking out from under white ones, and folksy, framed black-and-white photos on glowing terra-cotta walls.

The menu at this contemporary spot sizzles with color and creativity. Fresh figs and chestnuts, portobello and porcini mushrooms, fennel, sage, pecorino romano cheese and pancetta (Italian salt-cured bacon) are more prominently featured than tomatoes and mozzarella.

A complimentary hors d'oeuvre comes to the table immediately, a bit of pate of the Sicilian vegetable relish known as caponata. It's a little white bean and garlic pureed with some chopped tomato relish, all to be spread on pieces of grilled bread — the bruschetta of the title.

Pastas are prevalent here and offered in two portion sizes, as are the salads. And when it comes to salads, there simply are no boring ones. Two of the six choices are insalata verde (mixed greens with Gorgonzola, nuggets of fresh pear, roasted peppers and a vinaigrette made with a touch of red wine) and one in which grilled salmon, white bean and tomato relish and grilled tomatoes are enhanced with olive oil.

Chicken, seafood and veal dishes are all prepared here with elegantly earthy flair. Chef Frank Turner's style is typified by pan-roasted pheasant breast and leg confit with risotto, roasted garlic and fried sage; grilled swordfish with citrus and herbs; osso bucco (braised veal shank) and lamb ragout with roast peppers. Veal or chicken piccata with artichokes, lemon and capers is an especially nice dish.

Of course, if these people don't have it down pat by now, they never will. The Unique Restaurant Corp., employing more than 700 people, runs this and a passel of other restaurants, including Sebastian's Grill, Morels, Bruschetta Cafe, the new America and a deli or two.

Tres Vite

Tres Vite is a favorite spot for those who appreciate an urban cafe setting and its people-watching possibilities. Many of Detroit's best-known faces are frequently spotted in the glass-walled restaurant in the Fox Theatre building.

☆ ☆ ☆

2203 Woodward Avenue, Detroit.
(313) 964-4144

Hours: 11:30 a.m.-8 p.m. Tue.-Wed., 11:30 a.m.-11 p.m. Thu.-Fri., 5-11 p.m. Sat. Closed Sun. (except when the Fox Theatre has a show), Mon. and major holidays.

Nonsmoking: 95 percent.

Full bar.   Major credit cards.

Moderate.

The size of the place is just right: the L-shaped quarters don't overpower. And the fare is as bright and interesting as the setting.

The design reflects the history of the building. Walls have been left with their scars and imperfections uncorrected, but painted in a mottled pale brick shade. The huge windows, thick columns and high ceilings hint at the building's massive dimensions.

Old brass fittings have been polished and returned to the entrance doors off the Columbia Street lobby, and the metal staircase leading to the lower level lounges has been left as is.

The effect is striking, with the contrast of highly contemporary furnishings, including cherrywood-and-black Kim chairs. Black-and-white photographs of Paris in the '50s add to the bistro feeling, and the compact kitchen is open to view.

All of the cabinetwork is designed to look like slick furniture, and few extraneous details detract from the clean, crisp approach.

The Italian slant of the menu has taken a slight turn toward the American lately. You may have a burger at lunch, for instance. And not everything is polenta and pasta, but they are certainly there, as is pizza, with and without cheese, and such dishes as grilled marinated chicken breast, grilled salmon and swordfish.

Desserts include ice creams and sorbets, biscotti and creme brulee.

220

☆ ☆ ☆

220 Merrill, Birmingham.
(810) 645-2150.

Hours: Lunch, 11 a.m.-5 p.m. Mon.-Sat.;
dinner, 5-11 p.m. Mon.-Wed., 5 p.m.-midnight Thu., 5 p.m.-1 a.m. Sat. Closed Sun.
and major holidays.

Nonsmoking: 60 percent.

Full bar.   AE, MC and Visa.

Moderate.

Fans of the up-to-date fare at the Beverly Hills Grill were momentarily taken aback when they picked up the menu at the restaurant called simply 220 when it opened in 1994.

The Birmingham spot run by BHG proprietors Bill and Judi Roberts seemed at first to have taken a step backward in style of fare.

What's with this eggplant Parmigiana and chicken Marsala stuff? Where's the chevre and sun-dried tomatoes, the grilled salmon, the black bean chili, that intriguing food with an edge?

The Robertses have taken exactly the right tack, however. In the 1932-vintage building, a former Detroit Edison office and a relic of the days when the company handed out free light bulbs, retro dishes fit the setting. Besides, to have replicated their successful grill just two miles from the original would have been less than intelligent, something the Robertses have never been accused of being.

The menu does indeed include eggplant Parmigiana and chicken Marsala, as well as spaghetti and meatballs (part ground beef, part Italian sausage for a spicy kick), scampi with linguine, and baked penne. It's familiar, but what counts is the execution. And for the most part, everything is impeccably prepared in an open kitchen.

The Robertses brought chef Kevin Okuszka from the grill staff to be the head man in the 220 kitchen, with Ron Rebecca as sous-chef. Their challenge with that familiar menu is to bring it to full potential. And they're doing just that.

Arugula and mushroom salad with Parmesan, the bean-y rather than tomato-y minestrone, the spaghetti and meatballs, and the caper-dotted veal piccata are all top-notch.

Baskets of Italian bread (absolutely the real thing, and much of it from designer Ron Rea's favorite bakery, Cantoro's in Livonia) come to the table at both lunch and dinner. The white plates, some red-rimmed, some not, are part of that mix-and-match, we've-been-here-forever effect.

Colorful fresh vegetables and either a sliced roasted potato or parsley-dotted fettuccine are main course accompaniments.

The setting includes a convivially noisy bar in the front and a slightly more subdued dining room in the back. They are open to each other not only through two archways but also because the shelves over the bar are backless, to allow the rooms to flow together visually.

The decor, with its antique light fixtures and wall sconces playing up the Edison company origins, and the Barney Judge black-and-white caricatures of faces you may think you recognize (but they're actually "nobody," says Bill Roberts) looked comfortably settled from the first day.

As if to emphasize the retro effect, the restaurant's phone number is listed on the menus as MIdwest 5-2150.

Just don't ask for free light bulbs.

Under the Eagle

☆ ☆ 1/2

9000 Joseph Campau, Hamtramck.
(313) 875-5905.

Hours: 11 a.m.-7 p.m. Mon.-Tue., 11 a.m.-
9 p.m. Thu.-Sun. Closed Wed., Easter, July 4
and Christmas Day.

Nonsmoking: 50 percent.

Soft drinks only.　　　　　No credit cards.

Reasonable.

The brilliant pink beet soup, one of several earthy yet elegant soups at this ingenuous spot, is enough to reassure me about the kitchen. The friendly, unpretentious place has been around for 21 years, and has the kind of gentle prices that seems to survive only in Hamtramck.

For example, the combination plate of stuffed cabbage, pierogi, sauerkraut, kielbasa, applesauce-filled blintz, simple green salad, mashed potatoes and gravy, with good bakery rye, is in the $7 area. Little wonder no credit cards are accepted.

Tables are covered in vinyl cloth and the napkins are paper, but there are often fresh carnations in bud vases. The staff wears embroidered and spangled Polish dress to underscore the place's ethnic direction.

Union Street

☆ ☆ ☆

4145 Woodward, Detroit.
(313) 831-3965.

Hours: 11 a.m.-midnight Mon.-Thu., 11
a.m.-1 a.m. Fri., 5 p.m.-1 a.m. Sat. Closed
Sun. and major holidays.

Nonsmoking: 80 percent at lunch, 60 percent at dinner.

Full bar.　　　　　Major credit cards.

Reasonable to moderate.

Union Street draws one of the most eclectic crowds in town. Musicians from obscure rock groups rub elbows with symphony oboists. Professors and students hobnob with poets, attorneys, cops and off-duty bartenders. The owners like to say their midtown spot is "the house of sustenance to Detroit's cool, cultured and culinary hip" — and it's true.

Chef David Pillette not only became a partner in the enterprise with Greg Gedda and John Lopez in '94, but also presided over the construction of a new kitchen. It's a beauty — 2,000 square feet with white ceramic walls and a terra-cotta floor.

Diners, as always, may have a simple burger or something much more involved. The daily-changing menu is typified by such dishes as smoked salmon with bowtie pasta, whitefish sauteed with dill and shallots, duck liver *pate* and barbecued ribs. Pastas might include ravioli, shrimp linguine and chicken fettuccine, and seafood bisque and black bean are among the possible soups. A house salad and baguette come with entrees.

The setting is a great-looking Art Deco-influenced room that does get noisy on occasion. The cool, cultured and hip don't seem to mind at all.

Van Dyke Place

The well-preserved, circa-1900 West Village house makes an elegant setting for a restaurant. The house is small enough to be comfortable rather than overpowering, and in fact there is room for only 18 tables. The historic home of William Muir Finck is replete with needlepoint chairs, antique pieces and accessories.

Chef Keith Supian, who has been at Van Dyke Place for several years now, offers a small, select menu of traditional dishes with updated garnishes.

☆ ☆ ☆ ☆

649 Van Dyke, Detroit.
(313) 821-2620.

Hours: Dinner only, 6-9 p.m. Tue.-Thu., 5-9:30 p.m. Fri.-Sat.; lunch (in Dec. only), 11:30 a.m.-2:30 p.m. Tue.-Fri. Closed Sun., Mon. and major holidays.

Nonsmoking: 80 percent.

Full bar.   Major credit cards.

Expensive.

Entrees may include rack of lamb with chick pea crust and wild rice pilaf, sauteed veal medallions with risotto cake and wild mushroom Madeira sauce, grilled swordfish with roasted corn salsa and roasted duckling with fruit and toasted penne.

Desserts include "Sack of Apples," the most requested sweet ever at this spot, as well as individual, miniature berry pies with ice cream.

An option is Supian's special menu of traditional Jewish dishes adapted to more contemporary tastes. It's offered Tuesdays through Fridays and includes such selections as matzo ball soup, kasha meat loaf, roasted apricot chicken atop potato latkes (pancakes) and glazed beef brisket. The vegetarian chopped liver is made with lentils, eggs and carmelized onions.

Though not totally necessary, reservations are advised.

Victorian Inn

1229 Seventh St., Port Huron.
(810) 984-1437.

Hours: Lunch, 11:30 a.m.-2 p.m. Tue.-Sat.; dinner, 5:30-8:30 p.m. Tue.-Sat. Closed Sun., Mon. and major holidays.

Nonsmoking: 90 percent.

Full bar.   Major credit cards.

Moderate.

The three-story, Queen Anne-style Victorian house with tri-color paint job on its gingerbready exterior is on the state register of historic places. The authentic style of its rooms has the effect of transporting guests to that era.

Proprietors Lynne Secory and Vickie Peterson researched the patterns and colors of the time for their wallpaper and paint. They hung lace curtains veiled with the careful folds of draperies, plus mirrors and photographs. Even the coat racks are from the period.

The menu in the dining room changes on the first Tuesday of the month. Dishes are chosen "as the spirit moves us," says Secory. Certain things are popular enough to be regulars, however, like the grilled lamb rack with wine and herbs.

There are six entree choices, generally beef, seafood and poultry, and salad and vegetables are included. The only appetizer on the menu is soup. The two choices change constantly, maybe zucchini cheese, velvet tomato (that's cream of tomato to the less poetically inclined) or gazpacho.

Desserts change, too, and include "tortes, tarts, just gooey goodies," Secory says. Wines are emphasized of late.

Note that the house is a bed-and-breakfast, with four charming rooms up the graceful, balustraded staircase. A pub is on the lower level.

Vince's

Friendly and unpretentious, this Italian restaurant and pizzeria beats many spots at the pasta game being played all over town.

The house-made noodles with fresh, light tomato sauces, the solid veal dishes and the noted pizza with which the place started nearly 35 years ago all continue to draw people into southwest Detroit.

☆ ☆ ☆

1341 Springwells, Detroit.
(313) 842-4857.

Hours: 11 a.m.-10 p.m. Tue.-Thu., 11 a.m.-11 p.m. Fri., 2-11 p.m. Sat., 2-10 p.m. Sun. Closed Mon. and major holidays.

Nonsmoking: 50 percent.

Full bar.   AE, MC and Visa.

Reasonable.

The muraled dining room is bright and cheerful, its tables full of multi-generational groups. Notable dishes include pasta putanesca (noodles with tomatoes, black olives, anchovies and capers), manicotti with ricotta cheese and spinach, lasagna, and angelhair pasta with meat sauce and meatballs. Accompaniments are the house-made bread and bread sticks and simple green salads in vinegar and oil.

Vintage Bistro

Here's a place that dared to depart from the east side's seemingly obligatory Italian menu. Instead, Vintage Bistro treat people to a French-accented, grazing bill of fare.

East siders love it.

The all-day, a la carte menu of dishes ranges from light to substantial. It's not divided into specific categories, which allows for completely free-form ordering.

The menu changes frequently, but

☆ ☆ ☆

18450 Mack Avenue, Grosse Pointe Farms. (313) 886-9950.

Hours: Lunch, 11 a.m.-3 p.m. Tue.-Fri.; dinner, 5-9:45 p.m. Mon.-Sat. Closed Sun. and major holidays.

Nonsmoking: 90 percent.

Full bar.   AE, MC and Visa.

Moderate to expensive.

adheres to the bistro style. Ground sirloin with grilled bananas is a perennial favorite that stays when other dishes depart. Other selections might include whitefish and potato dumpling with mushroom beurre blanc, pheasant with brown sauce, stuffed rack of pork rack with currant demi-glace. Soups are typified by pumpkin bisque, potato and onion, and always a consomme.

Chef/proprietor Jon-Louis Seavitt, who works with sous-chef Tim Budzinski, encourages people to come in and graze, if they so desire. Small dishes are priced at $2-$10, with the more substantial, $12-$19.

Seavitt, his wife, Gloria, and their partner, attorney Richard Puzzuoli, had a very clear view of the atmosphere they wanted to create in this attractive building with its diamond-paned windows.

It's a simple setting with ivory plaster, polished dark woodwork and soft lights, subdued and attractive. You might slide into one of the high-backed booths in the tile-floored bar on the first floor of this immaculate place, or climb a flight of stairs to the slightly more formal dining room. From that vantage point you get a peek inside the kitchen.

While high-energy, upbeat, noisy restaurants may be more in style, there's something to be said for this approach — understated, quiet and comfortable.

Virginia's Mid-East Cafe

☆ ☆ ☆

**2456 Orchard Lake Road,
Sylvan Lake. (810) 681-7170.**

Hours: 11 a.m.-9 p.m. Mon.-Thu., 11 a.m.-10 p.m. Fri.-Sat., noon-9 p.m. Sun. Closed Christmas Day.

Nonsmoking: 100 percent.

Soft drinks only. AE, MC and Visa.

Reasonable.

Interesting ethnic cafes turn up frequently in suburban strip malls. Take this one, for instance.

The place opened quietly in 1990 and almost from the very beginning had the locals raving about the tabbouleh, hommus, chicken kebabs and baked or raw kibbee (ground beef and lamb mixed with cracked wheat, pine nuts and onion).

Virginia Daher Colvy also offers stuffed grape leaves, fatoush salads (toasted pita bread, herbs, onions, cucumbers, tomatoes and green peppers in house dressing), shawarma (beef or chicken marinated in herbs and served atop rice with sesame-seed sauce) and an excellent lemony lentil soup.

In addition to the Middle Eastern classics, Colvy has added several more unusual dishes. They include Greek-style spinach pies in phyllo, and acorn squash halves baked with a stuffing of chicken, almonds, walnuts and vegetables. For her potato chops, Idaho potatoes — she says they must be Idahos — are mashed and stuffed with meat or vegetarian fillings, then quickly deep fried.

The cafe seats just 32.

Wah Court

This is a restaurant to restore faith in the integrity of Cantonese fare. Watch as the succession of dishes goes by in the steady hands of the staff, and it is immediately apparent that care is being lavished where it counts — in the kitchen.

The menu is incredibly long, and as if 188 selections weren't enough, more dishes are part of a changing monthly menu. The array might include duck and pork in hot pot, pan-fried oysters with crabmeat sauce, silver bass with black bean sauce or fried salted shrimp.

2037 Wyandotte Street W., Windsor, Ontario. (519) 254-1388.

Hours: 11 a.m.-11:30 p.m. weekdays, 10 a.m.-11:30 p.m. Sat., 10 a.m.-10:30 p.m. Sun.; dim sum, until 3 p.m. daily. Closed on Canadian Thanksgiving and Victoria Day.

Nonsmoking: 50 percent.

Beer, wine, some mixed drinks.

MC and Visa.

Reasonable.

Dim sum is a specialty, and the assortment of dumplings, buns and other tidbits is served every day from opening until 3 p.m. On Saturdays and Sundays, dim sum carts roll through the dining room, and patrons are able to see the selection and choose what they want immediately. Other days, it is ordered from the laundry-list menus offering everything from steamed rice with ribs and minced beef noodle rolls to turnip cakes and sesame seed balls.

People cheerfully wait for a table on weekends to partake of dim sum in big family groups.

Water Club Seafood Grill

The biggest compliment of all to Chuck Muer's well-documented success in the food and wine business lies in the number of restaurants that are shameless copies of his ideas. Over the years, many of his employees have gone on to open thinly disguised pseudo-Muer restaurants.

39500 Ann Arbor Road, just east of I-275, Plymouth Township. (313) 454-0666.

Hours: 11 a.m.-10 p.m. Mon.-Thu., 11 a.m.-11 p.m. Fri., 4-11 p.m. Sat., 3-8 p.m. Sun. Closed major holidays.

Nonsmoking: 80 percent.

Full bar.   Major credit cards.

Reasonable to moderate.

When John Cleveland left the Muer fold after 14 years to open this airy spot, admirably he was not content to do just another Muer reprise. There *are* some little touches that are reminiscent of his mentor. That tart coleslaw, for instance, and the blue cheese-and-walnut-dappled mixed greens (but with strawberry vinaigrette rather than the Muer restaurants' raspberry, I hasten to add).

But Cleveland has come up with many of his own ideas — vegetarian paella (baked vegetables with saffron rice in a vegetable stock), for instance — to produce a very appealing menu. Another Muer alumnus, Michael Dopkowski, is his chef.

A wide range of seafood and fish is offered, both on the regular menu and the fresh catch list of eight to 12 varieties each day. Maryland crab cakes, a number of shrimp treatments, salmon with pesto, linguine with tomato basil sauce, chicken pot pie and barbecued baby ribs are all nicely garnished with fresh vegetables.

The whimsical decor is replete with fish cutouts in metal and wood — some made by Cleveland himself — and colorful fishing lures displayed in shadowboxes against bright blue walls. The waitstaffers wear fish-print ties.

Are we going to order chicken in a place like this? Certainly not me.

The Whitney

☆ ☆ ☆ ☆

4421 Woodward at Canfield, Detroit. (313) 832-5700.

Hours: Lunch, 11 a.m.-2 p.m. Fri. only; dinner, 6-9 p.m. Mon.-Tue., 5-9 p.m. Wed.-Thu., 5 p.m.-midnight Fri.-Sat., 5-9:30 p.m. Sun.; brunch, 11 a.m.-2:30 p.m. Sun. Closed major holidays.

Nonsmoking: 80 percent.

Full bar.   Major credit cards.

Expensive.

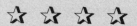

After nearly 10 years in its guise as a restaurant, the mansion built by lumber baron David Whitney in the 1890s is still a showstopper.

No matter how many times a person strolls through the high-ceilinged rooms replete with vintage glass, carved wood, marble and mosaic details at this amazingly well-preserved structure, it's still impressive.

The fare has been under the direction of chef Paul Grosz since the end of '91. His earthy yet elegant style is a good fit with the house.

The ever-changing dinner menu features such dishes as a tasting of three soups, perhaps spiced squash and apple; rock shrimp and lentil, and three-onion pheasant au gratin. Other main courses might include rack of lamb stuffed with veal, eggplant and spinach; peppercorn-crusted filet mignon, and a trio of grilled fish: salmon, whitefish and swordfish.

Sunday brunch is a particularly good time to admire the setting. Four courses are served to the tables, and the choices range from scrambled eggs with cheddar in brioche, poached eggs on English muffin with house-smoked salmon or bacon, and herb-marinated chicken breast.

Desserts at the Whitney are not to be missed. Like the rest of the menu, they change constantly, but almost always include the Chocolate Ugly cake with chocolate mousse frosting, a tasting of house-made ice creams, frozen lemon souffle and panna cotta (cooked cream) topped with caramel and fresh berries.

On Monday through Friday evenings, from 5 to 6:30, the Whitney offers a pre-theater dinner in the third floor bar. The fixed price, four-course meal is a value at $24.95, but lacks the full Whitney pizzazz found in the dining rooms on the first floor.

Xochimilco

This informal spot is popular for its pop-Mexican fare served virtually any time of day, 362 days a year. The first floor's three dining rooms often spill over to the rooms upstairs.

Specialties of the house include tacos, enchiladas, tostados, burritos, flautas and quesadillas (flour tortillas filled with melted cheese, guacamole and jalapeno peppers). Prices are so reasonable, it is hard to run up a check for two beyond $15.

☆ ☆

3409 Bagley, Detroit.
(313) 843-0179.

Hours: 11 a.m.-4 a.m. every day. Closed Easter, Thanksgiving and Christmas Day.

Nonsmoking: 60 percent.

Full bar.   AE, MC, Visa.

Reasonable.

An indication of the lack of amenities here is that you may be asked if you want a glass should you order a bottle of beer.

I guess that's considered an affectation.

Yau Hing

992 University Avenue W., Windsor, Ontario. (519) 252-0159.

Hours: 11:30 a.m.-10 p.m. Mon. and Wed.-Thu., 11:30 a.m.-11 p.m. Fri.-Sat., 11:30 a.m.-9 p.m. Sun. Closed Tue.

Nonsmoking: 35 percent.

Beer and white wine.   MC and Visa.

Reasonable.

Another of Windsor's interesting Chinese restaurants, this modest spot is the enterprise of Leung Chun Wong and his big family. The little restaurant has been modified since its opening three years ago. The former open kitchen has been moved to the back, giving the dining room a little more space.

Yau Hing is especially famous for the annual Chinese New Year's dinners it serves for six days around the holiday. The celebratory dinners are a mere $15 and people come from miles around to take advantage of the multi-course feasts.

The regular menu features an amazing 10 varieties of soup, and another 80 dishes. Some of them are twice-cooked fresh green beans tossed with bits of pork and hot spices, vegetarian spring rolls, pan-fried dumpling and chicken with garlic flavor.

The Yau Hing Special Shrimp is notable. Steamed shrimp are encased in a wrapper made from ground yellow beans, cut in chunks and deep-fried, then served with a sauce of Chinese lemons, ginger and vinegar.

And I love the drink list. It is simplicity itself: "Beer $2.50, Tsingtao Beer $3.50, white wine $3." That's it.

Zingerman's Delicatessen, Zingerman's Next Door

Ann Arbor's four-star deli, inside a 1909 red brick building on the corner of brick-paved Detroit Street and Kingsley, looks as if it has been there forever. It's been just a little more than a decade, however, since the debut of this interesting hybrid.

What sets Zingerman's apart is its insistence on top quality, as well as friendliness and service.

Top-of-the-line products sold at the retail counter include first-flush Darjeeling tea, obscure French mustards, Belgian cheeses and organic marmalade. The emphasis is on the products of small, proprietor-run companies. Zingerman's own bake house produces breads and Danish pastries, cookies, cakes and pies.

☆ ☆ ☆ ☆

422 Detroit Street, Ann Arbor.
(313) 663-3354
(313) 663-5282 (Next Door).

Hours: 7 a.m.-10 p.m. daily (until 11 p.m. daily Next Door). Closed Thanksgiving and Christmas Day.

Nonsmoking: 100 percent.

Soft drinks only.   AE, MC and Visa.

Moderate

Step up to the counter along the back wall if you want a great sandwich. The blackboard is lettered with the names and descriptions of a vast number of them, choices like Good Golly Ms. Molly (corned beef or pastrami on latkes, $8) or Louie's Box Lunch (roast beef, cheddar, lettuce, hot mustard on onion rye, $7.50). Those seeking other than smoked meats might consider such items as chicken salad, made from free-range Amish-raised chickens; three cheeses grilled on rye and served with Pommery mustard, and the ultimate peanut butter and jelly, $3.75.

Also offered are salade Nicoise and Caesar and Greek salads; potato salad, from old-fashioned to Dutch, German and blue cheese; coleslaw pepped up with caraway seeds, and the house's famous noodle kugel. Make your choice and hope there'll be an empty seat somewhere. Though the odds got better when a number of seats were added in the house next door.

The success of Zingerman's isn't surprising. Explains Ari Weinzweig, partner in the enterprise with Paul Saginaw, "We work really hard. It's a never-ending process. With people and food, perfection is not possible, but in some ways, we strive for it.

"We don't want 10 stores. This place has a personality to which everyone who works here contributes. Our values, our food and our people ... if we aren't here, you lose that."

☆ ☆ ☆ ☆

*More than 300 restaurants are reviewed in this 7th edition of Restaurants of Detroit,
and 24 earned the highest honor, four stars. Here are the best of the best.*

American

Acadia, *Auburn Hills*
City Grill, *Birmingham*
Hattie's, *Suttons Bay*
ONE23, *Grosse Pointe Farms*
Too Chez, *Novi*

Deli

Zingerman's Deli, *Ann Arbor*

Italian

Giovanni's Ristorante, *Detroit*

Japanese

Cherry Blossom, *Novi*

Mideastern

Steve's Back Room, *Harper Woods, West Bloomfield*

Mixed Bag

Cafe Edward, *Midland*
Cousins Heritage Inn, *Dexter*
Dusty's Wine Bar and Pub, *Okemos*
Emily's, *Northville*
The Lark, *West Bloomfield*
Opus One, *Detroit*
Pike Street, *Pontiac*
Rattlesnake Club, *Detroit*
Rowe Inn, *Ellsworth*
Tapawingo, *Ellsworth*
Van Dyke Place, *Detroit*
The Whitney, *Detroit*

Seafood

Joe Muer's, *Detroit*
Tom's Oyster Bar, *Grosse Pointe Park, Royal Oak*

Thai

Thai Bistro, *Canton*